JOHN OLSON'S BOOK OF THE

SHOTGUN

JOHN OLSON'S BOOK OF THE
SHOTGUN

by JOHN OLSON

J. PHILIP O'HARA, INC.
Chicago

Distributed by The John Olson Company
299 Forest Avenue, Box 767
Paramus, New Jersey 07652

J. Philip O'Hara, Inc. 20 East Huron, Chicago 60611 in cooperation with the John Olson Company. Published simultaneously in Canada by Van Nostrand Reinhold, Ltd., Scarborough, Ontario.

LC Number: 74–25387
ISBN: 0–87955–421–5 Casebound
ISBN: 0–87955–415–0 Paper

First Printing I

Dedication

This book is dedicated to the man who first introduced me to the wonders of nature and who taught me to love and respect the wildlife with whom I would so briefly share the forest. . . . my late father.

Contents

Acknowledgments

It would be impossible to produce a book of this kind without the help of a considerable number of sympathetic, knowledgeable and cooperative people. Unfortunately, now that it's done, I find it's hard to remember all of those who made a special effort to assist. So, if I've overlooked anyone in the following acknowledgments, please don't take offense.

Special thanks to Stan Slaten, Paul Westenberger and Richard Dietz for their invaluable assistance; to Bob Steindler for his photos and timely suggestions and to Emil Schwend and Richard Horlacher for their numerous contributions.

Thanks, too, to those unsung gentlemen of the trade who so kindly provided photos and "spec" sheets.

Finally, a special pat-on-the-back to my son, Bill, and to Russ Dunham and Bob Barr for posing before my camera. Also to Pat Olson for interpreting my "chicken-scratches," reducing them to a readable, typed, manuscript.

Introduction

Many books are written on shotguns and shotgun hunting but most fall into one of two categories: they're either too technical, dwelling on details that would not interest the average shotgunner, or they're too general, virtually lacking any basic technical material.

With this volume I've tried to tread that slender line between the two by offering useful technical data where appropriate, and by relating it to the target shooting or hunting concept under discussion.

Shotgunning embraces many gray areas, far more than the more exacting science of riflery, so the ardent and experienced shotgunner may find some new thoughts within these covers. On the other hand, the complete and basic format of the shotgun spectrum is presented for the beginning wingshooter.

In the final analysis, this entire volume is devoted to helping the reader bust more clays or bag more birds, and I sincerely hope that it accomplishes either or both of those goals for *you*.

CHAPTER 1

The Shotgun Barrel

There is much to discuss where the shotgun barrel is concerned because this is the heart of the gun: even an inexpensive shotgun can prove to be an outstanding performer if it has a good barrel, while a poor one can render a two thousand dollar custom model about as useful as a buggy whip.

Smoothbore shotgun barrels are made from a wide variety of steel alloys; some have even been made with steel bore-cores surrounded by aluminum or glass. They're also made in a wide assortment of lengths and gauges to fulfill an equally wide assortment of shooting requirements. At one time most were of a plain-round exterior configuration but, today, about half the shotguns marketed are equipped with barrels having some form of solid or ventilated rib—a device that aids sighting. Production techniques vary greatly from one manufacturer to another and dimensional specifications are likewise subject to considerable latitude. These factors, added to the many variables inherent to shotshell-making, explain why performance differs from one gun to another—even within the same make and model.

Until the late 1800s when the modern fluid steel barrel came upon the scene, shotgun barrels were made via the Damascus method: a rod of a size and shape that matched the desired bore dimensions was wrapped in a twist fashion with a number of narrow bands or wires of iron or soft steel. Subsequent heating and hammering welded the bands together. When the inner rod (referred to as a mandrel) was removed, the resultant pipe-like tube was fitted with accessory devices to facilitate mounting on a given action or frame. The exterior patterning resulting from this manufacturing process was often relied upon to provide an indication of quality which, as might be surmised, ranged from poor to excellent. Nevertheless, confidence in the Damascus barrel was cultivated over so many years that early makers of far superior fluid steel barrels were initially forced to artificially decorate them with Damascus patterns to gain market acceptance.

Damascus barrels still turn up from time to time, often when junior is turned loose in Grandpa's attic. Since these *cannot* be used safely with modern smokeless powder ammunition, one must be careful to have new discoveries examined by a qualified gunsmith.

Today, shotgun barrels are made by drilling and lapping a steel rod or by hammering a heavy steel sleeve. Because there are rarely less than five different internal dimensions, each manufacturer has his own favored technique for shaping the bore

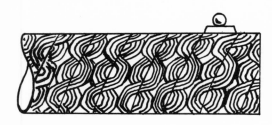

Damascus barrels were made from strips of steel, heated, twisted and welded together through hammering. Patterns resulted in the finished surface, such as shown in this artist's rendering. Damascus barreled guns should not be used with modern shotshells.

and this usually consists of a series of cutting and polishing operations which accomplish shaping of the choke, choke cone, bore, chamber cone, chamber and rim recess. With the comparatively new hammering process some shotgun plants simply shape the bore by cutting the external profile with the steps that are inverted through hammering. There is one special advantage to this method: the original straight and uniform bore hole lends itself to a simplified bore-lapping procedure that can result in exceptionally smooth barrel walls.

Manufacturing processes tend to bend the comparatively thin-walled barrel somewhat so barrels are straightened by highly skilled technicians after shaping has been completed. At times, too, barrels that do not shoot to point of aim will be "bent" to yield the desired result. This bending, of course, is usually so slight that it is not readily seen by the naked eye.

Special skills and care are required when fitting ribs to barrels or when joining two or more barrels for a side-by-side, over and under or Drilling-type shotgun because soldering tends to create strains and stresses that unfavorably influence bore alignment. With some expensive custom-made models the maker will fasten barrels (in the chamber area) and join the muzzles by means of a clamping device. The gun is test fired in this fashion and the clamps adjusted to achieve the desired result. Ribs are then fastened to the adjusted barrels in such a way that alignment is preserved. Barrels are aligned on popularly-priced shotguns by means of a jig.

At one time, barrels, ribs, etc., were fastened with soft tin-solder and, since this tends to melt if immersed in hot blueing solutions, tin-soldered assemblies had to be cold-blued. Silver-solder, the universally-accepted modern joining medium, has a considerably higher melting point and permits finishing via the much improved hot-blue process. On rare occasions when the harried gunsmith neglects to check the solder employed in an older model he'll find barrel components separated in his blueing tank. The re-assembly process is exceedingly difficult and time-consuming.

GAUGES

A four-gauge specimen in my shotshell collection serves to remind me of the many bore sizes that have been employed over the years. During the era of the market hunter, punt guns were so large they had to be anchored to the boat much the way a cannon would be employed. Fortunately, such destructive devices (and hunting practices) have been outlawed and present-day, conservation-minded hunters are limited to the 10, 12, 16, 20 and 28 gauges.

You'll note that I omitted the popular ".410;" while this is commonly referred to as ".410 gauge," its size was not arrived at by the usual gauge method. The .410 is really closer to ".410 caliber" since the bore diameter mikes .410 inches.

The gauge system of bore sizing was conceived by rather curious means: it seems the ball or projectile came first—during the days of muzzle-loading muskets—and the bore (or barrel) was developed to accommodate the projectile. If a one-pound ingot of lead was melted down to yield precisely twelve round balls of equal size, the

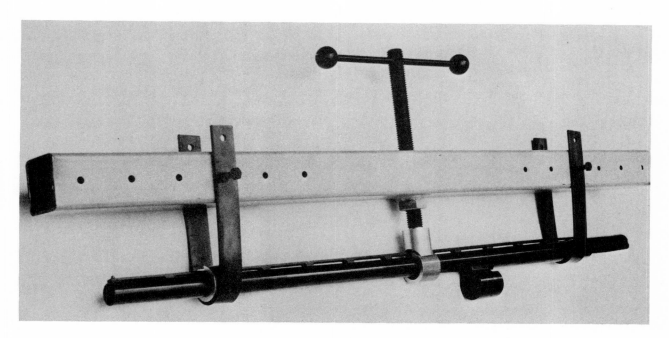

The barrel press, similar to this one by B-Square Company, is used by gunsmiths to bend or straighten barrels.

diameter of one ball would be ascertained and the resulting measurement was termed "twelve gauge." One pound of lead melted down into precisely twenty round balls of equal size would provide the measurement for "twenty gauge" and so on. Gauges, at one time, ranged from 1 to 32.

(Further details on individual shotgun gauges will be found in the ammunition chapter of this book.)

BARREL LENGTHS

Under the existing Federal Firearms Law the minimum legal length of a shotgun barrel is eighteen inches. Since the sportsman has little use, or need, for a barrel measuring less than twenty-two inches, this law—designed to thwart the gangland style use of sawed-off shotguns—is no impediment to the sporting application of shotguns. It should be noted, however, that some sportsmen

have innocently run afoul of the law by cutting down damaged barrels. One case that comes to mind involved a man who accidentally burst the barrel on his shotgun and who cut it down simply for convenience when packing the gun for shipment to the manufacturer to have a new barrel fitted. Under the law the manufacturer is forbidden to handle the weapon, instead he must immediately notify the authorities and surrender the illegal gun. In no time at all, our unlucky sportsman was visited by law-enforcement people who wanted to know "Why? When? Where?" etc.

Having established the average minimum length, let's take a look at the other extreme: what is the longest practical length of a barrel? Rifles and shotguns differ greatly in many ballistic areas—barrel length is one of them! A rifle develops higher muzzle velocities as the barrel is lengthened (to a point—depending upon caliber, powder, capacity, etc.). A shotgun, however, differs ballistically in this area. The scattergun develops peak velocity quickly and there are some experts who believe that maximum speed is at-

The four and eight gauges have all but passed from the scene; they're shown here only for comparison purposes. Left to right: 4, 8, 10, 12, 16, 20 and .410 gauges, with a pair of 9mm shotshells down front. Missing, is the 28 gauge.

tained in a barrel measuring twenty-seven inches. Others insist that thirty-one inches is the point at which velocity will start to fall off. My own opinion is that there is a strong correlation between the length of the barrel and the shell (or the powder) employed. With some loads, and some powders, the twenty-seven inch figure may be accurate. Nevertheless, I feel some slower powders and/or heavy loads require the extra barrel length to reach a total burn. When a barrel exceeds thirty-two inches in length I believe that it will start to reduce velocities *with most loads*.

Strangely, the velocity loss suffered when a barrel is shorter than the measured peak length is relatively insignificant; the shooter should not be overly concerned with this question. A number of laboratories have reported velocity drops of only forty to sixty feet per second when reducing lengths from thirty or thirty-one to twenty-five

inches. I could find no one who tested the effect of *longer* barrels on velocity, but I strongly suspect the loss would rapidly prove greater when the peak length is surpassed: for this reason I question the wisdom of shooters who seek barrels exceeding thirty-two inches in length. Trap shooters, handicapped out to twenty-seven yards, often look for trap guns with thirty-four inch barrels, but they're really looking for tighter patterns and a longer sighting plane. Small changes in velocity serves neither to help nor hurt their cause.

Insofar as the hunter is concerned, any barrel measuring between twenty-five and thirty inches will perform adequately. Handling qualities and chokes, patterns, etc., are far more important considerations.

During the years that I directed the marketing of a line of shotguns, I was given the task of selling a special magnum model equipped with thirty-two inch barrels. On our sales force at the time was a highly skilled and knowledgeable salesman, from Arkansas, who was also an excellent shooter and hunter. This man had a happy, gentle way about him and he could say things to people that, if at-

The Ithaca Model 66 Long Tom in 12 gauge with a thirty-six inch barrel.

tempted by anyone else, would elicit naught but a solid blow to the proboscis. Once, at a southern sportmen's show, we were engaged for the better part of a week in exhibiting our broad assortment of firearms. Almost without exception, those who visited our display were interested only in dove or quail shooting, so our shiny new 32-inch magnum sat in the corner of the rack collecting dust. Then, on the last day of the exhibit, a grizzled old timer spied the magnum and immediately plucked it out for a closer examination. Aiming it at selected targets on the ceiling he snorted, "This is what I've been looking for—a magnum! How long's the barrels?"

The salesman replied, "Thutty-two inches!"

"Aw, shucks," replied the old timer, "I gotta have at least thutty-four inches for the kind of shootin' I aim to do!"

"No problem," replied the salesman, "we can fix that!"

"How're ya' gonna do that!"

"Well, yuh see," said the salesman, now grinning broadly, "I'll give you a two-inch box to stand on while you're shootin' it!"

The man was a good sport and he laughed uproariously, but he didn't want the gun. No amount of explanation, ballistic data, or corraborative printed material would convince that particular shooter that the salesman was right. Except for two more inches of sighting radius, 34-inch bar-

rels would add no more to the performance of that gun than a two-inch platform under the feet.

There's a bag full of the same "ol' hunter's lore" encountered every day by those designing and manufacturing firearms and ammunition. Often, the valid advice of those *who know* (who work with the components every day—testing them in every possible way with sophisticated equipment) is rejected in favor of "good ol' Joe's" inexpert criticisms.

Getting back to barrel lengths, short barrels of from twenty to twenty-four inches are popularly employed only on riot guns (for police use), slug guns (for big game hunting with rifled slug loads) or on guns carried by those who have discovered the advantages of a short barrel and a wide open choke in heavy brush country hunting.

Knowledgeable gun authorities have long contended that the average American shotgunner uses a barrel that is too long with a choke that is too tight. Their advice is now being accepted by some adventurous souls and there has been a slow but steady shifting in sales figures towards shorter, more open-choked barrels.

Twenty-two and twenty-four inch barrels on slug guns, ironically, are intended only to facilitate handling in the field. These, cylinder bored, do not result in greater slug performance. In fact, repeated tests have indicated that the average slug performs best in a twenty-eight inch barrel having a modified choke.

The twenty-six inch barrel is usually bored with an improved cylinder choke or a skeet choke

Remington's Model 870 Pump Action Deer gun is available in the 12 or 20 gauges with a 22-inch barrel.

(which may be a bit more open). Some European makers use a length closer to twenty-five inches for this purpose. Hunters of quail, dove and upland game should favor the 26″ I. C. Barrel. It is especially useful to those who hunt with dogs.

I once shot a few rounds of skeet with a gun having a twenty-two inch cylinder-bored slug barrel. The result was such that I would favor further testing with this combination if I were seriously interested in pursuing this target-shooting sport.

For all around scattergunning the ideal barrel measures twenty-seven or twenty-eight inches and is bored with a modified choke. (Some barrels of this length are also full choked.) In double guns, for example, one barrel will be modified and the other, full. In a pinch, a shooter could use a twenty-eight-modified on the skeet range simply by substituting a "brush" or "scatter" load for the conventional skeet shell. Just don't attempt this in a registered match or tournament.

Thirty-inch barrels are intended primarily for open-country shooting of upland game or for waterfowl hunting or trap shooting. These barrels are generally full choked to keep patterns concentrated over the greatest possible distance. Barrels exceeding thirty inches in length may be found, occasionally, on shotguns designed expressly for certain forms of waterfowl hunting or trap shooting.

CHOKES

About one hundred years ago someone discovered that shot patterns could be regulated by means of constricting (or spreading) the muzzle of the shotgun barrel—much the way a garden hose nozzle regulates a stream of water. Since then, those engaged with the manufacture of shotguns, and shotshells, have experimented with many varied choking systems, adjustable choke devices, shotshell loadings, etc., etc. The result is that we are now blessed (?) with a highly complex

The Remington 870R Police Gun in 12 gauge. Note short, twenty-inch barrel.

and confusing lack of standardization in this area. As we pointed out earlier, the method employed for determining gauge sizes was rather crude to begin with, however, until you get knee deep into the study of chokes—"you ain't seen 'nuttin' yet!"

First, there are many different ways to constrict the muzzle of a barrel. Makers of inexpensive shotguns simply take a cylinder-bored barrel and swage the muzzle in a die of slightly smaller size. This compresses the barrel walls so that *both* inside and outside diameters are reduced. Crude? Yes—but often effective. Of course, the choke resulting from this method is quite short and creates a sharp inner edge that is quickly worn away. How much choke remains after a couple thousand rounds have been fired?

Makers of more sophisticated *American* shotguns employ a taper (or cone) from the bore diameter to the muzzle where the diameter is noticeably reduced to result in the desired constriction. Some, too, will take straight taper and relieve it a bit to form a slight radius—a cross-sectional view of the choke would then show a slight "dished taper" from bore diameter to muzzle.

English shotgun builders cut a straight taper from the bore diameter to some point short of the muzzle and then a choke section having parallel walls from that point to the exit. The parallel section is referred to as the "lede" while the tapered section is called the "cone." Sometimes referred to as the "standard choke system," the English method is practiced by many European makers and, I'm told, by a few American firms as well.

Except for special choking techniques which we'll discuss a bit later on, we've now established that there are three different types of choke currently in use—the "swaged choke," "American choke," and the "English (or standard) choke." The next question, then, is, "how are the various degrees of constriction identified?"

Again, Americans and Europeans went their separate ways. To simplify this for the sake of comprehension we've drawn up a chart that shows, at a glance, the approximate relationship of one type of choke to another, together with the *generally-accepted* amount of constriction required to achieve the desired choke. The reader will note that constriction is expressed in "points:" one point is equivalent to one one-thousandth of an inch (.001″) and a constriction of thirty points, in a twelve gauge barrel having a bore diameter of .729″, would indicate that the choke, at the muzzle, has a diameter of .699″.

American Chokes	European Chokes	Constriction in Points	Choke Length*
Cylinder Bore	Cylinder	none	0
Improved Cylinder	¼ Choke	10	⅝″
Modified	½ choke	20	1¼″
Improved Modified	¾ choke	30	1⅞″
Full	Full	40	2½″

*(Choke length)—this dimension varies greatly from one maker to the next and is largely dependent upon the choking method employed. These dimensions are offered for illustrative purposes only.

In the above chart will be found a choke specification that is rarely found in U. S. guns though popular in Europe. This is the improved-modified, which represents a degree of constriction between modified and full and is frequently employed on double-barrel (or over and under) guns that are intended for International Trap Shooting—the two-barrel combination being improved-modified and full. Some pigeon guns also make use of it in an improved-cylinder, improved-modified combination.

Other chokes, conspicuous by their absence from the chart are: "spreader," "skeet," and "extra-full."

A "spreader choke" is actually not a choke at all because this is made by removing *all* constriction and, instead, tapering the bore diameter in a reverse pattern so that it is actually larger at the

The Ithaca-Perazzi Single Barrel Trap gun is available in a choice of barrel lengths, i.e., 30", 32", or 34'.

muzzle. The intent of course, is to hurriedly expand patterns for a wider distribution of shot at close range.

Skeet chokes: every skeet gun manufacturer has his own special interpretation of this. If possible, he would like to have his skeet guns steal all the honors on the skeet field, so he experiments with barrels, chokes and patterns until he gets consistently good results from a given combination. When building two-barreled guns, it naturally follows that he'll create two different skeet chokes to better cope with the doubles-shooting inherent to skeet; with single-barrel guns (pumps and automatics) he usually refers to the choke simply as "Skeet choke." With side-by-side doubles, or over and under guns, he'll often call the chokes "Skeet #1" and "Skeet #2."

It is then apparent that skeet chokes lack uniformity, they can range all the way from a cylinder-bore dimension to a constriction exceeding that of a modified choke. I wouldn't fret over this though, because manufacturers are anxious to produce winners and the shooter can be pretty much assured that his new skeet gun will throw fairly good patterns at skeet distances.

The term "extra-full choke" makes me wince because this implies that it is possible to constrict a barrel beyond normal full choke dimension.

Referring back to the choke chart, it will be seen that a full choke is associated with a constriction of forty points (.040"). This is about the *maximum* amount of constriction possible. In practice, most barrels throwing full choke patterns of 70 to 80% have *less than forty points of constriction.* Some, hardly more than half that!

When a choke is too tightly constricted it tends to *blow the pattern,* spreading it erratically—almost as if a spreader choke were being employed. So, you see, one can't obtain an "extra full choke" by simply reducing the bore opening beyond full choke limits! Nevertheless, because some barrels inexplicably produce patterns of 80% or more; they can, and should, be labelled "extra full choke."

What I am driving at here, is that the proof of a choke is in its patterning: no one can predetermine a pattern percentage by mechanical means or precalculation. (There's considerably more info on this coming up a little later, in the chapter entitled "Patterning.")

JUG CHOKE

This is not a form of choking employed by the manufacturer but, rather, a gunsmith's answer to the problem created when a barrel has lost its choke. The choke section of a barrel is cut off when an adjustable choke device is installed and barrels are easily burst, at the muzzle, when fired while inadvertently plugged with snow or mud.

The gunsmith faced with a shotgunner who has lost the choke end of his barrel will often *attempt* to save the barrel by cutting a jug choke—a recess

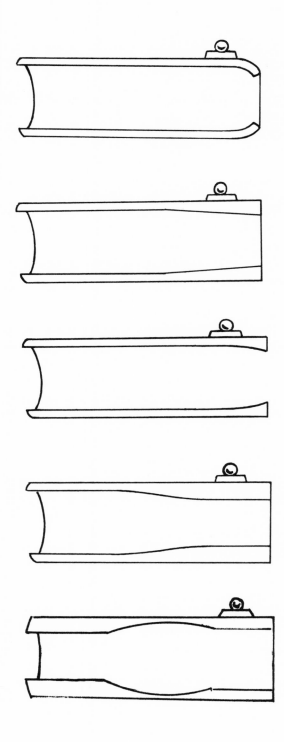

Diagrams of the four conventional choke systems. Top to bottom: the swaged choke, the American choke, a variation of the American choke and, finally, the English or standard choke. (Drawings are exaggerated for illustrative purposes.) The fifth choke, at the bottom, is the new and highly acclaimed "Tula choke" designed specifically for skeet shooting. This is the choke employed in the Rottweil Olympic Skeet Gun which won the last Skeet Olympics at Munich. With the Tula, the choke dimensions at the muzzle— directly under the sight—is actually larger than the bore dimension. This, theoretically, lengthens the shot column because the leading pellets escape the bore without interference. Following pellets tend to detour into the jug-like recess, delaying their departure from the muzzle.

in the bore. For some strange reason (one that I've never found a suitable explanation for) enlargement of the bore diameter, slightly inside of the muzzle area, tends to tighten patterns. The process is one of trial and error: repeated cutting, polishing and testing, until a satisfactory pattern is achieved.

Some degree of improvement is possible with jug-choking—over the alternative cylinder-bore pattern—but rarely can the gunsmith achieve the density of a good modified pattern by this means.

Summing up this dissertation on chokes, the shooter should bear in mind that the choke is simply the mechanical means by which one expects to distribute the shot charge most advantageously. Yet, like a fickle woman, the choke doesn't necessarily behave in the anticipated manner. Any change in the shotshell, or its components, can greatly affect patterning qualities. Consequently, one can't assume that a barrel stamped "modified" will produce 60% modified patterns at 40 yards with any given shell or shot size—*and the manufacturer can't really be criticized if it doesn't.* Through their continuous testing programs gunmakers determine a given choke formation with dimensions that will *generally* yield the desired result but, it is impossible for them to deal with all the possible variables short of patterning and customizing every barrel produced (and shooters wouldn't sit still for the gun prices that such customizing would necessitate.) Furthermore, even with customizing, one would only be assured of getting the desired pattern with a shotshell of *one given make, load and shot size!*

THE BORE

While the inner surface of the entire barrel is properly referred to as "the bore," we are concerned, here, only with that portion situated between the chamber cone and the start of the choke. This is the straight walled section that everyone examines closely when peering through a barrel—and usually the only thing the untrained eye can learn from such an examination is whether or not the barrel is smooth or rusted and pitted. The real measure of a barrel lies in those things that *can't be seen* by the unaided eye!

When looking through a barrel the chamber and chamber cone appear as dark shadows, as does the choke cone. It's the dimensions and alignments of these that are important and these things cannot be determined without measuring and/or test-firing.

The trained eye, however, will look for a few other telltale signs when scrutinizing a barrel: for one, it'll peer down the *outer* walls of the barrel looking for irregularities in the exterior finish—shallow dents, slight bulges, polishing depressions, etc. The smoother and more even the exterior finish, the better the quality!

The trained eye will also look for inexplicable shadows in the bore which would indicate bulges, defects, etc. in the barrel walls that may have been disguised on the outside.

A highly knowledgeable friend of mine once showed me a very expensive double gun that he had picked up in a trade. He was most anxious to get this piece and made an especially attractive offer to the former owner—who must have laughed all the way home! My friend was so excited about the prospects of acquiring the gun that he failed to examine the bore carefully. When he showed it to me, I found a very heavy suspicious shadow in one wall that didn't encircle the entire bore (as most ring bulges do.) It quickly became apparent that the barrel had been badly bulged at that point and that the former owner had simply peened the bulge down from the outside and smoothed it over with abrasive cloth followed by touch-up blue. The portion of the bulge that I spotted lay under the rib, and, since this was a side-by-side, that area couldn't be peened (or seen) from the outside. Subsequent disassembly of the barrels indicated that the barrel had to be replaced because inexpert peening had cracked the wall in the bulged area.

The trained eye will also look for streaks of lead deposits called "leading" in the bore area immediately beyond the chamber cone. Leading here also indicates heavy leading in the choke area which would tend to disrupt patterns. This is not a serious problem because such deposits are easily removed with a stiff wire bore brush and solvent; I mention it only for the benefit of those who would shoot in competition.

To prevent a lead build-up when shooting in competition, I try to run a bristle brush through the bore after every round.

One of the reasons why choking is so unpredictable is that there is a correlation between the bore diameter and the choke diameter that influences patterning. Strangely, it is often possible to change pattern-percentages by simply polishing the bore, *without touching the choke area.* Exceptionally tight full choke patterns have been achieved, in this manner, by increasing the bore diameter ever so slightly.

Some imported 20 gauge guns kick like steers simply because European bore dimensions for the 20 gauge are slightly smaller than ours.

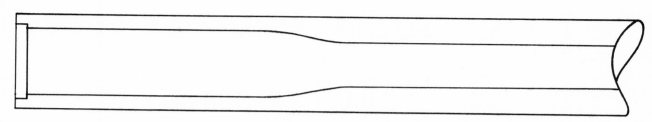

Varying bore dimensions are so gently tapered they're difficult to detect. We've had the artist magnify the differences here to demonstrate how the chamber flows into the forcing cone and the cone into the bore.

CHAMBER CONE

This is a tapered portion of the bore that is designed to provide the step between the differing diameters of the chamber (which is larger) and the bore. Actually, there is no clearly defined step in the cone area—rather, it is a gently flowing taper from one dimension to the other.

Cones are made to various lengths, depending upon the experience of the individual manufacturer. Some Europeans cut a two-inch cone; most English and American makers use cones that are shorter.

When a shooter accidentally loads a shell that is too long for the chamber of a given gun, it's the cone area that points the telltale finger—it develops a severe ring bulge that completely encircles the barrel.

Finally, the cone acts as a funnel, gathering the shot as it exits the fired shell and feeding it into the bore.

THE CHAMBER

The chamber, of course, is designed to house the loaded shell and is meticulously dimensioned to accept all shells of the proper gauge *and length*.

At one time, for example, most 12 gauge shotshells measured 2½ inches. In England, I believe, many still do. Then someone came up with a 2⅝-inch shell and this was subsequently increased to

2¾ inches (in the U. S.) during the early 1900s.

The smaller 16 and 20 gauges were a bit slower "growing-up" but they, too, now measure 2¾ inches.

As we explained earlier, when discussing chamber cones, it is important to match the shell to the length of the chamber. If, for example, one should fire a 2¾-inch shell in a gun having a 2½-inch chamber the barrel is sure to be bulged, *at the very least*.

Loaded shotshells incidentally are *always* shorter than the chambers they're designed to fit, simply because length is ascertained when the crimp is open and fully extended. For this reason, they'll invariably load easily into shorter chambers in spite of the fact that they're the wrong size.

Many a fine old gun is found with a 2½- or 2⅝-inch chamber; it can easily be modified to handle 2¾-inch shells, assuming that it is in otherwise good condition and the barrels are of fluid steel. A gunsmith will simply re-cut them with 2¾-inch reamers. This is easily accomplished and the cost is not prohibitive.

While one cannot use shells *longer* than the length of a given chamber, one can safely use shells that are *shorter*. A 12 gauge 2½-inch shell, for example can be used in a 12-gauge 2¾-inch chamber. A 2¾-inch 12 gauge Magnum shell will fire safely in a 3-inch 12 gauge Magnum chamber but the 3-inch shell CANNOT be used in a barrel cut for 2¾-inch shells.

Factory loaded shells differ somewhat in diameter depending upon materials used, wad sizes, crimp pressures, etc., and for this reason, gun makers have to provide some tolerance in chamber diameters. Thus, chambers are usually cut two thousandths of an inch larger in diameter than the maximum acceptable diameter of the newly loaded cartridge. Any greater tolerance could easily lead to trouble; split cases, escaping gases, etc., etc.

Upon firing, the case is instantly expanded to seize the walls of the chamber. Internal pressures then stretch the head of the case slightly rearward until it is stopped by the resistance of the breech face. As soon as the pressure recedes, the case will shrink slightly, releasing its hold on the chamber walls and facilitating unimpeded extraction and ejection.

(This is one of the reasons why tired reloaded cases often split in the area where the case body joins the metallic head. The other reason for failure in this area is that the powder charge generally lies directly under this junction and the heat of the burning charge is concentrated here.)

HEADSPACE

The rim recess, cut in the very end of the chamber, serves to stop the forward motion of the shell as it is loaded. It is the depth of this recess, determined by the thickness of the rim of the shell, that constitutes that oft-misunderstood term, "headspace." Too little tolerance here will prevent the breech from closing on a loaded round. Too great a tolerance can result in split cases and extreme gas leakage: possibly even greater difficulty, depending upon the severity of the condition. Break-open type shotguns of the side-by-side or over and under types, designed with non-retracting firing pins, will often discharge prematurely, as the gun is being closed, when headspacing is inadequate.

One small point worthy of mention here, is that the convergence factor common to double barrel guns results in some distortion of the case head upon firing because the shell is angled slightly to follow the alignment of the bore while the breech face is flat and straight. Reloaded shells, having once been fired in a double gun, will often fail to load subsequently in other types of actions. By the same token, and rare though the occurrence is, shells fired in one barrel of a double gun will sometimes fail to feed, when reloaded, in the *other* barrel of the same gun.

It's a good idea to try newly acquired empty fired cases in the chamber of a given gun before loading them. Jammed cases can damage extractor mechanisms.

BARREL LIFE

Every time a shot charge travels down the bore it tends to polish the barrel walls a bit and while the amount of steel removed is ever so slight, continued polishing will have a cumulative effect on the barrel; after a sufficient number of rounds, walls will be considerably thinner than they were to start with.

We are not concerned with the chamber area, where pressures are the greatest, because this portion is not subjected to wear. The choke portion, especially the cone, *is* subject to wear but barrel design in this area naturally results in heavier wall thickness to begin with. That portion of the barrel lying between the two—the bore—is where noticeable wear can be expected and since the barrel is made with some breech-to-muzzle taper, walls are usually thinnest just before the start of the choke.

Here we show six different methods employed for joining the barrels of double guns. In diagrams A, B, and C, the lugs and rails are separate components that are brazed to the breech ends of the barrels. In diagrams D and E, the lugs are forged as part of the barrels and/or dovetail joined. Diagram F shows a form of monobloc as it is used for an over and under gun. A heavy steel block is forged, milled and drilled to encompass the chamber ends of both barrels; lugs are cut into the heavy lower surface.

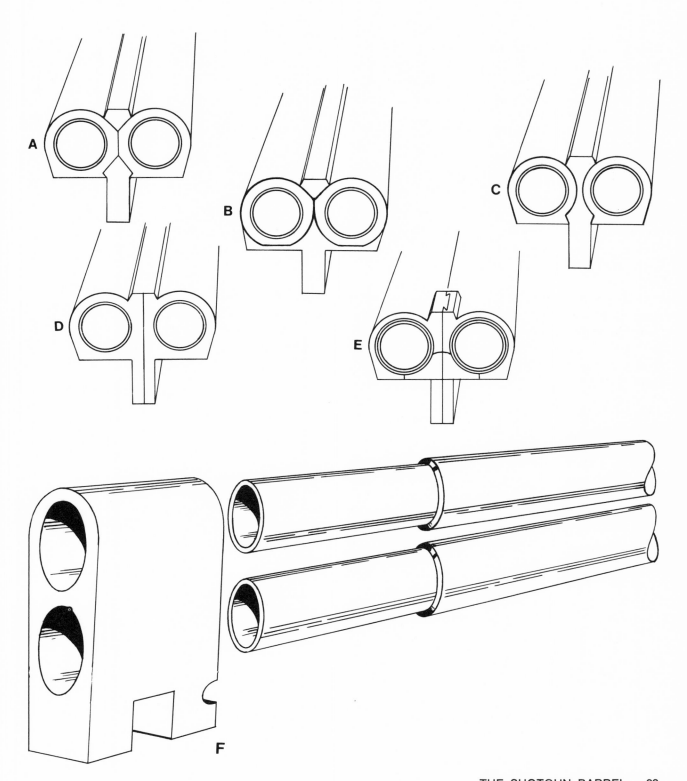

Fine old guns, handed down from father to son, have been known to suffer ruptured barrels on occasion and, while not usually dangerous to the shooter, such mishaps can be dangerous to those in close proximity.

I mention this phenomenon only to caution shooters in the use of obviously well-used relics. All such firearms should be checked carefully by a qualified gunsmith before being put into service. When substantial wear is evidenced in barrel walls it would be prudent to retire the gun or, at least, use it only with the lightest possible loads.

CHAPTER 2

The Shotgun Action

Present-day firearms designers are often amazed to find that some supposedly new concept was attempted a hundred or more years ago by an obscure gunsmith in a remote European mountain village. Had the state of the art in related fields been more advanced at their time, there's no doubt that many of those pioneer gunmakers would be more prominently mentioned in our firearms history books today. This should give the reader some idea of the number of shotgun designs that have come down the pike over the years—the serious student would be hard pressed to count them all. And yet, if we gathered up the bulk of our modern specimens, reducing them to basic patterns, we'd arrive at a total of six!

The Galef Single Barrel Companion Gun folds almost in half.

THE SINGLE-SHOT SHOTGUN

The simplest of shotgun designs is the fundamental break-open type having a barrel that is hinged to expose the chamber for loading. This is commonly employed on inexpensive single-shot models as well as on side-by-side and over and under guns; however, for our purposes, we'll treat the latter two types as separate entities under double barrel models.

The hinging action dates back to the first attempts to create a breech loader. It has a comparatively simple construction consisting of barrel, fore-end, receiver and buttstock. The receiver contains a hammer, sear, firing pin, trigger, guard, lock and top lever together with appropriate springs and pins. Some are designed with an internal hammer that is cocked by the opening ac-

Ward's Westernfield Model M150C is a .410 gauge bolt action model with a 3-inch chamber. An ideal beginner's model.

tion of the barrel. Others are made with an external hammer for manual operation. To facilitate removal of fired shells the barrel is designed with a crescent-shaped extractor which is cut into the rim recess at the base of the chamber. A rod-like extension of this is channeled through the lug area into the knuckle of the hinge in such a way that it is activated by the opening action of the breech.

Single barrel guns of this type have been produced in large numbers and in every possible gauge. As a boy I once spent a very painful afternoon shooting crows with one in 10 gauge magnum.

In .410, 28, or 20 gauge they can provide some excellent sport for those with limited finances. In 16 and 12 gauge they can be a bit rough on the shoulder because they weigh so little. With one of these I'd try to weight the buttstock and add a recoil pad.

The single barrel trap gun should probably be included in this grouping but it is such a sophisticated version of the single barrel break-open design that there is no room for other than rudimentary comparison. Trap guns, like side-by-sides and over and unders are made with refined locks, triggers, ejectors and wooden components.

THE BOLT ACTION

Next step up the ladder is the bolt action shot-gun—a type of scattergun that has started many a wingshooting career.

These are not unlike their rifled cousins. While most bolt action shotguns are made with the conventional box or clip magazine, tubular magazines are also occasionally encountered.

Savage, Stevens, Marlin and Mossberg are considered specialists in producing bolt action shot-guns although just about every maker of long guns has taken a crack at this market at one time or another.

Found in all popular gauges the only real complaint one will hear about the bolt is that it is too slow. Most wingshooters feel they have to have a rapid second shot.

For those who desire to hunt big game with slugs, the bolt action is probably an excellent choice. I'd choose one with a 28-inch modified barrel for this purpose.

Bolt action shotguns are very easy to clean and maintain and they readily accept rifle-type sighting accessories.

THE PUMP GUN

There's little question that the slide action shot-gun is, and has been, the mainstay of American shotgunning for almost a century. It is the most efficient of the manual repeaters, can take a lot of abuse, is easy to clean and maintain, is highly reliable and has always been offered at prices within reach of the modest pocketbook. If that weren't enough to assure its continued popularity, it's surprisingly fast and there are some who claim it can be cycled faster than the old recoil-operated automatic (in skilled hands, of course).

Early models of the pump gun were made with external hammers: when the slide was activated it would open the breech and cock the hammer while simultaneously ejecting the fired, empty casing. Hammerless versions operate in a similar fashion but are designed so that the hammer is entirely contained within the receiver.

The magazine and feeding mechanism of the pump gun is a splendid example of mechanical genius; the basic pattern is used with only slight modification by virtually all makers. Interestingly, the tubular magazine and feeding mechanism of current autoloading shotguns has been modeled from that of the traditional pump; it's difficult to improve on a design that has proven so reliable against the acid test of time.

In the tubular magazine, shells are loaded through the bottom of the action and arranged end to end so that all crimp ends point toward the muzzle. Care must be taken to push each cartridge fully into the tube so that the last shell loaded will be engaged by the shell latch or—as some refer to it—the cartridge stop.

Ejection in a pump gun is achieved just before the slide and bolt reach their rearmost position and then, as the action is about to reverse, a pawl engages the shell latch releasing one cartridge from the magazine. The spring loaded action of the follower pushes this shell onto the carrier which then swivels upward to align the cartridge in front of the bolt for chambering. When the slide has been returned to its forward, battery, position, the shell is fully chambered and the bolt is locked behind it by means of a swiveling locking bolt that engages a recess in the inner receiver wall. The carrier, too, is returned to its lowest attitude where it is aligned for the next loading cycle.

Most pump guns are made with an ejection port in the right side wall of the receiver. When some makers started producing slide actions for left-

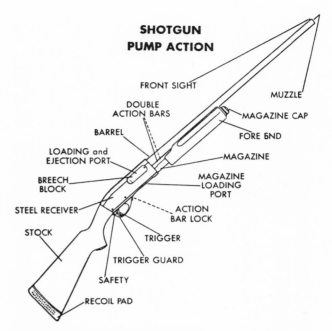

SHOTGUN PUMP ACTION

FRONT SIGHT
MUZZLE
DOUBLE ACTION BARS
MAGAZINE CAP
BARREL
FORE END
LOADING and EJECTION PORT
MAGAZINE
BREECH BLOCK
MAGAZINE LOADING PORT
STEEL RECEIVER
ACTION BAR LOCK
STOCK
TRIGGER
TRIGGER GUARD
SAFETY
RECOIL PAD

Diagram of Remington Pump Gun.

handers they moved this to the opposite wall for left-side ejection.

Unique among pump guns is the Ithaca Model 37 which has no side wall ports. This model ejects through the bottom of the action, as did early Remington pumps.

The timing of a bottom-ejection pump is fascinating—I once sat with a model 37 on my lap so that I could study the action through the lower port. By moving the slide rearward very, very slowly I expected to follow the sequence of mechanical functions. Ha! Suddenly, just as the slide approached the turn-around point everything happened at once! The action was simply too fast for the eye to follow. My first thought was that timing was so critical the action would have to be trouble prone. However, I soon realized that both Remington and Ithaca had devoted years to the development of this design and that literally hundreds of thousands of bottom-ejectors were in popular use. There's no doubt that they had perfected the system.

Steel billets, weighing between 8 and 9 pounds each, are stacked awaiting machining. More than half their weight will be cut away before the Savage pump gun frame results.

Much smoke is generated over the number of action bars a given model of pump gun employs; some firearms salesmen, describing guns with two parallel bars, would leave one with the impression that a single bar is a noisy, weak and vulnerable member of the pump fraternity. Horseradish! In twenty-five years of handling, shooting and working on both types, I've never seen an example of weakness in the bar area other than that which could be attributed to normal wear (in bolt-engaging surfaces) and this would affect both single and double bars alike.

Unlike the hunting rifle which can rarely expect to handle more than a few thousand rounds in the course of an entire shooting career, shotguns are generally subjected to hard usage: some scatter-gunners claim they burn up in excess of ten thousand rounds a year. Maintenance is therefore important to the shotgunner and headspacing adjustments can have some special significance as

A big Cincinnati milling machine is shown here shaping the top surface of the Savage receiver.

the consumption of ammo approaches six-digit figures. One or the advantages of a pump gun is that headspacing is easily adjusted (by qualified gunsmiths) to compensate for any wear in the chamber or breech area. At times the correction is made by simply replacing the barrel bushing. (Some makers produce oversized bushings for this purpose.) When a new bushing won't do the job the gunsmith can often re-face and re-thread the barrel to the frame at just a bit more expense. At times, too, a new breech bolt will restore dimensions. Autoloading models have a similar feature but headspacing adjustments in double guns are usually very tricky and costly.

SOLID FRAME vs. TAKE-DOWN MODELS

Solid frame pump gun designs are those in which the barrel is fastened to the receiver in a non-detachable manner. With take-down models, barrels—and often magazine tube assemblies— are designed for easy removal and re-assembly.

Savage is a firm believer in steel receivers. Here we show the receiver in its four phases of production, from solid block to finished, blued sheel.

Winchester's Model 1200 Pump Gun with plain barrel equipped with interchangeable "Win-Choke."

The advantage of the take-down model is that a number of different barrels may be interchanged on the same receiver. For example, one could switch from a 26-inch improved-cylinder to a 30-inch full choke barrel in a matter of minutes. Often no tools at all are required to do the job. In this way it is possible to adapt the gun for skeet, field or trap use by simply affixing the appropriate barrel. True, differing stock dimensions are recommended for these three forms of scattergunning, but a shooter accustomed to one stock, action and trigger, would have little difficulty compensating for the differences. When a pump gun is purchased with this intent, and with three interchangeable barrels, it is suggested that a field stock be chosen since neither skeet nor trap dimensions are as flexibly suited to all-around use.

Foreign gun makers are reluctant to compete in the pump gun market simply because this is a typically American firearm that has never really caught on elsewhere. At this writing I can only think of two foreign sources. It is also possible that the fierce competitiveness of American producers (which tends to deflate prices) is enough to discourage foreign involvement.

Before the heavy influx of foreign made over and unders (and before Remington released their Model 3200 O & U) the pump gun dominated trap competitions; it probably still does, though not so decisively. At one time, too, the pump was popular among skeet shooters. Now, however, the gas-operated automatic appears to reign supreme on the skeet field in spite of the fact that it is endlessly challenged by other types.

For all-around hunting use, the pump gun is hard to beat!

THE AUTOMATIC SHOTGUN

There are two distinctly different types of

Left-handers used to have a problem, but makers, today, are turning out left-hand models. This is a Remington LH 870.

An unusual import was this Swedish "T-Gun"—a pump action shotgun made from stainless steel and designed with top loading and top ejection. Bob Steindler, noted gun scribe, is shown here putting a T-Gun through its paces.

automatic shotgun produced today: the first is the traditional recoil-operated design that John Browning invented about the turn of the century and which was originally made by Remington in the Model 11. When the original patent expired, many other U. S. and foreign makers added the recoil-operated auto to their lines.

The second is the newer gas-operated automatic that has attained popularity over the last ten years. Actually, gas-operated firearms designs were first experimented with back in the late 1800s by the Hotchkiss Company. Then in 1926, Garand patented his famous gas-operated rifle. Scattergunners had to wait until the late 1950s to get a really efficient gas-operated shotgun.

Let's discuss the recoil-operated shotgun first: with the conventional Browning version the barrel is designed to move back and forth in the receiver. To accomplish this, while simultaneously providing the proper breech seal and bore alignment, the barrel is fitted with two special, though integral, appendages. The first of these is a long barrel extension which is fitted to the chamber end in such a way that it is enclosed by the shell of the receiver when the barrel is properly mounted in the frame. When in a firing attitude, the breech block nests tightly within the extension and is solidly locked into position by a swiveling breech bolt, one that engages a mated recess in the top surface of the extension. These two components then, when joined, comprise the breech of the gun—the receiver or frame is simply a shell or housing designed to keep the bolt and barrel in alignment through the firing, ejecting and loading cycle.

When the recoil-operated shotgun is fired, pressure on the face of the bolt drives it rearward in the receiver. Since the bolt is locked to the barrel extension, the barrel moves with it to a point of disengagement somewhat short of the peak stroke position. The extractor, fitted to the right face of the bolt, tends to hold the rim of the empty shell casing as the barrel reverses direction. The ejector, which is fitted to the barrel extension, then strikes the opposite side of the rim as the crimp end of the shell clears the chamber and the combined action forcibly swivels the spent casing out through the action port. An entirely separate function, occurring about the time the bolt and barrel separate, causes the shell latch to release one new

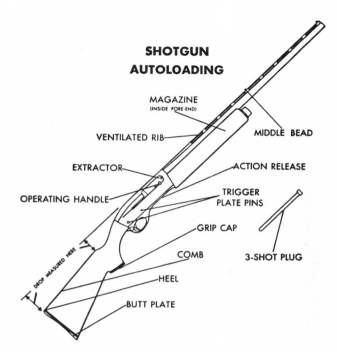

Diagram of Remington Automatic Shotgun.

round from the magazine so that it is fed onto the platform of the lifter. As the barrel regains its battery position the lifter swivels upward aligning the loaded shell in front of the bolt for chambering. A link attached to the rear surface of the bolt is then spring operated to close the bolt and lock it into position behind the newly chambered round.

Franchi recoil-operated autoloader.

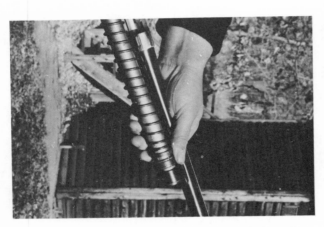

One arrangement for friction ring and friction piece in a recoil-operated model.

Small, almost insignificant, rails on the underside of the barrel extension control the timing of these related functions. When these are damaged, or worn excessively, jams result.

The second barrel appendage is a ring that is brazed to the underwall of the barrel (toward the forward end of the magazine tube when the barrel is in battery). This encircles the magazine tube and provides the bearing surface for the friction ring; it also serves to guide the barrel through its reciprocating travels. The brass friction ring, encircled by a tough steel friction spring, is mounted on the magazine tube so that its leading beveled edge engages the bevel of the barrel ring. Behind this is usually mounted a steel friction ring followed by the recoil spring. The combination of these rings and springs, together with the surface condition of the outer magazine wall, are the factors that determine the reliability of the recoil action. If the rings fit too tightly, or if the magazine

wall is rusted or coated with a sludge-like oil, or if the rings are not arranged in their proper order, the shotgun will not function properly. Another little-known factor affecting recoil-operated designs is that the butt of the gun requires some resistance from the shoulder of the shooter. If the gun is fired too quickly, before it is properly shouldered, it is almost certain to jam. By the same token, shooters who are unusually small or light often encounter difficulty with all but the heaviest loads simply because they are unable to offer the required resistance to the recoiling action.

When jamming occurs with the recoil-operated shotgun, the friction ring alignment should be checked first. Each manufacturer has his own particular recommendations on this point; settings differ according to the type of loads employed and no attempt should be made to interchange shells of varying velocity with one particular ring setting. It is possible, of course, to set friction rings for the lightest loads and to push all manner of hotter loads through the action, but the shooter will experience unreasonably heavy recoil and the practice will no doubt damage the shotgun if prolonged.

Assuming that jamming continues with the rings properly aligned, the shooter should next check to see if the bevels of each ring are facing in the proper direction. With high velocity loads the bevel, or bevels, of the brass ring should be engaged by the bevels of the barrel ring, on one side, and the steel ring, on the other. When using light loads, try to avoid mating bevels—at least on one side of the brass ring—because this forces compression of the friction piece against the wall of the magazine tube. Sometimes the wall of the magazine tube is simply too dirty or, perhaps, even rusted. Cleaning is accomplished with steel wool, oil and/or a fine grade of emery cloth. This surface should be smooth, clean and *virtually dry*. After oiling, it should be wiped with a clean dry cloth so that only the thinnest of coatings remains.

An unusual lightweight autoloading shotgun once offered by Armalite.

In very cold weather it's best to avoid using oil altogether. Continued balkiness can sometimes be corrected with a *trace* of graphite applied to the magazine tube.

Another idiosyncracy of the recoil operated shotgun is that it has little tolerance for recoil-reducing devices—either the ventilated adjustable choke or the recoil suppressant that is built into the stock. As we stated earlier, shoulder-resistance is important to functioning so this eliminates the stock suppressant entirely. The adjustable choke device should be employed *without* the customary ventilated sleeve. While a good gunsmith can often make adjustments in the friction pieces, to facilitate functioning with a vented choke device, I frown on the practice because it is bound to damage the action if it's done to work reliably with *all* types of shotshell loads.

Summing up the recoil operated automatic shotgun, special consideration should be shown

toward the recoil spring of these models. This is the heavy coil spring that encircles the magazine tube, under the forearm. When storing the gun for long periods, remove the fore-end cap, the barrel and the forearm so that the spring can lie in storage at its natural length. A continually compressed spring loses tension and requires frequent replacement.

THE GAS OPERATED AUTOMATIC

The reader will note that I use the term "automatic" both here and, earlier, when referring to the recoil operated shotgun. Actually, better terms would be "semi-automatic" or "autoloading," however, the sporting fraternity commonly uses the inappropriate designation "automatic" and I must bow to tradition. In military circles the term has an obviously different significance.

The gas-operated automatic shotgun was slow in "making the scene" simply because shotshells

Browning's new Model 2000 gas-operated auto shotgun with loading port on the left side of the receiver.

Remington's Model 1100 Autoloading Shotgun is popular on the skeet range as well as in the bird field.

The Beretta AL-1 gas-operated autoloader.

Winchester's Model 1400 gas-operated autoloader with a ventilated rib and Win-choke.

A bright, new addition to the Winchester line is the Super-X Model gas-operated auto. This one is in Skeet grade.

had a contaminating quality that would plug up gas ports, pistons, etc. Only since the introduction of plastic components have shotshells proven clean enough for reliable performance in a gas assembly. Before the introduction of plastics, shells were made with a rolled paper sleeve, a paper base wad, a cardboard over powder wad and fibre filler wad. And, when a roll crimp was used, there was even a cardboard wad lying over the top of the shot charge.

When paper, fibre, lead, powder and carbon residues found their way into the gas cylinder, as they were bound to do, it was just a question of time before they plugged the mechanism.

Essentially, the gas-operated automatic is very similar to the older recoil-operated version with but two important differences: the barrel doesn't move—it remains in a fixed position and, two, the entire breech mechanism is powered by a piston assembly that draws its energy from the gases that propel the shot charge. A small hole, drilled through the lower barrel wall between the chamber and the muzzle, serves as a gas port. (Sometimes there are more than one.) When the shot column and wadding pass this point, a portion of the propellant gas enters the port and travels into a cylinder containing a piston. A connecting rod links the piston with the breech bolt and, as the piston is driven rearward, the bolt is unlocked and powered to the full open position. A heavy coil spring opposes this rearward motion and serves to return the piston to the closed position when pressure subsides. The magazine cap of gas operated models is usually vented to release the gas that is caught in the cylinder well. For this reason the long-armed shooter must be careful to avoid placing his forehand over the magazine cap.

Extraction, ejection and reloading operations are similar to those found in the recoil-operated automatic.

Early gas models had to be cleaned frequently

TOP: a diagram of a typical bar action side lock; lock is cocked for firing with hammer poised (top-center) for release.

CENTER: a form of back-action side lock produced on a plate profiled in the bar action pattern. Hammer, here, is in the fired position.

BOTTOM: a back action side lock made on a plate contoured in the typical back action manner.
The primary difference between the "bar action" and "back action" lock systems is the location of the mainspring. Note how it projects forward in the bar action lock and how it lies to the rear of the hammer in the back action lock.

THE SHOTGUN ACTION   37

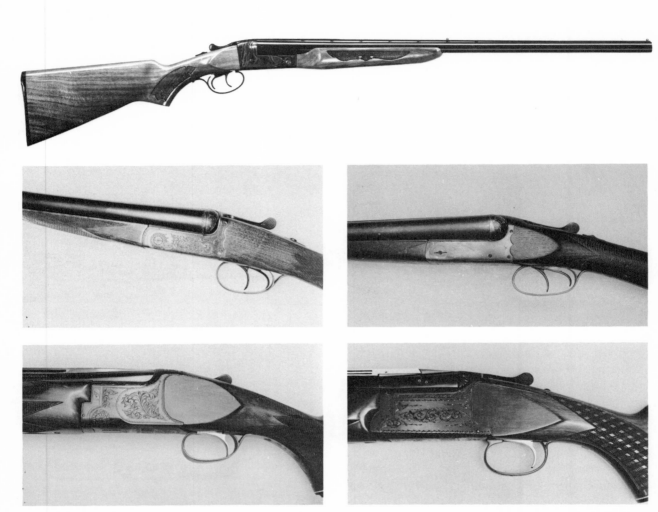

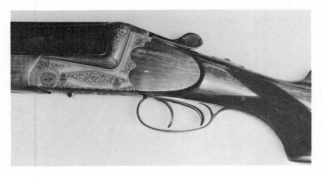

These are some fine examples of both the box lock and side lock systems.

At the top we illustrate six box-lock models, starting with the Savage-Fox Model B, followed, in sequence, by a Churchill 12 gauge, a Purdey 20 gauge ejector model, a Miroku 12 gauge Trap model, a Nikko "Shadow" 12 gauge Trap gun and an Austrian Ferlach over and under.

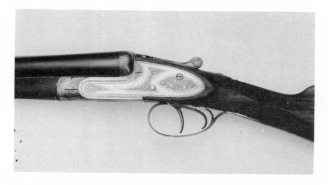

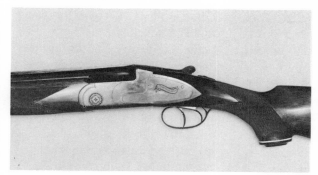

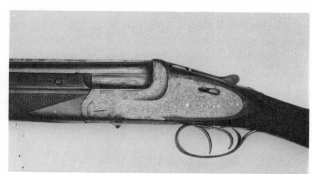

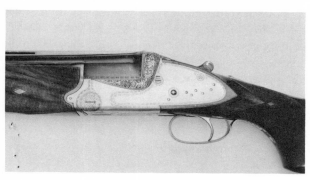

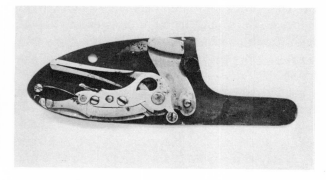

because of the plugging and jamming problem. The introduction of plastic shotshell components helped greatly but extensive design improvement was still required before Remington came up with their now-famous Model 1100. Gas ports were made either larger or more numerous and attempts were made to create a self-cleaning action. Today, efficient gas-operated models are made by Remington, Winchester, Browning and numerous European and Japanese firms.

Next, in order, are side-lock models: a "Novotny, Prague" auto ejector, a "Castellano, Brescia" over and under 20 gauge, an "Aya, Eibar" auto ejector (custom made for Richard Horlacher,) a "Lebeau-Corally, Liege" over and under, an "Antonio Zoli, Gardone" 12 gauge O&U, and, finally, an internal view of a back action side-lock.

DOUBLE BARREL SHOTGUNS

When we speak of side-by-side double guns we are really concerned with only two basic patterns;

the box-lock and the side-lock. Outwardly, these two forms of shotgun action have the same general contours, though there are some differences visible to the eye; internally, they differ considerably. (See accompanying photographs.) One can't rely on outward appearances, however, because it has long been a practice of some gunmakers to dress up a box-lock gun with dummy side plates. This isn't done to mislead anyone (makers invariably describe such guns as a "box-locks") rather, this is done only for decorative purposes.

The side-lock action has long been regarded as the ultimate in double gun designs. It is certainly more costly to produce. The design consists of two separate and detachable side plates mounted behind the standing breech so that they are partially inlettered into the receiver and partially encircled by the stock. Each plate houses the firing mechanism for one barrel and components are often finished in a watchmaker's fashion—highly polished and jewel-indexed. When the simpler and less costly box-lock first appeared, there were some who were quick to find fault with it by claiming it wasn't as strong or as reliable. They pointed to the hammer that protruded from the side of the action (in close proximity to the sharp angle formed by the breech face and bar flats) stating that this weakened the action at its most critical point. They also objected to the extensive channeling of the breech. Nevertheless, the box-lock has survived for more years than I'd care to count and if there's ever been an epidemic of box-lock failures, I've never heard of it. Double guns, of both types, have had to overcome a number of other problems that far overshadow any complaint that can be found in this area. Let's discuss these:

First, double guns of both the side-by-side and over and under types require considerable hand fitting. The design is such that it tends to thwart modern mass-production techniques. For the best possible result, barrels still have to be joined by hand and individually fitted to each frame or receiver. This requires the services of a truly expert gunsmith who devotes hours to the task, painstakingly fitting, filing and testing. The fact that the upright portion of the breech does not lie at perfect right angles to the action bar flats makes the job even more difficult. Then, too, the hinge pin and lugs must be fitted simultaneously if the action is to close up tightly. Hinge pins, incidentally, are subject to considerable wear. Eventually sloppiness is detected in the fit of the barrels to frame and, in extreme cases, a separation appears between the tail surface of the barrels and the flat of the breech face. To correct this, gunsmiths will generally attempt to fit the frame with an oversized hinge pin (refitting the barrel lug to the new pin). At times, when this is not possible, other more costly remedies are required.

When an experienced double gun shooter is examining a used model he'll invariably remove the fore-end, brace the butt against his upper leg, grasp the small of the stock in both hands, and shake the gun vigorously. Any looseness in the fit of barrels to frame is easily detected by this means. On occasion it is also possible to see the slop that has developed in a well used specimen by holding the gun, sidewise, against a light source. A sliver of daylight peering through the breech-and-barrel joint waves the telltale flag. An old friend of mine (an ardent double gun enthusiast) practiced the "paper test." He'd lay a thin piece of paper against the breech face as he closed the barrels. If the barrels locked home, his eyebrows would shoot up and a scowl would darken his countenance. And, if he was subsequently able to slide the paper out of the closed and locked breech, you wouldn't need anyone to translate his acid comments.

English gun makers, who have long been considered the masters of double gun design and fabrication, have experimented with many assorted devices to enhance the double gun's strength and durability. Their first and most obvious step in this direction was to try to eliminate any weakness in the size and contouring of the frame itself— particularly in the area of the near right angle between the action bar flats and the standing breech.

James Purdey's double under lugs, made with rearward-facing squarish recesses, was a substantial improvement over earlier locking systems. A sliding bolt, activated by an elliptically shaped top lever shaft, was made to engage the lug recesses with a slight wedging action which provided a constant solid engagement—one that would tend to draw the barrel flats snugly against the action flats. Any reasonable wear in the mechanism was also cleverly anticipated by the wedge-fit of bolt to lugs so that the shooter would notice only a bit more right-to-left travel of his top lever upon closing. At worst, the top lever would lock up slightly left of center.

This design was created over a hundred years ago and is still found in most modern double guns.

Other gun makers acknowledged the excellence of Purdey's design but still felt that some strong bearing surface was required *above* the axis of the bore to complement the under locks. The famous old firm of Westley-Richards was of this school; their search for a top lock—one that would help contain pressures against the breech face (rather than simply holding the barrels in firing attitude) resulted in their now famous "doll's head extension." At first glance this doesn't look like much —a simple knob at the end of an extended top rib. However, when this is properly fitted to grip the top surface of the breech it is quite effective. Other European gun makers were quick to use it when the original patent expired.

W. W. Greener was on a similar quest when he developed his now famous "Greener cross bolt." He, too, fitted the breech end of the barrels with an extension that homed into a recess at the top of the breech. His extension, however, is square cut and drilled with a round hole through its center. A sliding cross bolt, running horizontally through the upper breech area, is operated by the top lever to engage the hole in the barrel extension. The trick here is to provide a very snug fit between the cross bolt and the hole in the extension —no easy task. Over the years there have been countless doubles made with what appeared to be a "Greener cross bolt" but, lacking any real contact between bolt and extension, such devices served only to impress a poorly informed buyer. With the cross bolt, as Greener makes it, the extension hole is very slightly tapered to accept a similarly tapered bolt. This is the only way the bolt can be made to function reliably in spite of the inevitable erosion through wear.

Interestingly, some gun makers elect to use a square-cut cross bolt, something that never fails to arouse my suspicion; if the round bolt is difficult to fit properly it would seem, to me at least, that the square one would be impossible! The square hole in the extension doesn't sit quite right with me either since the apprentice gunsmith is taught, from the very outset of his metal-shaping lessons, that sharp-cornered right-angle configurations are the most vulnerable. L. C. Smith used a bar-like cross bolt on quite a few models, but this was rounded fore and aft.

Today the shotgunner will find a wide variety of lugs, locks and extensions of assorted sizes and shapes. When examined closely, however, it will be found that virtually all of them are based on the original designs of the old English gun makers.

With over and under guns it will often be found that two barrel extensions are employed, one on each side of the upper barrel. Mechanically the only real difference between an over and under and side-by-side, is the position of the barrels and contouring of the receiver. Otherwise the design features you'll find in the side-by-side are also found in the over and under though somewhat modified to fit a narrower, vertical breech. It makes no sense to separate the two for our purposes here.

(Double gun barrels are covered in the chapter on shotgun barrels so we won't repeat that information here.)

DOUBLE GUN FIRING PINS

Firing pins can be especially troublesome to makers of double guns for a number of reasons: first, rigidly chambered shotshells quickly bear against the firing pin aperture in the face of the breech as the gun is being closed. If a firing pin should project a bit too far (as they sometimes do when poorly designed or installed), a premature discharge can result. Dirt, too, is often responsible for interfering with the movement of a firing pin. Finally, breech designs—particularly in some over and under models—are such that firing pins must be *angled* sharply to strike the center of the shotshell primer. If not done properly, the angled firing pin will wear faster and suffer considerably more damage.

In the cheapest guns, the firing pin is sometimes fitted directly into the face of the hammer and a cross pin is used to retain it. A firing pin so fitted will often have some loose movement which permits it to center easily in whatever channel is provided for its passage. Strangely, some very fine doubles are also made with the firing pin in the hammer, though they are invariably mounted rigidly—oftentimes designed and produced as an integral part of the hammer itself.

Other inexpensive models will simply "float" the firing pin in a hole in the breech so that its tail surface is exposed to the hammer. These are most susceptible to jamming and breakage.

With finer guns, firing pins are invariably made with a light *rebounding spring* that restores the pin to its rearmost rest position.

Finally, in better quality doubles one will find firing pins that are fitted into the action *through the face of the breech*. With these, the firing pin is fitted, tail end first, into a hole in the breech face. Then a light rebounding spring is slipped over the pin and followed by an escutcheon that is *threaded* into the breech face. The center of the escutcheon is drilled through to receive the nose of the pin. Two other small and shallow blind holes—one on each side of the firing pin aperture—accept the spanner wrench that is used to install the escutcheon. This system facilitates replacement of broken or worn firing pins quickly and easily since the entire action doesn't have to be disassembled to get at them. As you've no doubt surmised, most firing pins are installed from the opposite direction, where they require considerable labor to replace.

Careful fitting of replacement firing pins is especially important to the double gun—a job for the experienced gunsmith.

DOUBLE GUN EXTRACTORS AND EJECTORS

Double gun terminology may be a bit confusing to the newcomer so we had better start by defining the terms used by the firearms trade to describe the assorted devices employed for the removal of fired cases.

Extractors—the simplest form of chamber emptying device—partially withdraws *both* hulls from their chambers as the gun is opened, whether or not the cases have been fired. Removal is completed by hand.

Ejectors—forcefully expel both chambered shells each time the gun is opened, again, whether or not the shells have been fired! Sometimes referred to as an "automatic ejector" or "non-selective automatic ejector."

Selective Automatic Ejectors—a device that

Selective automatic ejection—note fired shell in the air at point of arrow. The unfired shell remains in the lower chamber of the gun and is only partially extracted.

forcefully ejects *fired* hulls but which simply extracts *unfired* shells so that they may be removed by hand.

Extractor mechanisms are found in the least expensive break-open type guns, including the single-barrel, single-shot models. Ejectors are a bit more complicated and more costly. Selective automatic ejectors, understandably, run to even greater expense.

As a result of the dramatic growth in the practice of handloading, some makers of fine target-class shotguns have advertised a form of delayed selective ejector that permits manual extraction of empty hulls if so desired. Retrieval of fired hulls

from a conventional ejector model is not difficult, however, because the shooter instinctively learns to cup his free hand over the opening breech. At least one maker, too, is offering an over and under gun with a selector device on the side of the frame that permits the shooter to choose between an extracting or an ejecting function.

In side-by-side double guns, extractors and ejectors are operated by push rods that are channeled between the barrels into the knuckle area. While extractors generally require only a camming surface in the knuckle, ejectors—especially selective ejectors—are invariably operated by an elaborate mechanical assembly partially housed in the fore-end. With over and under models the push rods are most often positioned on the sides of the barrels.

COMBINATION GUNS

Designs for combination guns having rifle *and* shotgun barrels (often more than two) are really based on standard double gun patterns modified to accommodate the added bores. The variations encountered in these elaborate mechanisms are virtually unlimited so it is impossible to describe them in detail here, nor would such an attempt serve any useful purpose.

TRIGGERS

The trigger mechanism of a double gun often makes or breaks its potential sale, and gun makers are painfully aware of the fact. No other facet of

Remington's Model 3200 over and under has selective automatic ejectors.

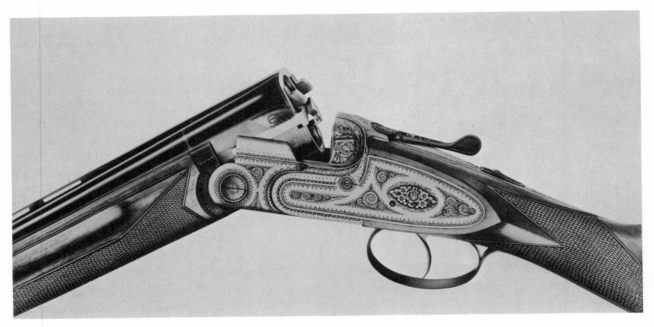

A high grade Beretta (Model S02) over and under with a selective single trigger.

the double is so acutely dependent upon the whim or fancy of the individual shooter and for this reason a survey of ten different models will usually turn up ten completely different mechanisms. There's only one way to tackle a question as complex as this so let's start at the beginning:

The Double Trigger—is the simplest, least expensive and most reliable of trigger designs, but any firearms marketing man who would attempt to sell a quality shotgun so equipped on the American market would soon find himself pounding the pavements with the want ads under his arm.

Double trigger units consist of two completely independent firing mechanisms—two sears, springs, levers, etc.—rarely will both malfunction at the same time. On the minus side, they require considerable spacing between the trigger levers to facilitate movement of the trigger finger. Consequently, the trigger guard itself is a bit oversize. Another common fault is that there is no real

uniformity to the two trigger actions, or pulling weights.

In combination guns having three or more barrels, two triggers are the rule rather than the exception. Sometimes one trigger operates both shotshell barrels and the second trigger—the rifle barrel. At other times one shot barrel is fired by each trigger and the rifle barrel, or barrels, only come into play when a selector button is activated.

The Non-Selective Single Trigger—is another very reliable form of firing apparatus but since it unvaryingly fires the barrels in the same sequence (open choke first, tighter choke second), it has little appeal among American shooters. This one is so rarely encountered in our market that anyone desiring it would probably have to search for a cooperative distributor to handle his special order.

The Selective Single-Trigger—this is the "king of the realm"—90% of the doubles sold on the U.S. market are equipped with one and, while they often look alike, there is little similarity under the surface.

The selective single trigger is tricky and damnably difficult of manufacture: its presence in a given model is therefore certain to be reflected in costs. For one thing, until recently, the selective single trigger was traditionally designed with an "inertia block," a delicately balanced device that is operated by the recoil of the first shot to set up the sear engagement for the second. With such a trigger the firing-sequence selector serves only to determine which barrel is to fire first.

When testing the inertia block single trigger, the selector is set and the trigger activated to snap (on an empty chamber or snap-cap.) The gun *should refuse* to snap on a second pull of the trigger. A sharp blow, delivered to the butt of the gun by the open hand, should then set up the inertia block for the second shot.

Even the best of designs, assembled and fitted by the most expert craftsmen, does not assure reliability in the inertia block system. This is an exceedingly difficult mechanism to produce and it is one that is inherently trouble prone. Happily, it appears that gun makers have scored a breakthrough in this area in recent years. A purely *mechanical* selective single trigger is contained in Remington's new Model 3200, and—while I haven't had an opportunity to disassemble one of their models—I suspect that Krieghoff's Model 32 also has a mechanical unit. These would have to be more efficient and reliable than the inertia block trigger.

Some selective single triggers are made with selectors that are combined with the sliding tang safety; when moved from the "safe" to the "fire" position, the safety can be swiveled right or left to set the trigger for the desired firing sequence. Others are built into the trigger area where a laterally-operated button determines the firing order. Selectors will also be found behind the trigger itself operating with a forth or back movement, and then, too, there are some mounted on the tang, designed to operate in a "U" track. Krieghoff's selector lies in front of the trigger and consists of a simple lever that pivots from one side to the other.

A recent innovation found among expensive custom-class over and unders is the interchangeable trigger which offers the shooter a variety of types and pulling weights.

THE RELEASE TRIGGER

Though not especially common to any single type of shotgun, there is another unusual form of trigger that is encountered with increasing frequency, especially on the trap field, and I mention it only for safety's sake: this is a gadget called the "release trigger." With this, a normal rearward pull on the trigger lever *does not fire the gun*. Instead, the shot falls as the trigger is released! Why?—because some target shooters feel that it helps them to overcome a flinching problem or that it corrects their natural tendency to yank on the trigger (disturbing the aim). If someone competes regularly he can no doubt get accustomed to this form of trigger but this old conservative takes a dim view of the theory; I don't like the device for rather obvious reasons!

SHOTGUN SAFETIES

Little has to be said on this subject because safety devices are rather obvious, even to the novice.

I mention them only to call attention to some special safety devices that are useful in special circumstances. For example, the left-hander will have no difficulty with the sliding tang safety typical of double guns. On the other hand, with a pump or automatic he'll often find that the push button safety (generally located in the trigger guard) operates in the wrong direction—the process of moving it from the "safe" to the "fire" position is awkward. To overcome this objection, some gun makers design safeties that are reversible—simply ask your local gunsmith to turn it around. Williams Gun Sight Co. makes left-hand safety devices for many irreversible models and the local dealer often has these in stock.

Some shooters object to the small safety buttons found in some pumps and autos, because—they claim—they're hard to locate especially with the gloved finger. Again, the Williams Giant-head safety will eliminate the problem. These can be had for right-hand operation as well as left!

CHAPTER 3

The Shotgun Stock

The shotgun stock is considerably more than simply a handle with which to hold the gun; accuracy and performance are largely determined by the way it is designed and fitted to the shooter. As you will discover later, in the chapter on wingshooting, we are concerned with an *exacting* fit of the stock so we'll discuss the fitting process first before going on to cover designs.

The shotgun must be fitted so that, when properly shouldered, it will automatically come into alignment, pointing as naturally as the extended finger. This takes a lot of doing! A shooter's general build, height and weight, arm length, neck size and length, facial shape and even the clothing he wears, influence gun fit.

To a lesser extent, the shooting stance or style may have something to do with this, even though it shouldn't.

The first step in fitting a shotgun, surprisingly, is for the shooter to decide which shoulder he will shoot from; the obvious answer doesn't always apply because it is possible to be right-handed and left eyed, or vice-versa. One eye invariably dominates an individual's vision and the shooter must ascertain which eye that is! With both eyes open, carefully aim a pencil, or your finger, at a selected target about 15 to 20 feet away. Hold the aim as steadily as possible: now close your left eye. If the aim remains true, if the pencil is still pointing directly at the selected target, you're right eyed and should be shooting from the right shoulder. If, on the other hand, upon closing the left eye, the pencil or finger suddenly seems to shift so that it appears to be pointing about two feet to the left of the target, you're *left eyed*—and should be shooting from the left shoulder. Try it again, to make sure!

If your dominant or master eye matches your dominant hand, you're in good shape and can simply go on from there. However, if you discover that you're left eyed and right-handed (or vice-versa) you've got a serious problem. One can't shoot well from the weak-eye side. This is because wingshooting is best accomplished *with both eyes open*. The triangulation effect of two-eyed shooting aids depth perception, facilitates tracking, improves the target speed read-out and flight-path data that is being fed to the brain. The best advice I can give the shooter with an eye problem is to learn to shoot from the opposite shoulder—the one that matches the dominant eye. This is difficult but not impossible. Those who can't adapt to the switch have only one other alternative and that is to wear a patch over their master eye. They simply

Bob Brownell's Pull and Drop Gauge is a handy tool for measuring stock lengths and drops.

won't have a chance if they try to line the gun up under the weak eye with both eyes open—they'll see more of the side of the barrel than they will of the top surface.

Having decided which shoulder to shoot from, the next step is to fit the stock to the shooter. This is not an easy task because several critical dimensions must be determined—specifically: length of pull, cast-off, drop of comb, drop of heel, and pitch.

By far, the best way to gather this information is to visit a good custom gun house where a "Try Gun" is employed for fitting purposes. Try Guns are very costly gun maker's tools designed with fully adjustable stock components. Most are non-firing pieces but some—extremely costly—are shootable and fitting-while-shooting would be the preferred method.

Years ago, when I first started to develop a real interest in the shotgun sports I wasn't overly concerned with any detail of stock fit other than length of pull. Then, one day, I had the good fortune to visit Holland & Holland's famous Shooting School in the outskirts of London. There, a man by the name of Rex Gage put me through a short course with a shooting Try Gun. Before I left he made a record of my measurements (for Holland & Holland's file) and gave me a copy. Shortly thereafter, I had a customized trap gun stock built for

me by Frank Pachmayr—the famous Los Angeles custom gun maker. Frank followed the H & H dimensions (except for the usual trap gun modifications) and, when the finished gun arrived, I promptly entered a trap competition with it—and didn't miss a bird! You can bet your faithful old bird dog that I've been fussy about *all* stock dimensions ever since!

For those who can't locate a custom gun shop equipped with Try Gun, there are other ways to arrive at these stock dimensions. Such methods are a bit slower and involve a lot of trial and error but, if supervised by a knowledgeable gun man the resultant measurements would be just as valid as those taken from a Try Gun.

LENGTH OF PULL

This is the measurement taken from the center of the butt plate to the center of the trigger. (With double-trigger guns, use the forwardmost trigger.)

Most production-line shotgun stocks are made with a length of pull approximating fourteen inches. These will fit most shooters of average build, i.e. 5′ 10″ tall, 160 to 175 lbs.

To get this measurement one needs only a yard-stick or an 18″ ruler. Stand erect with the shooting hand hanging naturally at the side. Now, while maintaining the upper arm in the relaxed vertical position, bend the elbow until the forearm is at right angles to the upper arm. Turn the palm up with the fingers extended. Lay the ruler on top of the forearm and measure from the joint at the elbow to the first joint of the trigger finger. Subtract about ¼ to ⅜ of an inch from this dimension and you'll probably have the right length of pull for you! (The thickness of your shooting clothing can influence this measurement so be sure to wear the appropriate outer garments.) I say "probably" because adjustments in this dimension are sometimes dictated by the length of the shooter's neck: a long neck would require a slightly longer stock, and vice-versa.

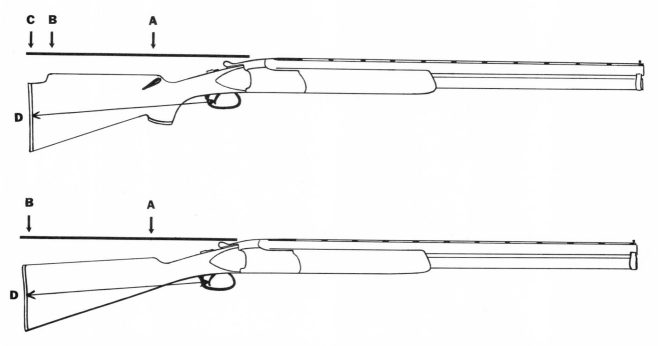

Length of pull ("D" in diagrams) is the most critical dimension in stock fitting. Comb dimensions are next most important. Assuming tne sight line is continued at the same level over the buttstock, in the above diagrams "A" shows where the measurement is taken for "drop at comb," "B" represents the location for "drop at heel," and "C" indicates the position for measuring "drop at Monte Carlo."

Models containing more than one trigger have length of pull dimension determined from the leading, or forwardmost, trigger.

Some shooters would also be fussy about the grip location in pistol grip stocks, furnishing a measurement for the spacing between the bottom-leading edge of the grip to the center of the trigger. (Note that lower diagram illustrates an English-style straight grip stock.)

DROP AT COMB

The accompanying diagram shows at a glance, how this measurement is taken to indicate the level of the comb below the sight level of the gun.

When the gun is properly mounted and cheeked, the shooting or aiming eye should be approximately one-half to one inch behind the leading edge of the comb. If it is not, the length of pull is incorrect! Assuming that question had been resolved, let's go on:

Assume a good shooting stance and mount the gun by tucking the butt under the armpit and subsequently sliding it up into the hollow of the shoulder. Aim at a selected target and cheek the stock firmly. It's best to close your eyes when doing this so that you won't adjust for improper sight alignment. Maintain the position of your head and open your eyes. What do you see?

You *should* see only the center of the top of the receiver with the front sight centered above it.

With a ribbed barrel it is also acceptable to see just a trace of the rib.

When only the tail surface of the receiver falls into view, the comb on that particular stock is too low. If, on the other hand, you can see a large portion of the rib, or top surface of the barrel, the comb is too high.

Most specialty gun shops sell comb pads having adhesive backings. These come in assorted thicknesses and are easily fastened to the stock to compensate for a slightly low comb. When the required adjustment exceeds ⅜ of an inch, there's little choice but to discard the stock or have a gunsmith add an unsightly block to the existing one.

When the comb is too high, it is much easier to correct by simply planing the *entire* top surface, rounding the edges carefully and sanding. Any removal of stock material, however, should be done cautiously, cutting only a fraction of an inch at a time and testing each cut carefully to avoid overdoing it. Be sure to round the edges. Stop cutting a whisker or two before reaching the desired level to allow for the material that will be lost in finish sanding.

The drop-at-comb dimension is very important so don't handle this question nonchalantly; work at it, until you're absolutely sure of the measurement required for *you!*

Production line field models are generally made with a 1⅝-inch drop at comb, to fit the average shooter. With skeet models the drop is generally 1½ inches. Trap guns have the highest combs, measuring barely 1⅜ to 1 ⁷/₁₆ inches. If you come up with a dimension that differs greatly from these figures, the chances are you're doing something wrong—unless, of course, you have some unusual physical proportions.

DROP AT HEEL

When in a shooting attitude, the sighting eye will naturally seek a position somewhat higher than the level of the shoulder pocket receiving the butt of the gun. For this reason the stock is designed to angle slightly downward from the grip area. When a straight edge is laid along the line of sight and subsequently compared to the line of the comb, this down slope is immediately apparent.

Earlier we discussed the drop at comb and thereby arrived at the starting point; if we now measure from the line of sight to the rearmost level of the comb, we will find the "drop at heel." (See illustrations.)

There is a very subtle relationship between the heel and comb measurements that is sometimes overlooked by those fitting stocks, so some care must be given this detail, especially when transferring dimensions from one stock to another. For example: the sighting eye is never positioned directly over the leading edge of the comb (the point from which the measurement is taken) instead, it is located slightly to the rear of that point. If the second dimension, the drop at heel, differs appreciably from that of the test gun, it stands to reason that the comb angle will change and the relationship of the eye position to the line of sight will be ever so slightly affected. Similarly, variations in stock length will alter the angle causing difficulty even when comb and heel drops are identical.

It is important, when fitting stocks, to first accurately measure the length of pull and to keep this dimension constant throughout the fitting process. Also, that casual changes are not made in the drop at heel without testing their effect on the comb and eye position.

There is another way to get around trouble in this area, a method that target shooters frequently employ: it's called the Monte Carlo stock. I would not, however, recommend this solution to the hunter because it often creates other problems.

The true Monte Carlo stock has a comb line that is perfectly parallel to the line of sight. In theory, no matter where the shooter positions his eye over such a comb, he will achieve a proper sight picture. To compensate for the difference between the levels of the eye and shoulder, the stock is simply relieved in the butt area. This results in a rather decorative scoop or cut out in the tail section of the comb. Unfortunately, this decorative quality has led to some misinterpretation of the meaning and purpose of the Monte Carlo design. Very often one will find *apparent*

Monte Carlo stocks having combs that do not parallel their lines of sight. On shotguns such stocks are next to useless unless accompanied by a cheek piece. (Though they can often be employed advantageously on rifles.)

Generally, on non-custom guns the drop at heel dimension will be one inch greater than the comb measurement. If the comb measurement is 1½ inches, for example, the heel dimension will approximate 2½ inches. Whenever a fitter comes up with a heel dimension that differs greatly from this one-inch standard, the dimension should be re-checked.

CAST-OFF, CAST-ON

This particular facet of stock fitting is something of an enigma but, before we go on to explain that, we had better define these terms: a "cast" is the angle traced by the center line of a stock *when it angles away from the center line of the barrel or barrels*. If this stock line tends to point toward your right shoulder, as the gun is sighted, the stock is "cast-off" for a right-hand shooter. If it angles in the opposite direction, it's "cast-on" for a left-hander. The intent is simply to facilitate the positioning of the shooter's eye so that it aligns properly behind the front sight when the stock is correctly cheeked.

It is a popular belief that all shotgun stocks have some degree of cast. Actually, most American guns have no cast whatsoever—they're perfectly straight! The need for a "cast" is really dictated by the shape or design of a given stock and/or the peculiar requirements of a shooter who has some unusual physical quality—one that demands consideration.

Cast can be determined by centering one side of a straight edge over the middle of a shotgun barrel (or barrels) so that a large section of it will overhang the stock. By sighting along the straight edge one can compare it with the center line of the stock and estimate the extent of cast, if such is present.

Most stocks for field guns have a decided sidewall taper which is narrow at the grip and flaring towards the butt. Such stocks really don't have to be cast to fit the average shooter if they have sufficient drop and slender combs.

When the comb is broadened (for shooting comfort) or when a cheek piece is added, some cast is generally required. Thus, the question is to determine whether or not a cast is desirable and, if so, how much?

For most facial shapes and neck sizes the average stock can range from straight to a cast of ⅛ of an inch. However, those with very prominent cheek bones, or heavy broad faces, or short stout necks, may need considerably more cast in order to align the shooting eye over the axis of the bore.

When cast-off is inadequate, the right-handed shooter will tend to shoot to the left of his target. Too much cast-off will cause him to shoot to the right. With cast-on, for a left-handed shooter, the opposite would apply.

While the individual shooter can, without assistance, do a creditable job of determining length of pull, measurements for cast, drop and pitch should only be attempted with the help of one who is well versed in the technique of gun fitting. Nevertheless, we'll go on to demonstrate some of the improvised methods that can be substituted for Try Gun fitting.

While stock dimensions should remain fairly constant from one gun to another, regardless of type (double, pump, automatic, etc.) there is one peculiarity I've found common to improvised measuring methods: it's often possible to come up with differing dimensions when changing from one type of shotgun to another. Consequently, it is strongly recommended that one work with a pump gun if that is the type of gun one is attempting to fit. Select a specimen having a length of pull closely approximating your own requirements.

Stand with the feet fairly close together, heels about ten inches apart, and face about thirty degrees to the right of an imaginary target some twenty yards distant (if you are a right-handed shooter). Tuck the butt under the appropriate armpit while gripping the stock in a shooting attitude. Concentrate your attention on the target. Next, without moving your head, close your eyes and shoulder the gun by sliding it out, up and back, into the hollow of the shoulder pocket. Try to point it directly at your imaginery target while your eyes are closed. When the gun is properly cheeked, open your eyes and carefully note where the muzzle bears in relation to your selected target. Guard against the natural tendency to do some sight-aligning as you open your eyes. If the gun points to one side of the target, you want to know *where* it's pointing. Repeat this test three or four times to make sure you're coming up with the same answer consistently.

After making sure that the gun is unloaded, one experienced in gun fitting will often ask you to point the gun at him so he can sight back over the front sight to determine the position of your aiming eye. Working alone, you can sight into a mirror and come up with some fairly valid observations.

Okay, suppose you've determined that your lateral alignment is poor. What then?

Recheck the drop at comb that we described earlier and decide whether or not a change in comb height was overlooked. When the comb is too high it tends to make one believe that some cast is required. A comb that is too low can encourage one to think that he's working with a stock that has too much cast. *Finally,* make sure you are cheeking the gun correctly—that you're not canting your head over the comb in an exaggerated fashion.

When satisfied that it's the cast that needs modification, you have only three alternatives: one, test other guns until you find one that fits and have that stock measured by a professional gunsmith for catalog comparisons; two, determine that the extra cast required is a very small one that can be accomplished by simply slimming the stock through the cheek area; or finally, having determined that you need a major change, visit a professional and have a stock custom made. Of course, if you find a stock with too much cast, there's little that can be done with it, other than building up the side wall of the stock via laminating or simply having a new stock made.

The custom-made stock, obviously, can be exceedingly costly.

For whatever it's worth, in my twenty-five years of experience in the firearms field I've only come across three individuals who had to have radically cast-off stocks. Two of these men had necks the thickness of telephone poles!—the third had unusually large and protruding cheek bones!

Ninety-nine times out of a hundred, shooters asking for cast stocks have impossible shooting stances. With proper gun mounting and a reasonable shooting stance problems seem to melt away.

For the benefit of those who are inclined to practice a little home gunsmithing, I have some special words of wisdom: small, almost insignificant changes in stock dimensions result in dramatic differences in the way a gun points. Work slowly! When removing material do so by degrees and test repeatedly to make sure you're not cutting away too much.

PITCH

When referring to this some prefer to use the more complete expression, "pitch down;" but, however you refer to it, pitch is the dimension determined by the angle of the butt and relates to the position of the muzzle when the stock is comfortably shouldered.

(The accompanying illustration reveals how the pitch is measured *at the muzzle.*)

The physical characteristics of the individual shooter and, to a lesser extent, his peculiar shooting style or stance, dictate the amount of pitch required. Target shooting pitch, too, will often vary from that which is required for hunting purposes. For this reason the same shooter may have a field gun with a 3-inch pitch and a trap pitched less than half as much. Barrel length, too, gets into the act here because the difference between a 26-inch barrel and 30-inch barrel is rather obvious. One can't measure a 26-inch barrel and apply the resultant dimension to a new 30 incher.

Go back to your imaginery target to determine pitch. Working with a stock having the proper length of pull, mount the gun with both eyes closed. Then, when in a comfortable aiming attitude, open your sighting eye and see where the gun tends to point—high, low or on target. (Lateral deviation was discussed earlier when we covered cast-off, cast-on.) If the gun tends to point too high, it doesn't have enough pitch; too low, and it needs less. In either case, determine how much the muzzle would have to be moved to bring it on target. Then have the butt cut and the plate remounted. If considerable material is lost via the cutting process, there's little alternative but to install a recoil pad and/or spacers. It is for this reason that I dislike the practice of offering shotguns with factory fitted recoil pads. What happens to the poor guy who needs more length of pull or a drastically different pitch? It's easy to cut material away and doggone difficult to add. The factory pad indicates the stock has already been shortened and this will often rob the shooter of the ability to economically custom fit his stock.

Once you've come up with a desirable pitch dimension make up a small block of wood of the appropriate thickness and a second block about 2-inches thick and 6-inches long having parallel side surfaces. Then, with the aid of an assistant, stand the shotgun vertically against a wall with the butt

If the butt of the gun is placed flat on the floor, and the shotgun located against a vertical wall so that the topmost point of the receiver makes contact, the "pitch" can be determined by measuring the distance between the muzzle and the wall at point "A.'

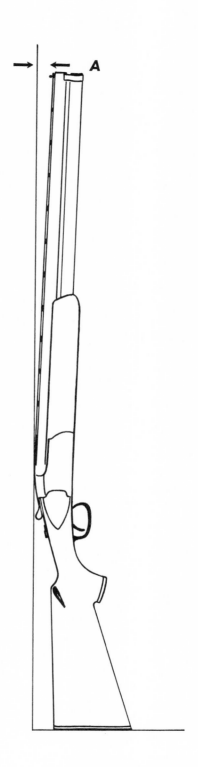

in firm contact with the floor and the highest point of the receiver in contact with the wall. (See illustration.) Next, place the first small spacer block between the muzzle and the wall, tipping the gun slightly to wedge the block against the wall.

Now, make sure that the highest point of the receiver is still in contact with the wall when the spacer block is in place. This should cause one point of the butt to lift off the floor (the toe, if you're reducing pitch; the heel, if pitch is to be increased).

Your assistant now lays the 2″ × 6″ block flat on the floor, alongside the butt of the stock. With a grease pencil, he draws a line on the stock, parallel to the top surface of the block. This, now, indicates the desired *angle* of the butt. *It does not, however, indicate proper length of pull.*

The next step, obviously, is to measure for length of pull, placing a dot in the center of the stock side panel. Transfer the desired angle, from the line drawn earlier, by means of a flexible plastic rule having parallel sides.

If the stock will prove too short when cut to the new angle, the only logical solution is to fit a recoil pad or spacer. Measure the thickness of the pad, subtract that dimension from the length desired, mark the stock, transfer the angle line, and you're ready to cut the butt.

This business of pitch can be confusing to the novice so I strongly suggest that the newcomer enlist the professional aid of a competent gunsmith.

Those who believe they are capable of handling the fitting on their own would be wise to test new pitch angles before putting blade to wood. Remove the butt plate and insert a makeshift spacer block under the appropriate point; fasten the plate and spacer to the stock with masking tape and try the new angle.

Bear in mind that a zero pitch factor exists when the front sight and the high point of the receiver are in contact with the wall while the butt is bearing flat against the floor. If the *heel* of the butt

were raised off the floor when the other two reference points were in contact, you'd be dealing with a *reverse* pitch—a most unnatural condition that is to be avoided at all cost.

As a rule of thumb, pitch should rarely measure less than one inch, nor more than three! Keep this in mind and, by maintaining a dimension within that range, you won't go far wrong. While there are some exceptions to the rule, even small deviations from the standard are very, very seldom encountered.

FOREARM DESIGN

Some shooters attach a great deal of significance to the shape of their fore-ends. My own experience, however, has indicated that there is little need for extraordinary consideration of this detail. The primary concern, here, is to have a fore-end of a size and shape that complements the lines of the gun and one that satisfactorily contributes to overall balance.

Long-armed English shotgunners commonly employ a hard leather sleeve for fore-grip purposes. This is moulded in a broad "U" pattern and simply slides over the barrels of the double gun, providing a gripping area in front of the normal wooden fore-end. Such shooters don't use the wooden grip at all! This should tell us something about the importance of forearm shapes and sizes.

Pumps and automatics generally come through with forearms of generous proportions because of their magazine tube construction. Balance is good and there is little cause for complaint. Over and under guns are likewise unique and can easily be fitted with forearms of varying size. The controversy centers around the side-by-side double gun. Americans dislike the English style splinter design; they contend it's too small—an inadequate handle. The semi-beavertail and full beavertail designs are more to American tastes. Actually, forearm design should be dictated by the balance requirements and intended purpose of a specific gun, not by any arbitrary aesthetic thinking. To my mind, it's foolhardy to equip a light upland bird gun with a cumbersome beavertail forearm. This would prove self-defeating because speed and maneuverability suffers. Such a gun should really be made with a light, slim, straight-grip English style stock and splinter forearm. If you've never tried one of these in the field, don't laugh—they're a pleasure to handle, especially in the smaller gauges.

Beavertail fore-ends are more appropriately mounted on heavy magnum class shotguns or on those pieces specifically designed for target shooting. I'd never accept one on a general purpose field gun.

In short, don't think of the forearm as a handle, more appropriately it's a simple forehand platform.

STOCK DESIGN

We've pretty much covered the importance of stock dimensions earlier in this chapter while discussing stock fittings. It follows, that under the limitations of dimensional needs, designs are highly restricted. Thus, we have flexibility in only two areas: Cheek pieces—most shooters feel that these are intended to provide a comfortable resting place for the cheek. In reality, they are designed to facilitate the unvarying placement of the cheek so that sighting-eye position remains constant from shot to shot. Cheek pieces are truly effective only when they are custom fitted to the individual shooter and then only when intended for use on a target shotgun. In the field, where gun handling is not so premeditated, they often cause trouble because they cannot be cheeked as indiscriminately as a straight-walled stock.

The Europeans, especially the Germans and Austrians, favor small cheek pieces but they shoot differently, with their heads erect, rendering our objections invalid.

GRIPS—one would assume that there exists a great variety of these but the entire selection can be reduced to four basic patterns: straight (English) grip, semi-pistol grip, full pistol grip, and target grip.

Some complain that the straight grip is awkward. However, where speed and maneuverability are criterions, it's hard to beat.

The semi-pistol grip is sometimes referred to as a "modified" grip. It's neither fish nor fowl, lying somewhere between the straight grip and the full pistol grip. To some, this pattern serves to eliminate the awkwardness of the straight grip but I think this is just wishful thinking. Hand position is really not altered to the point where one would detect it. The full pistol grip is something else again. This one positions the trigger hand comfortably and locates the trigger finger ideally for a near straight-back pull. The problem lies in the fact that the full pistol grip makes for a rather large and heavy buttstock. The shotgun would have to provide enough front end weight to yield proper balance. Overall weight would, of course, be a shade on the heavy side. The full pistol grip is perfectly suited to target and waterfowl guns. Light weight is too highly valued in a general field gun to be so compromised, yet there are some who don't seem to mind it and opt for the big grip without reluctance.

I hesitated to bring up the target grip because these are really custom versions designed to accommodate the whims of the individual shooter. Some are very elaborate and at times, grotesque. There's really little need for anything other than a conventional full pistol grip on a target stock in spite of the fact that some shooters insist upon near 90° grip angles, thumbrests, Wundhammer swells, etc., etc. If the truth were known, I'd bet most would do as well, and perhaps, better, with a less extravagant grip.

Insofar as grip construction is concerned, elaborate grip endings are easily damaged if not capped by a separate durable material. Flared

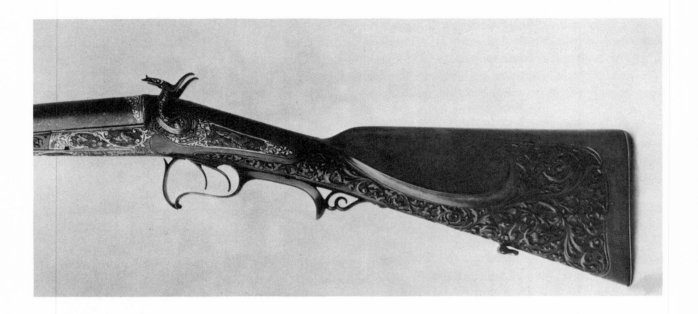

A pin fire double barrel shotgun based on the Le-Faucheux system made by Springer Erben of Vienna. (Photo, courtesy of Deutsches Waffen Journal)

grip ends are especially vulnerable. The simpler the lines, the better. The rounded-end semi-pistol grip is often looked upon with disdain by Americans, but there's something to be said for such a shape—it can certainly take more punishment than a non-capped design utilizing sharp or flared edges.

CHECKERING, CARVING

For many years all but the least expensive shotguns were produced with hand-checkered panels on their grips and fore-ends. Today, costs have gotten so out of hand that a pattern cut in the traditional fashion would add something close to one hundred dollars to the cost of a given gun. Manufacturers have been forced to look for alternatives to the slow, hand-produced job and impressed machine checkering has resulted. First attempts

in this direction were, admittedly, rather crude until firearms engineers had a chance to refine their equipment. Now, they've developed such a high degree of sophistication in this area that impressed checkering is often more attractive and flaw free. Not only that, but they've found it possible to introduce decorative little touches (resembling carving) to impressed patterns. Unless one is prepared to pay for a genuine hand-checkered job, there's little sense in complaining about stamped checkering. Bear in mind that a two hundred dollar shotgun would cost you 50% more if you insisted upon having the original checkering job. Don't look for it on any model retailing for less than $500.00—it's simply not practical to employ it on less costly specimens.

When you do spring for a deluxe job flaunting hand-checkered surfaces, examine the checkering carefully. Diamonds should be uniform, sharply pointed and neatly shaped. There should be no "run-overs" at the edge of the pattern. Lines should be perfectly parallel and cut to a uniform depth.

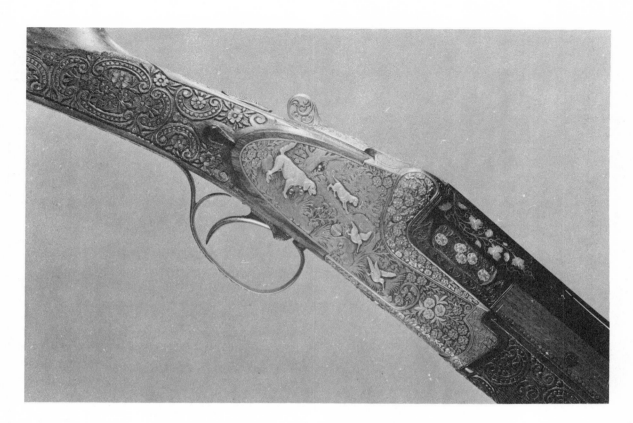

A high quality over and under shotgun with a beautifully hand-carved stock, apparently made for a feminine shooter. (Photo, courtesy of Richard Horlacher.)

WOODS

Shotgun stocks are generally made from walnut: American guns from American black walnut and European models from a great variety of woods stemming from the English walnut tree. There's really no qualitative differentiation to be derived from the terms "French walnut," "Circassion walnut," etc., etc. They're the same tree, only their geography differs. Some believe that European walnuts are denser, more closely grained than ours. Assuming this is true, it would only seriously concern the hand checkerer—fine checkering patterns (22 lines to the inch, or more) cannot be cut attractively in coarse grained woods.

Structurally, differences are otherwise relatively insignificant.

Because most shotguns are made with two separate wooden components (buttstock and fore-end) an occasional model will turn up with mismatched pairs. Compare fore-ends and buttstocks for color and grain when making a new purchase.

Straight, plain grained, woods are the most stable and most durable. Surface flaws plague the seeker of fancy-grained stocks and gun makers are forced to do some rather tedious filling and touch up work to make these presentable.

Laminated stocks, usually consisting of a mix of light and dark woods, are considered ugly by most in spite of the fact that they've been proven strong, durable and stable.

With some inexpensive "popularly priced" models, beech wood is substituted for walnut, particu-

Production models today are machine inletted and shaped. This is a tape-controlled inletting machine working a stock at the Savage Arms plant.

larly in the smaller gauges. Color and grain may not be too satisfying but beech wood components are acceptable in most other respects.

STOCK FINISHES

Manufacturers find it difficult to market the plain, old, garden-variety dull oil finish. They've had to come up with slicker, glossy finishes to sat-

isfy current market tastes. Only the epoxies have proven acceptably durable in this pursuit. If you've ever tried to repair a damaged epoxy finish you'll understand why I prefer the traditional oil. With a few extra home-workshop applications and a little elbow grease, one can build a fairly attractive velvet gloss from a dull oil start.

RECOIL PADS

A recoil pad is used to replace the customary hard rubber or plastic butt plate for one of two reasons—recoil is objectionable or the shooter

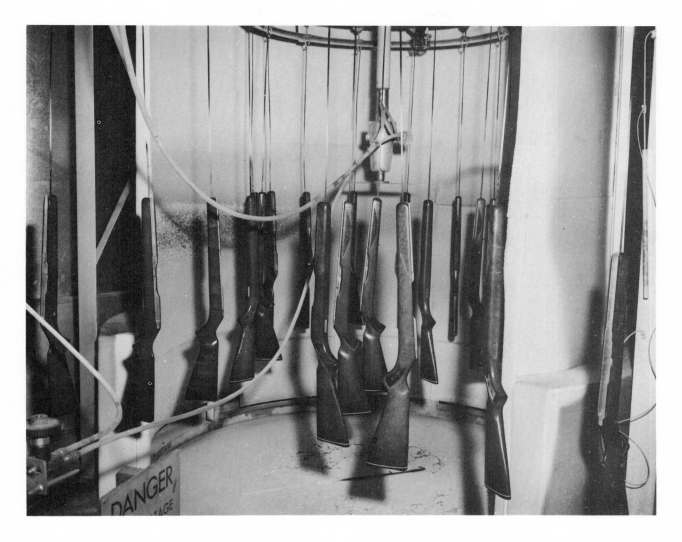

The new Savage Arms stock finishing system: The prepared stock passes through a chamber where the finish, charged with 16,000 volts, is spun off a disk, forming a mist that penetrates the wood pores, giving it an even, deep, protective coating. It is then baked for a lustrous, durable finish.

requires some added length in the buttstock. The variety of types and sizes available are almost unlimited: choices range from half-inch thick solid rubber pads to some measuring over an inch in thickness.

Special purpose pads are also available for skeet and trap shooting. Some, too, are made with goat skin coverings so that they'll slide easily into position against the resistance of the clothing. The broad variety manufactured by Pachmayr Gun Works will be found in most specialty gun shops.

Installing a pad properly is something of an art. Stocks come in such a great variety of shapes and sizes that pads are made oversized and fitted to the individual piece. If the value of the gun is not to be impaired, this work should be done professionally:

Baked and finished Savage stocks heading for the final assembly area.

most gunsmiths will charge from $10.00 to $15.00 for the job and tailor the length of pull and pitch to the shooter in the bargain. For those who are talented in the use of hand tools, we have included step-by-step instructions for pad installations in the gunsmithing chapter of this book.

STOCK MAINTENANCE

The wooden components of a shotgun must be cared for as diligently as the metal. Oil finished stocks should be rubbed down before and after each outing with boiled linseed oil. (G-B's Linspeed Oil is specifically designed for stock finishing and maintenance.) Stocks finished by other means (including epoxies) should be coated with a good grade of paste wax and buffed to a nice sheen.

All gunstocks are designed to carry a small moisture content of about 8 to 10%. If they are stored for any length of time in a drier atmosphere, they'll shrink a bit and this can lead to small cracks and eventual splitting. By the same token, stocks will swell when exposed to moisture-laden atmospheres, resulting in swelling which can also cause cracks.

With each new firearm, rifle or shotgun, it pays to check the stock carefully before taking it out in the field. If either swelling or shrinking is apparent, it would be best to consult a local gunsmith so that appropriate adjustments can be made to prevent subsequent damage.

No matter how well a stock is sealed and finished, some interchange of atmospheres is inevitable. A hot-air heating system in the home, for instance, will tend to dry out a gunstock causing it to shrink. A humidifier added to such a system will do much to prevent trouble.

Stocks designed with a longitudinal stock bolt should be carefully hand tightened before the start of each shooting season and checked periodically as the season progresses. Automatics and pumps are usually made with such a stock bolt.

Side by side and over and under guns can create headaches in this area because their stocks are often intricately fitted. Side lock models are especially troublesome. With these, an early trip to the gunsmith is in order: ask him to coat interior surfaces with a thinned epoxy.

Any form of damage to a buttstock or forearm (nicks, gouges, scratches, dents, etc.) should be repaired immediately. These minor faults eventually develop into major problems if ignored.

CHAPTER 4

The Shotshell

So much emphasis is placed on the primary tool of scattergunning—the shotgun—that one tends to overlook the total contribution of the second essential component—the shell! Yet, one is as important as the other, and, in the end, it is *only* the careful mating of the shell with the firearm that assures consistently good performance.

Here we will attempt to avoid boring our readers with a lot of dull history by offering only the most pertinent details in the evolution of the shotshell. The sketchy history we do present is intended only to demonstrate how and why components have arrived at their present state:

The earliest form of scattergun dates back centuries to the time when grape shot was employed in cannon-like devices and, except for technological developments that raised the levels of component-sophistication, little was done to change the basic composition of the shotload: great-grandpappy stuffed his fowling pieces much the same way the cannoneers did in the fifteenth century—a priming charge, propellant charge, wad, shot and over-shot wad or seal.

Then, in the 19th century we were catapulted into the industrial age and science leaped ahead in all areas. In about the time it took us to go from Kitty Hawk to the moon, the firearms industry moved from flintlock muzzle-loaders to breech loaders firing self-contained cartridges.

GUN POWDER

The basic ingredients of black powder might have been taken from "Greek Fire," specifically sulphur, charcoal and saltpeter. Formulas varied considerably and, at times, other ingredients were tried in an effort to simplify manufacturing processes or gain higher pressures. The greatest difficulty confronting powder makers was found in simply putting the ingredients together safely to achieve granulations that were serviceable. It was quickly learned that fine granulations resulted in accelerated burning rates and somewhat higher pressures. The problem cropped up when attempts were made to granulate the dehydrated cakes resulting from the blending processes. Black powder, it must be remembered, is extremely sensitive to flames, sparks, and even static electricity. Since there exists a delicate relationship between bore size and the size of powder granulations, newly manufactured powder was grated, sifted and sorted to result in a variety of granulations from Fg through FFFFFg; shooters referred to these as "Fg," "2Fg," or "3Fg," etc., etc. Fg was the largest employed in hand-held firearms and was generally used only in guns having large bores. FFg was a bit finer and used in large bores of approximately 50 to 75 caliber. Triple-Fg was commonly employed in smaller rifle calibers and 4Fg and 5Fg were generally used only for priming purposes, though they sometimes found there way into handguns.

Needless to say, in that era everyone had a healthy respect for black powder, most especially the people who made it, so it was just a question of time before experimentation would turn up a more stable propellant. Black powder was also considered to be rather inefficient because roughly only half its volume would give off the gases required for propulsion. The other half would yield primarily sludge, carbon and debris which tended to foul the bore. Any attempt to extend the effective range of a given projectile was naturally linked to an effort to increase velocity and this, logically, was associated with an effort to get more powder behind the projectile. With black powder, however, this sequence of progression could only be followed to a point, beyond which a continued effort resulted in a diminished return. When the ideal balance was passed it took progressively more powder to attain proportionately smaller increases in velocity.

The goal of powder makers then, was to develop a substance that would have a much higher rate of efficiency, preferably a powder that was non-hygroscopic, offering a minimum of waste together with greater stability.

During the period from 1860 to 1900 many experimenters set out to achieve this goal, among them the famous inventor of dynamite—Alfred Nobel (who eventually contributed to the formulation of the now famous English powders "Ballistite" and "Cordite"). The earliest breakthroughs, however, came from experiments with nitrated hardwood pulp. Schultz, a Prussian artillery officer was one of the first to try this and he was quickly followed by an Austrian named Volk-

mann and the American, Lindsley—to name but a few. Nitrated wood, however, was not the ultimate solution and after a period of "semi-smokeless" powders the first of the cellulose or modern smokeless powders appeared. Interestingly, just about every reference book you'll find on the subject of gun powder will take pains with the semi-smokeless era cautioning the reader to avoid contact with a DuPont powder called "Lesmok." This, it is stated (usually in italics) was far more sensitive and dangerous than the black powder it was designed to replace. (If anyone should find a canister of this stuff, I'd suggest they dispose of the powder and save the canister. With the hullabaloo that it apparently caused, the canister should one day prove to be a valued collector's item.)

One of the first successful smokeless shotgun powders was "DuPont's Bulk Shotgun Powder" which was introduced in 1893 and which has only been recently discontinued. This was a very stable propellant, one that served a number of uses and, because it had loading characteristics similar to those of black powder, was ideally suited to the transition period. Today we have a large variety of smokeless shotgun powders to choose from; these are often designed for specific case capacities and specific velocities, so the handloader must be careful to match a powder type to a given case and load. American powders *cannot* be blended or mixed with each other in any manner because the outcome of such a duplex charge is entirely unpredictable. Handloaders must take special care to clean powder hoppers and measures when changing from one powder to another.

European shotgun powders, incidentally, differ considerably from ours—not only do many of them retain the square-cut flake shape of the early nitrated-wood powders, but they often have the low density structure that is common to bulk powders. During one European jaunt I made a tour of small firearms shops and was surprised to discover that some had retained the tradition of custom-loading shells for their better customers. These, packaged in elaborately monogrammed boxes, are supposedly tailored to a particular gun or a particular form of shooting. At first, I was appalled to find gunsmiths mixing and blending powders to make up their special loads: then I surmised that they were dealing with powders having a common base and were simply mixing *granulations* to vary burning rates. (*This is something an American handloader should never attempt with our powders.*)

Loading the Powder—with bulk shotgun powders it was often necessary to pressure the powder charge under the over-powder wad. For this purpose early shotshell loading tools were made with simplified pressure gauges. Modern high-density powders and the further development of wad materials have all but eliminated the pressure phase of shotshell loading. Today the handloader simply seats his plastic wad snugly against the powder charge. Pressurization of some of our powders would do more harm than good.

Black powder is still used today, in muzzle-loading guns and in some special purpose factory loads. Damascus barreled guns and muzzle-loaders, whether modern or antiques, should *never* be used with anything other than black powder.

Anyone taking up handloading will quickly discover that all powders are labelled for "rifle," "shotgun" or "pistol." Operating pressures differ considerably between the three. Since the shotgun functions with one of the lowest operating pressures it would be decidedly foolhardy to attempt any form of substitution, our best advice on this point is "don't experiment!"

Because it took a considerable volume of black powder to attain breech pressures required to propel a given load, black powder was measured by dram:—a unit of weight in which one dram equals $\frac{1}{16}$ of an ounce. Average shotshell loads ranged from two to four drams, depending upon gauge. From this it is obvious that black powder was, and

is, a low density propellant in spite of its sensitivity. A few grains one way or the other would not have much effect on the load so, consequently, shooters used volumetric powder measuring devices.

When smokeless powders came along, manufacturers retained the dram ratings that they printed on casings and shell cartons to serve as indicators of the performance or velocities that the shooter could expect. Actually, however, they were loading shells with smokeless powders of considerably greater density and a very small measure of smokeless equaled a considerably larger charge of black powder. Smokeless powders have to be weighed carefully, by grain—not dram— and the volumetric slide bars currently employed by a loading tool manufacturers have to be very carefully calibrated for a *specific type and weight of powder*.

You'll find more on this subject in the chapter on handloading.

LEAD SHOT

The grape shot of the 15th and 16th and 17th centuries was not the round-ball type that we know, rather it often consisted of random pieces of assorted sizes and shapes. The uniform round lead ball that we call "shot" didn't appear until the mid-1700s when the English found a way of pouring molten lead through a sieve to form teardrop shapes; these were then placed in a drum and spun to result in a near round shape.

Then in the early 1800s, an Austrian improved on the manufacturing process (and the roundness of the individual pellets) by pouring the molten lead through a sieve from the top of a tower. At the base of the tower he placed a large catch basin and filled it with water. Rounder shot resulted because the individual pellets tended to spin as they fell—eliminating the teardrop tail. Water served to harden the pellets quickly and cushioned them as they came into contact with each other at

Some early examples of Remington-UMC shotshells that came into the author's collection from a case labelled "1917." The "Arrow" shells are loaded with buckshot. (Note tracer shell.)

the bottom, thus minimizing deformation. It was quickly discovered, however, that the distance of the drop had some influence on concentricity. Small shot could be dropped from a tower of only 100 feet but some larger sizes had to be dropped from 250 feet or more. Shot made by this method was commonly called "dropped shot."

Later, someone found that a small percentage of arsenic, added to the mix, would not only harden the pellets but would also help the molten lead to flow smoother. Arsenic content ranged from .2% in the small shot sizes to .5% in the largest sizes. Eventually arsenic gave way to antimony as a hardening agent. Shot so hardened is referred to as "chilled shot" and is still produced via the shot tower method today. Remington's famous shot tower is a landmark in the city of Bridgeport, Connecticut.

In recent years another manufacturing process was developed that eliminates the need for a tower. With the newer system, molten lead is poured into a trough that has a series of small holes in its lower wall.

Only two to three feet below the trough there is positioned a sloping board that is continuously covered with a light film of flowing water. As the pellets form and drop through the perforations, they land on this board and immediately start to roll in the direction of the slope.

With this method the heat of the pellet combines with the water to form a vapor shield and this, combined with the rolling motion across the surface of the board, results in near-perfect roundness. Falling off the edge of the fairly narrow board, the shot lands in a water-filled catch basin.

PLATED SHOT

Why such a fuss over hardened shot? What's wrong with plain old lead?

There are two reasons for the interest in

hardened shot. First, it is believed that hard shot will survive the trip through the bore with fewer deformities resulting in a lesser number of "flyers" and more shot in the effective pattern. Secondly, it is felt that hardened shot achieves greater penetration after impact. The problem has always been that hardening agents tend to reduce the weight of the individual pellet thus changing flight characteristics—velocity diminishes at a faster rate and impact energy is drastically reduced. Effective range also suffers.

One method devised to circumvent the problem was that of coating soft lead pellets with a harder metal. This resulted in copper-coated or nickel-coated shot which, for years, was loaded into shells used for waterfowl. Also, for a time, coated shot was used for some forms of target shooting but has since been banned on American skeet and trap fields. Apparently, this prohibition doesn't apply to international trap matches because the most recent Winchester-Western ammo catalog lists a nickel-plated international trap load.

STEEL SHOT

In recent years an objection to lead shot has been raised by various conservationist groups. Their claim, which has some validity, is that a percentage of our waterfowl is lost each year through lead poisoning. Birds that are lightly wounded and which fly off to suffer a lingering death are not the primary concern, as one might suspect. Instead, it's the puddler types that ingest lead shot from the muddy bottoms of marshes and ponds. This shot, taken into the crops of the birds, with the grit that they need to render their food digestible, eventually poisons them.

Estimates of the number of birds lost annually via the lead poisoning process vary greatly; it suffices to say that it is a small though significant percentage. Like all other sportsman-hunters I am concerned with preserving our waterfowl but I am also concerned with the positions taken by some of the groups that have proclaimed themselves "conservationists" and "protectors of our wildlife." These days, whenever anyone takes a bead on the hunter or shooter, for whatever reason, valid or invalid, he is immediately joined by a significant number of newly sympathetic, energetic and outspoken allies professing the same interest and objective. Actually, many of the latter-day joiners are really members of that hysterical group that would ban firearms, hunting and shooting. They're so damned intent on accomplishing their goal that, stymied in one arena, they'll jump on anyone's bandwagon if it appears to provide an oblique angle for attack. The hunter then is in the ridiculously difficult position of trying to work out a solution with an honest element that is surrounded by a fringe of fakers who have an entirely different goal in mind. So it is with the lead shot question.

For the record, the hunter and shooter is largely responsible for the currently enjoyed levels of our wildlife population and, most particularly, the hunter has done much to improve the lot of our ducks and geese. He's the only member of our population that has continuously backed up his words with deeds—with money, in plain language, through license fees, self-imposed excise tax and outright donations to organizations like Ducks Unlimited. When anyone takes the approach that our waterfowl hunters are simply crude, insensitive, cold-blooded killers of ducks and geese, he's barking up the wrong tree!

In dealing with the question of steel vs. lead shot, one must not lose sight of a few other related facts: by far more ducks and geese are lost through landfill projects, polluted waterways and farmland pesticides than are lost through lead poisoning! This is not intended to justify the loss incurred through hunter's lead, for any loss is deplorable. Rather, it is meant to establish a prospective at the heart of the issue: sportsmen have always worked diligently to preserve wildlife and we certainly don't need any prods from "Johnny-come-latelies" at this juncture. If "they" want to do something for waterfowl, put them to work on the land developers who systematically destroy waterfowl habitats. Have them roll up their sleeves and join the ecologists who are diligently striving to eliminate the pollution of our waterways. Dry-land "enthusiasts" can scrutinize pesticides and spraying programs. *Professional state and federal conservation officers working with hunting and shooting organizations and the firearms industry will solve the lead shot problem!*

But steel shot, I feel, is not the answer!

Steel shot is too light, doesn't perform adequately and certainly cannot approach the ballistic qualities of lead. Beyond 30 yards it's virtually useless and how often can you coax a duck or goose in closer than 30 yards? Not only that, but repeated tests have shown that steel shot literally destroys the average shotgun barrel—it scores the bore and peens the choke into oblivion. There has to be a better answer and I'm convinced the firearms industry will find it. Almost without exception, manufacturers have joined with hunting and shooting groups, professional conservationists and game biologists to come up with a solution. Considerable time and money has already been spent.

Even this author has gotten into the act: I've suggested that they test a new shape of lead shot—one that is not round but, rather, pointed at both ends, like a fleschette. I feel that ducks and geese only pick up lead shot *because it is round*: I've never found pointed objects in any of the crops that I've examined. Such a shape wouldn't be hard to manufacture, though it may be a bit difficult to load initially. Ballistically, I think it would be comparable to common round shot but that theory would have to be tested.

So much for the question of shot; keep your guard up and don't let anyone sell you on the idea of accepting steel shot until all of the alternatives have been exhausted.

WADS

Whenever one seeks to propel lead shot (which has a low melting point) with a powder charge, some protective material must be introduced between the two to prevent the heat and flame of the burning powder from softening or otherwise deforming the shot. Furthermore, most gun powders have to be tightly confined to achieve operating pressures. In shotguns, the wad column serves both purposes.

With granpappy's black powder gun only a tightly fitted filler or spacer wad was really necessary. Later, with self-contained ammunition a double wad was found to offer the best in performance. With these, ammo makers placed a heavy "nitro" card wad over the powder, under pressure, and followed it up with a shot-cushioning filler or spacer wad consisting of assorted materials such as fiber or felt, etc. Then plastic cases came into being and with them, we got a new one-piece plastic wad designed to fulfill a number of functions: with a cup-like base it served to contain the powder charge and prevent the passage of gases into the shot column. The center of the wad is made in a form of compressible design so that the initial impact of the powder charge will not overly damage the shot and, finally, the wad extends forward encircling the shot charge. This shot reservoir cushions the shot column of its trip through the bore—again helping to prevent damage to the ball-shaped pellets. The result is that we have more working shot in today's patterns, fewer flyers and improved performance.

The old rule of thumb, applying to the wads used in black powder specimens, was that a wad would equal in length what it measured in diam-

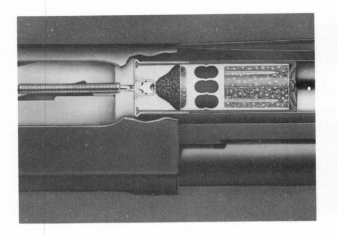 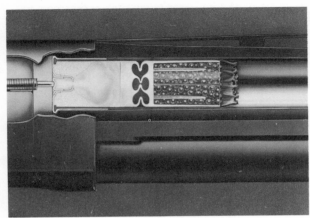

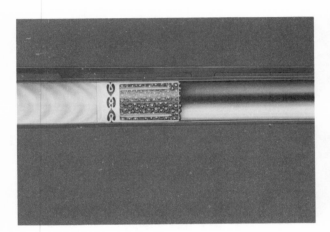 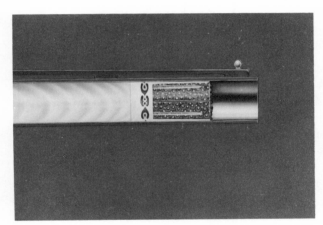

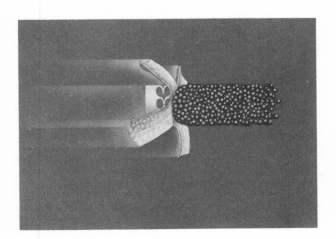

These photos illustrate the travel of a modern shot load using the one-piece plastic wad. Top to bottom: chambered shotshell; crimp opens at instant of ignition; shot charge in the bore; shot charge negotiating the choke and; finally, wad separating from shot column after clearing the muzzle. (Photos, courtesy of Remington Arms Co.)

eter. Examination of our modern plastic wads reveals that we're still using wads that are close to the rule.

If there is any disadvantage to the modern one-piece shot reservoir type, it is that it may be tightening patterns, inducing modified choke barrels to pattern like full chokes and improved cylinders to shoot like modifieds, etc. Whether there is any truth in this remains to be seen because, as I stated earlier, there is less *wasted* shot from such an arrangement and, naturally, pellet counts will climb on the patterning board. Reloaders who feel they're getting patterns that are too tight, or too dense (and these are differing problems) should go back and try the paper case wad system, i.e., a nitro card wad over the powder and a filler wad between that and the shot charge. This can be used safely in plastic cases so there's no reason to show any reluctance for the test. Also, it is possible to simply cut the shot-encircling fingers off a one-piece plastic wad and there are some simpler short plastic wads (made for certain makes of cases) which lack the shot cup. If you can break more clays or bag more birds with the older wad column, by all means—use it!

Another solution, one that I'd employ only as a last resort, would be to have a gunsmith simply open the choke a bit. This doesn't take long, nor cost much, but it would pay to have it done via the trial and error method: remove a little choke material, pattern the barrel, polish a bit more and test again—until you achieve the type of pattern you think you'll do best with! (This can't be done with barrels having chrome-lined bores.)

OVER-SHOT WADS

These are common only to brass case loads or paper cases that are roll crimped. On occasion, they're also used for buckshot loads. Anything placed over the shot column tends to compromise patterns. Knowledgeable shotgunners will invariably avoid roll crimped shells for this reason—

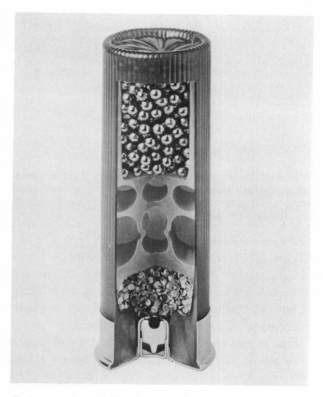

Cutaway view of Remington-Peters target shell.

especially any shells that are loaded with small sizes of shot. With buckshot loads the over-shot wad has little apparent effect.

THE CASE

The first step in the direction of an assembled shell for the shotgun was probably the simple paper

The well-known gun writer, Roger Barlow, contributed these Russian shotshells to the author's collection. They're made with lacquered paper cases and roll crimps, as ours used to be.

wrapped load, twisted at the ends. Then, with the advent of breechloaders more substantial forms of cased loads evolved. At one time or another shotshells have been made with brass, aluminum, or alloyed casings. Later came combinations with paper or plastic tubes.

One would probably surmise that a full length brass shotshell would be ideal—but it wasn't, and isn't! These can't be made to perform as well as crimped paper or plastic and they'd prove excessively expensive today. They're really only useful to the handloader who enjoys tailoring loads for one particular shotgun.

For quite a number of years, paper cased shells with brass heads were the rule. These were produced by stamping flat, round discs from a belt of brass. Roughly the size of a quarter, the flat discs were then punched into cup form and subse-

quently drawn into the desired shape, thickness, and size to form the case head. The tube, or body of the paper case was made by rolling a wide ribbon of suitable paper stock tightly around a temporary core. A thin but durable adhesive was applied during the rolling process to result in a tube of near cardboard thickness. Rolled sections, a number of feet in length, were then lacquered or varnished and waxed.

After drying, the tube was cut to appropriate length, inserted into a brass case head and wedged into position by a rolled paper base wad. At times a canneluring operation was added to firmly lock the brass head to the paper tube. Finished cases were then stacked for the loading operation.

When the first plastic cases appeared they were not without flaws. With most anything new, it takes a little time to work out the bugs and ammo factories had their fair share of headaches.

Plastic cases were first used by European producers who had succeeded in developing a casing that was entirely plastic, without a brass or alloyed

An international assortment of paper cased shotshells.

head covering. And, with their forms of plastic, their guns and their types of powders, they enjoyed considerable success. American firms that negotiated for the use of foreign patents quickly discovered problems when working with American materials and, most especially, when substituting some forms of resins popular here.

The American market, for example, must cater to the reloader's needs because handloading is so widely practiced in the U. S. The all-plastic case couldn't withstand the rim abuse to which it was subjected from the extractors and ejectors of pump and autoloading shotguns. (Europeans use side-by-side or over and under guns almost exclusively so they weren't too cognizant of the problems we'd have in this area.) American producers were therefore forced to cover case heads with the traditional brass, at considerably greater expense.

Then, with some American components, it was found that heat and breech pressures caused a softening in the plastic tube which would transmit a very light film to the walls of the chamber. This would build up under repeated firings to the point where cases would not extract or eject properly and, in extreme cases, new shells would not chamber properly. Complaints poured in until shooters learned to clean their chambers to remove such deposits. Needless to say, our manufacturers went to work on these faults as soon as word trickled back to them and within a year or so they had found plastics that would not break down in the chamber. Today, our plastic shells are as good, or better, than those found anywhere.

Plastic cases and wads have proven considerably cleaner than the paper and fiber they replaced and are largely responsible for the success and popularity of the gas-operated autoloading shotgun.

Crimping, of course, differs considerably between paper and plastic but six and eight segment crimps were developed for plastic that are easily

European ammo makers were the first to use plastic cases. They seemed to favor the see-through feature of clear plastic.

managed by the handloader.

PRIMERS

Not too many years ago there existed only two American sizes of primers for shotshells: the Winchester 209 and the Remington 57. If my memory serves me correctly, the Federal Cartridge Co. used a primer comparable in size to the 209 and which was easily interchanged with Winchester's.

Today, we have a broader assortment to choose from including a number of magnum types. Also, because our battery-cup shotshell primer is rather costly—by handloading standards—someone came up with the idea of replacing only the primed cap, retaining the original battery-cup sleeve and anvil. Tool makers responded with devices that would remove and replace only the fired cap. While this did save the reloader a few cents per box, it was a time consuming process and one that

many handloaders were unwilling to add to their busy schedules. The practice quickly lost its appeal.

Modern shotshell primers offer considerable latitude in ignition intensities and care must be taken to match a specific primer to a specific powder charge. One doesn't substitute one brand or type for another without carefully checking and testing the new combination. Magnum primers, particularly, can bring dramatic changes in pressures if placed behind the wrong charge. Handloading manuals are careful to stipulate the make and size of the primer along with powder data.

Primers are easily contaminated by water, oil, cleaning solutions and what-have-you, so some care must be taken to avoid exposing loaded shells to these liquids.

The shotshell is a highly complex shooting ingredient, many different factors combine to determine its effectiveness. Overall pattern size is one consideration; pattern density, another. Velocity

American plastic shells are invariably fitted with a metallic head covering. Note that none of these foreign shotshells are so equipped.

and pellet size establish impact energy while, conversely, the size of the shot has a bearing on the air resistance to which it is subjected in flight. The length of the shot string also influences the question of shot volume at any given target point in its flight; relate this to the speed and size of a right angle crossing target and suddenly some of those inexplicable misses are no longer quite so "inexplicable." Add some wind gusts to the path of a shot string and matters are further confused.

Velocities, fortunately, vary only slightly. Magnum loads zip along at close to 1400 f.p.s. and standard field loads are only a few hundred feet-per-second slower. The real difference between magnum and field shells is found in the amount of shot each throws.

Having cleared the muzzle, the shot load will immediately start to lengthen because individual pellets do not travel at a uniform velocity. Slight variations in size, weight and shape will cause some to move faster than others; also, the position of a pellet within the string has a bearing on its speed. Pellets bearing against barrel walls will tend to suffer flattened surfaces on the trip through the bore and often will fly erratically, separating from the pattern. Shot strings, therefore, tend to lengthen progressively as they gain distance from the muzzle.

In spite of the apparent complexities that an overall view of these variables presents, there's little need for the shotgunner to go into a detailed study of ballistics: an understanding of a few basic rules will suffice.

First, because velocities differ so little, the shooter is not hard pressed to make adjustments by leading targets more or less when changing ammo. The stringing characteristic of the shot charge in flight is another compensating factor as well.

The patterning board is not the ultimate mea-

Seven different crimping methods. A roll crimp is used on the two paper cases at left (though one has a clear plastic window). Third from the left is a paper case with a star crimp. Fourth and fifth are six-segmented crimps on plastic cases. The sixth—a foreign shell—has a solid plastic over-shot wad recessed into the mouth of the case. At the extreme right is a segmented plastic-case crimp of German origin.

sure for performance—neither for the barrel nor the shell! (More on this subject will be found in the chapter on "Patterning.") The patterning board is a flat target-like surface set up at one specific range where it is struck by *all* of the pellets in the string. It can't indicate the length of the string nor the density of the shot at any given point.

It is apparent that *all* shot sizes are fairly effective on thin skinned game, at *reasonable ranges*—say, up to thirty-five yards. Beyond thirty-five yards one must weigh the advantage of having a lot of shot in the pattern (small shot size) against the disadvantage of a shot charge that is rapidly losing impact energy. Larger shot sizes come into

their own at ranges of forty yards or more, especially on heavily furred or feathered targets. There is a point, however, at which even the largest sizes of shot will run out of adequate impact energy.

While ten different shotgun authorities would no doubt compile ten differing tables to illustrate the maximum effective range for each size of shot, the differences, I'm sure, would be minor. The reason why gun scribes avoid this particular endeavor, is that gauge and pattern density are related to the question of effectiveness. Studies have shown that a goose, for example, must be hit with a *minimum* of three pellets to be put down for keeps. We could state that #2 shot is effective at 80 yards, but we'd have to add the qualifiers, "if your gauge, barrel and shell are such that they can put three #2 pellets into the vitals of fast moving goose at that distance." (Only a tightly choked 10-gauge magnum could be expected to put enough shot in the air to accomplish this and then not with any real consistency.)

Thus, ammo makers and firearms writers simply recommend certain sizes of shot for each game bird or target and leave it to the shooter to weigh these recommendations against the gauge and choke to be employed. Following is a typical chart:

Game	Shell	Shot Size
Ducks	Hi-Vel	#4, 5 or 6
Geese	Hi-Vel	#BB, 2 or 4
Pheasant	Hi-Vel	#5 or 6
Grouse, Partridge	Std. or Hi-Vel	#5, 6, 7½ or 8
Dove	Std. or Hi-Vel	#6, 7½ or 8
Quail	Std. Vel	#7½, 8 or 9
Woodcock	Std. Vel	#7½, 8 or 9
Squirrels	Hi-Vel	#5 or 6
Rabbit	Std. or Hi-Vel	#4, 5 or 6
Turkey	Hi-Vel	#BB, 2 or 4
Fox	Hi-Vel	#BB, 2
Deer, Bear	Hi-Vel	Buckshot or Slug

When studying such a chart one must assume that it was intended for the twelve-gauge shotgun which dominates the scattergun scene. With smaller gauges, favor the larger shot sizes and avoid excessively long shots. The .410 shooter should limit his shooting to targets under 35 yards. With the standard 28 or 20 gauges, the maximum range should be about 40 yards. Those who use 20-gauge magnums or 16-gauge models can approach the twelve but have to show some reluctance for attempts beyond 45 yards. Finally, these estimates are based on the use of tightly choked barrels. Those equipped with short open choked barrels can deduct five or more yards from the estimates offered.

Brenneke slug shells (for big game hunting with the shotgun) together with a couple of loose slugs. More on slug shells will be found in Chapter XIV.

NO.	9	8½	8	7½	6	5	4	2	1	BB
SHOT SIZES Diameter in inches	.08	.085	.09	.095	.11	.12	.13	.15	.16	.18
BUCKSHOT Diameter in inches			No. 4 .24	No. 3 .25	No. 2 .27	No. 1 .30		No. 0 .32		No. 00 .33

LEAD SHOT PELLETS PER OUNCE (Approximate) Shot shells are loaded by weight, so small shot means more pellets in the load. For steel shot charges, see page 5.

Size	Pellets	Size	Pellets	Size	Pellets
9	585	7½	350	4	135
8½	490	6	225	2	87
8	410	5	170	BB	50

Chart of shot sizes (Courtesy of Federal Cartridge Co.).

CHAPTER 5

Patterning

For a number of years it has been the fashion of some gun scribes to sit down at their typewriters and hammer away at the desirability of patterning the shotgun in a thirty-inch circle at a distance of 40 yards. If I accomplish nothing else with this book, I'd like to put an end to this folly!

Why?—because it's a waste of effort to attempt to prove anything with most gauges via the 40-yard method!

The "40-yard, 30-inch" formula is strictly a manufacturer's yardstick for gauging the excellence of barrel designs and manufacturing processes. It's about as useful to the average shooter as a cinder in the eye! Is there anyone out there who seriously believes there is any real uniformity or density to the pattern of a 20 gauge at forty yards, *even if one did manage to throw a 70% full choke pattern at that distance?*

Would the man who plunks down his hard-earned cash for a costly 10-gauge magnum expect nothing more than 12-gauge performance from it?

Would it be any consolation to the unfortunate wing shooter who can't hit a darned thing with his new custom-super-blooper to find that it patterns beautifully at forty yards?

There are four other factors vitally more important to the shooter than those revealed through the literal application of the popular 40-yard patterning method. These are: point-of-aim *accuracy,* overall pattern *size,* pattern *density* and *uniformity* of shot distribution.

This patterning business is greatly misunderstood—let's restore some perspective to the practice!

The first question one should ask himself upon unpacking that new gun is, "Does it shoot where it's aimed?" It can throw the most uniform patterns you've ever laid eyes on but, if it doesn't center those patterns where you want them, you're in for considerable disappointment.

Gather a couple of large pieces of paper, paint a four-inch black circle in the center of each and set these up at ranges of 20, 30 and 40 yards. Then, line up the sights carefully and squeeze off one shot at each target. Shoot at least three targets for each range because one shot could give you a false impression. (Also, do not attempt this on a windy day.) While all shotguns should shoot a wee bit high, what do you do if it shoots low, or left or right? The next logical step would be to try another type of shotshell, a different shot size, or load, or even another brand. Of course, if you're testing a skeet or trap gun you're restricted to the use of target loads. *Usually,* a shotgun that deviates

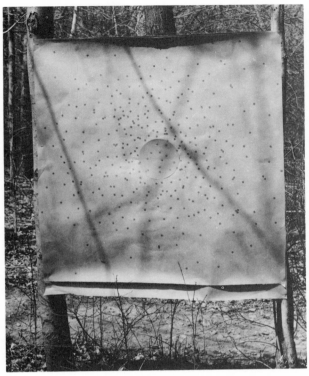

(Attempts to illustrate actual patterns were frustrated because the small holes in the patterning sheets were almost impossible to see in the finished photographs. Thus, the author's daughter was put to work pasting small circles of dark paper over each hole.)
The excellent pattern at left was fired from a modified trap gun barrel at a range of 32 yards with #8 shot.
The pattern at right, while hitting the target, heavily favors the right side. If fired from a single barrel model, at the proper distance, this barrel should be corrected by bending. A similar pattern would result from firing a side-by-side double at the wrong distance. Off-center pattern could also indicate a poor stock fit. When checking patterns align the sights carefully. If checking stock fit, point and shoot quickly, as soon as the butt is shouldered.

from point of aim will do so consistently regardless of the shells employed but, every once in a while, it's the shell that's causing the trouble.

If experimentation fails to turn up a shell that hits point of aim you'll have to take the gun to a good, qualified gunsmith, or write the manufacturer. (In the "Gunsmithing" chapter of this book we describe the process for making *small* corrections in point of impact so consult that material if the correction desired is a minor one.)

With pumps, automatics, and other single barrel guns, assuming that each target shows approximately the same margin and *direction* of error, the barrel can often be bent to shoot on target. There's nothing wrong with this procedure—factories adjust about every barrel via the bending process. Double guns are something else again: at close range a side-by-side should be *expected* to print slightly right or left of the target because their barrels are aligned to provide some convergence so that patterns will be superimposed at a range of about 35 yards (in 12-gauge guns). Over and under guns, by the same token should be expected to shoot a little high or low, depending upon which barrel is employed.

Obviously, twin-tubed shotguns are far more difficult to correct if they show considerable deviation from point of aim. For this reason, I strongly recommend that the shooter with limited finances restrict his new-gun thinking to single barrel shotguns, like the pump or automatic, rather than attempt to pick up a "bargain" grade double. Often, that "good deal" is no bargain at all! Good double guns are costly and there's no way around it. Incidentally, double guns in smaller gauges should be expected to superimpose both patterns at shorter ranges, depending upon the gauge.

One of the reasons I object to the 40-yard patterning system, is that 40 yards does not accurately reflect the average range at which most game is shot—or targets broken!

Some years ago I decided to conduct a little study on the trap field so, at a local club having a number of trap fields arranged side by side, I sat in a trap house on one field and watched birds being broken on the adjoining field. Between rounds I'd go out and position stakes to indicate the boundaries of the area, or range, at which 90% of the birds were being broken. I then measured the position of these stakes from the trap house and added sixteen yards. To my amazement, I discovered that 90% of the birds were being broken between 32 and 34 yards. To satisfy my own curiosity, I then gathered up five of the best shooters in the club and asked them to shoot together as a squad. They agreed, and I went back out to the observation point. The result, this time, showed that the greatest number of birds were being broken at 30 to 32 yards—the "hot shots" were a bit faster! Later, in discussing this with the boys in the club house, I learned that three out of the five were using modified choke barrels from the 16-yard stations in spite of the fact that most trap shooters insist upon full chokes. This little experiment proved that those using modified barrels were on the right track. Also, in light of this result, wouldn't it make far more sense for the 16-yard trap shooter to pattern his gun at thirty-two yards?

Similarly, the skeet shooter rarely shoots at anything beyond 25 or 26 yards, in fact, most of his shooting is done at shorter ranges: station eight targets, for example are taken at a scant 18 feet. Skeet shooters would be wise to discard that pattern-percentage formula and simply look for the *largest* possible pattern at 21 yards—a pattern that is very evenly distributed so that dimes couldn't be placed between pellet holes.

Upland game hunters often talk about those distant, high-flying birds but if they were to put up a target at forty yards they'd discover it's a hell of a long way off. Suddenly, they'd realize that most of their birds are taken between 30 and 35 yards. When hunting over dogs the shooting range shrinks down to about 20 to 25 yards. Most hunters, too, would be wise to do their patterning at 30 yards—examining the *overall size* of patterns and their uniformity.

Waterfowl hunters are something else again. For them the forty-yard pattern board bears some validity. For one thing, they're using big gauges (as a rule) with large shot-capacity shells. Also, they have fewer shots at ranges under 40 yards unless, of course, they excel in the use of their decoys and bird calls.

Nevertheless, even to them, the uniformity of the pattern is more important than the percentage of shot in a 30-inch circle.

To add a little conservation note to this, magnum shooters should put up some patterning targets beyond forty yards to see what the shot pattern looks like out there. It would also help to paint these with life-size silhouettes of ducks to

Author's experiments have indicated that the trap gun should be patterned at a range of 32 to 34 yards, when intended for 16-yard competition.

learn the range at which it becomes difficult to place *three* shot pellets in the *vital* areas of a simulated bird. Fish and Wildlife Department experts have indicated that it invariably takes a minimum of three good solid hits to drop a duck or goose for keeps. We'd have fewer cripples and lost birds if we'd study shotshell performance at extreme ranges and *learn when not to shoot!*

Forty-yard patterning is best limited to twelve gauge (or larger) guns, and only those models that are intended for open-country upland shooting or waterfowl hunting. The only exception to this would apply to the 3-inch 20-gauge *magnum* which has loads roughly equivalent to the standard 12 gauge.

From the foregoing it will be seen that the average shooter buys a gun for a type of shooting that rarely exceeds 35 yards. No one competes in trap shooting with anything but a twelve gauge and only the waterfowler is seriously interested in shooting anything beyond 40 yards with any consistency. It stands to reason that the average waterfowl hunter is not going to buy anything smaller than a 20-gauge *Magnum,* standard 12 gauge, or a 10 or 12 Magnum for his particular sport.

Patterning performance is greatly affected by changes in shotshell ammunition or changes in shotshell components. For example, a given barrel will often pattern one size of shot very poorly and the next smaller or larger size, beautifully.

When using paper case shotshells, made with cardboard and fiber wads, one will notice a dramatic change in patterns when simply switching to the newer one-piece plastic wad. The full-length shot-encircling plastic wad will bring about further change, as will the switch to modern plastic cases. Primers and powders, too, often contribute to variables.

If one understands how the traditional paper

The Skeet gun should be patterned at 25 yards.

case is loaded, he will realize that a large percentage of the shot charge is in direct contact with the barrel walls from the time it clears the casing until it exits the muzzle. This contact results in considerable deformation of pellets. A large flat area in a normally round pellet would, of course, cause erratic flight and result in a "flyer" printing outside of the normal pattern. For all practical purposes, flyers are wasted pellets. Since factory patterns are measured by the number of hits within the traditional 30-inch circle, a large percentage of flyers would sufficiently lower the count to result in a modified classification instead of a full—for example.

If one would take the same barrel and shotshell and substitute a full-length shot-reservoir plastic wad, the pattern would suddenly turn up with a larger percentage of hits in the 30-inch circle. Why? It's the same barrel, the same choke, same shot size, etc?

Actually, because the plastic wad acts as a cushion between the shot and the barrel walls, there is far less pellet deformation attributable to this loading; i.e. fewer "flyers" and a heavier concentration of shot in the 30-inch area. Suddenly, that modified barrel is shooting full-choke patterns—or is it? If we rely on the customary "40-yards and percentage of hits in a 30-inch circle formula," it is! But now we've brought out the third big fallacy of test-patterning as it is customarily preached: the procedure fails to take into consideration the amount of shot that can be wasted—or *saved,* for that matter!

By way of review, the shotgun should be tested in a logical, common-sense manner: With this renegade's system, one should pattern the various gauges at the distances indicated below:

All skeet guns	21 yards
.410 and 28 gauge field gun	25 yards
20 gauge field gun	30 yards
16 gauge field gun	35 yards
12 gauge field gun	35 yards

12 gauge trap gun*......................32 yards
20 gauge Magnum waterfowl gun...........40 yards
12 gauge (2¾") waterfowl gun............40 yards
12 gauge (3") Magnum..................45 yards
10 gauge (3½") Magnum................48 yards

*For trap guns intended for 16-yard shooting: when handicapped, add handicap yardage to 32 yards, i.e. when shooting from 22 yards, test patterns at a range of 38 yards.

Make sure the bore is clean (unleaded) when doing this, and pick a calm day. Check, first, for point-of-aim accuracy, then look at the overall *size* of the pattern, uniformity and density of shot distribution. Shoot at least five patterning sheets with each load and shot size. Experiment with different makes of shells and various loadings to learn those best handled by your particular shotgun. In short, test the gun at the distance that best represents the *average range* anticipated for most of your shooting.

Save your test sheets and take them to a local gunsmith if you're unable to make head or tail of 'em. Barrels that throw irregular (oblong) patterns can often be corrected. Also, patterns that are obviously too small can be improved by opening the choke a bit. Another alternative here, is to try Brush loads of number eight shot.

Follow these recommendations and you won't make this classic mistake:

A skeet shooter bought a new skeet gun from a local gun shop and, after pattern-testing it at the conventional 40 yards, complainingly returned it to the dealer.

The dealer turned the gun over to his gunsmith who tested the gun at 21 yards with assorted skeet loads. Upon subsequent examination of the test sheets, the gunsmith was amazed by the excellent large and uniform patterns the gun threw. He reported back to the customer that this was about the finest skeet gun he had ever seen. The customer wouldn't hear of it and demanded another gun, or a refund.

To make a long story short, he got a new gun. But the gunsmith, being a skeet shooter, bought the gun he rejected—and he's been burning up skeet fields with it ever since!

For those who are interested in computing the percentage of shot in a given area, we've created the following chart which indicates the approximate number of pellets, of a given size, to be found in a given weight of shot charge. (It should be noted that all shot sizes are not generally found in the full range of loads.)

For those who want to compare pattern-percentages with manufacturer's standards for the various chokes, the following table applies:

Percentage of Shot In a 30" Circle at 40 Yards

Cylinder bore	25 to 35%
Skeet #1	35 to 45%
Skeet #2	45 to 55%
Improved Cylinder	45 to 55%
Modified	55 to 65%
Improved Modified	65 to 70%
Full	70 to 80%
Extra Full	80% or more

Note: Percentage rules are not rigid. Skeet #2 chokes can exceed 55% and modified chokes often throw close to 70% patterns, depending upon the ammo used. Cylinder bore patterns are largely dependent upon the bore diameter of a given barrel.

Quantity of Pellets per Given Weight of Shot Load

Shot Size	Dia. of Pellet	Approximate Number of Pellets per Charge										
		½ oz.	1 1/16 oz.	¾ oz.	⅞ oz.	1 oz.	1⅛ oz.	1¼ oz.	1½ oz.	1⅝ oz.	1⅞ oz.	2 oz.
BB	.18	25	34	38	44	50	56	62	75	81	94	100
2	.15	45	62	68	79	90	101	112	135	146	169	180
4	.13	68	93	101	118	135	152	169	202	219	253	270
5	.12	85	117	128	149	170	191	212	255	276	319	270
6	.11	113	155	169	197	225	253	281	337	366	422	450
7½	.095	175	241	262	306	350	394	437	525	569	656	700
8	.09	205	282	307	359	410	461	512	615	666	769	820
9	.08	292	402	439	512	585	658	731	877	951	1097	1170
12	.05	1192	1640	1789	2087	2385	2683	2981	3577	3876	4472	4770

To use this chart, determine the shot size and the weight of the charge found in a particular shotshell, and read the corresponding pellet count from this table. For example—a charge of 1⅛ ounces of size 7½ shot consists of approximately 394 pellets. Count the number of pellets that have penetrated the area in question and divide that figure by the load count to determine pattern percentage, i.e. using 1⅛ ounces of #7½ shot 276 holes are counted in the pattern area. Divide 276 by 394 to arrive at a percentage of 70.

CHAPTER 6

Handloading the Shotshell

Horse racing has always been referred to as the "Sport of Kings." Until the early 1950s, skeet and trap shooting shared the same prestigious classification—both were very expensive leisure-time pursuits! Handloading has changed all that.

Today the handloader can re-use his spent cases at an investment of about $1.50 per box of twenty-five. Factory new shells range from $4.00 upwards.

Significant developments in shotshells and their components have helped bring this about; however, in my eyes, the real breakthrough came when a man by the name of Puth invented a greatly simplified and efficient shotshell loading tool for the hobbyist. Prior to the introduction of Puth's Acme Loader, shotshell reloading was fumbling through its dark ages: tools were crude single-step types and procedures were painstakingly slow. Only a handful of the most dedicated scattergunners attempted to "roll their own."

"Is shotshell loading dangerous?"

No, not for anyone who comprehends what he reads and who is willing to follow instructions. It is important, however, that the would-be reloader resign himself to the task of following directions in a precise and methodical manner. Experimentation is for the experts—the professional laboratories of the ammo makers. I've been reloading rifle, pistol and shotshell ammo for close to twenty-five years and have never had an accident. By the same token, I'd never attempted to deviate from tried and tested formulas.

Incidentally, modern smokeless powders are not as dangerous as you might have been led to believe. In loose form they simply burn—much like lighter fuel or gasoline. They need the confinement of a tight and rigid casing to develop any real energy.

"What kind of tools are required and what do they cost?"

This would depend upon how much loading you'd care to do and how much time you'd care to devote to it. The Lee Loader is a simple, inexpensive (about $10.00) hand tool that does a creditable job. It is slow however, because each of the seven primary steps must be accomplished seperately.

The next step up in tool sophistication will deposit you in the middle of an unlimited field. Here you'll find lever operated presses offered by Lyman, Pacific, Ponsness-Warren, Bair, Herter's, MEC, Texan, C-H, etc., etc. Prices start at about $48.00 and range up to $500.00. Actually, the $48.00 press will do everything the more expen-

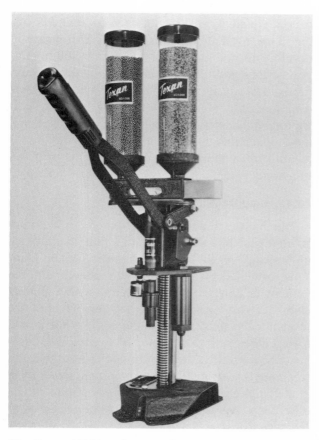

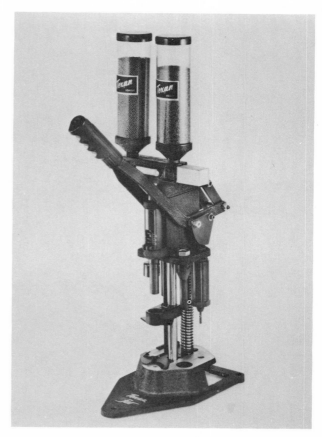

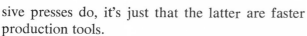

The Texan LT Shotshell Loading Press may be had for all standard gauges and retails for only $49.95. It is a very efficient and inexpensive tool.

The Texan FW is a bit more sophisticated and goes for $184.95.

sive presses do, it's just that the latter are faster production tools.

When loading for rifle or pistol the handloader needs a wide assortment of accessory tools in addition to his press and dies. Generally, with shotshell loading one needs only the press (which comes with dies for one gauge) and a supply of components. The biggest problem you'll have with the shotshell tool is that it is generally offered with a slide bar measure (for powder and shot) *designed for one specific load.* You'll need to order extra (interchangeable) bars for every other load that interests you. These are generally supplied at mod-

est cost so it shouldn't pose a barrier. A change of *gauges,* however, requires a complete new set of dies and these can be expensive. Many reloaders simply buy a second complete press for any additional gauge and have both set up for convenient, easy use. This is great—for those who can afford it!

Before we go on to discuss reloading procedures, there is one added point that should be made here: in spite of the improvements made in shotshells, components and loading tools, the handloader cannot expect to duplicate the quality of a factory-new round. The shotshell reloader

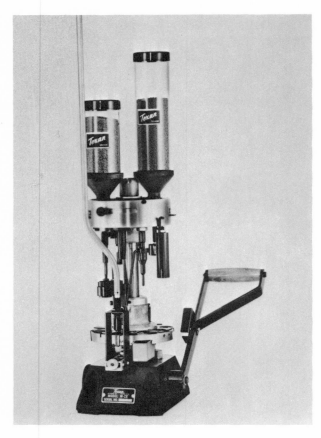

The Texan M IV is a production-type tool commonly referred to as a "progressive loader." This one sells for about $300.00 and will turn out a finished shell with every pull of the lever.

is only interested in saving money. Even if the rules permitted (and they usually don't) I would never think of competing in a trap or skeet match with handloads. In the course of shooting a hundred birds, or so, with reloads, I've often found my score impaired by one or two inexplicable misses. Scores shot with factory rounds point up this subtle difference.

As to the "why" of it, I can only state my opinion—both paper and plastic cases are weakened in the crimp area each time they are fired and they get progressively softer with each successive loading. The shotshell requires a good, firm crimp to develop normal operating pressures. Some shotgun actions add to the problem by distorting case heads; this would be true of side-by-side doubles, over and unders and automatics. In short, uniformity influences performance and the shotshell handloader finds it difficult to achieve the degree of uniformity that is enjoyed by the rifle or pistol handloader.

DRAM EQUIVALENTS

During the black powder era manufacturers labeled each box of shells (and, often, the individual casings) with the dram capacity of the load. This served to give the shooter some idea of the velocity of a particular shell. When ammo makers changed over to smokeless powders (which are measured in grains), they determined that is was a Herculean task to re-educate the nation's shooters. Consequently, they continued to use the dram reference based on the equivalent attained by a given smokeless charge. This was in spite of the differences between the loading characteristics of the two powders—a heavy dram load of black powder could be matched, pressurewise, *by a much smaller charge of smokeless powder*. There was nothing wrong with their thinking until we arrived at the modern age of handloading. Now, if the handloader were to attempt to charge a shell *with drams of smokeless powder* he'd soon be a candidate for the local pill palace. In loading shotshells, disregard all references to "drams," use *only* the charges recommended in a specific, professionally compiled loading table and be sure you're working with a *grain* scale. Fortunately, modern loading presses, with their bar measures, are set up to throw proper loads of smokeless powders and this has served to eliminate much of the confusion. It's only when the reloader gets caught up with the old black powder data that matters get out of hand.

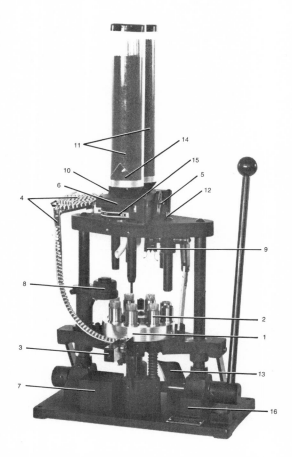

SIZE-O-MATIC 800B

THE ULTIMATE IN
SHOTSHELL RELOADING

1. CYLINDER INDEXES AUTOMATICALLY. A factory perfect shell is produced with every pull of the handle.
2. ABSOLUTE RESIZING Shells remain in full length, precision die through entire operation, eliminating feeding and chambering problems and assuring increased case life.
3. UNIQUE AUTOMATIC PRIMER FEED SYSTEM is dependable and completely safe.
4. EXTRA LARGE PRIMER TRAY AND TRACK can be filled in a few seconds.
5. SHOT AND POWDER are charged automatically and with complete safety.
6. PRECISION BUSHINGS can be easily changed to vary shot and powder loads.
7. SPENT PRIMERS collect in convenient metal container.
8. CAM-OPERATED WAD CARRIER swings out to receive all types of wads.
9. SIX AND EIGHT POINT CRIMP STARTERS are ball-bearing lined to assure perfect crimp alignment automatically.
10. WAD PRESSURE can be varied from 10 to 130 lbs. with a single screw adjustment.
11. EXTRA LARGE SHOT AND POWDER RESERVOIRS.
12. CRIMP may be set to any desired depth with handy adjustment screw.
13. FINISHED SHELL is automatically ejected by knock out rod down convenient chute at rear of machine.
14. SHOT AND POWDER BAFFLES assure consistently precise loads.
15. SHUT OFF SWITCHES enable operator to stop flow of powder or shot at any time during cycle. Switches include a drain feature which permit complete draining of reservoirs.
16. RUGGED ALUMINUM CASTINGS are finished in a handsome baked-on black wrinkle varnish.

A schematic of the elaborate Ponsness-Warren Size-O-Matic 800B Progressive loader. This speedy tool runs about $500.00 in cost.

CASE VARIATIONS

The terms "high brass, low brass" and "high base" and "low base" are used rather indiscriminately by non-reloaders, often erroneously. The fact is, one can't judge the capacity of a given casing by the amount of brass that encompasses the head. *Usually,* a high brass sleeve will indicate a *low interior base*—extra room for a heavier charge, thus heavier and faster loads. But this is not always the case; oftentimes brass height is determined by manufacturing needs and bears little relationship to internal base dimensions. Cases must be sorted by make and type and then measured, *internally,* to determine if they are acceptable for a given load. When one tries to put a light skeet or trap load into a case designed for a duck load, he'll invariably have trouble filling the case for an adequate crimp. On the other hand, it's next to impossible to squeeze a duck load into a case originally intended for a light target shell.

Another point the reloader must bear in mind, is that once-fired shells are not always interchangeable in the chambers of other guns of the same gauge. Initially, the new loader should take pains to load only casings that have been fired in his own shotgun. Later, when he has gained some experience, he can go on to make use of the assorted empty hulls that are offered at bargain prices.

When difficulty is encountered on this score—when reloaded shells give chambering difficulties—it is often possible to write to the press manufacturer for a smaller full length sizing die.

Before we get into the specifics of the loading procedure, we must declare that it is impossible for us to provide *all* of the information the reloader should have in this book. For this reason I strongly suggest that the new enthusiast obtain a book on this subject alone and, of all those currently offered, I feel that Lyman's new "Shotshell Handbook" is by far the best for the beginner. In their first complete edition Lyman has provided a complete table of loads for just about every currently manufactured hull one will encounter and these cover the spectrum, from 10 gauge all the way down to the 28 and .410. (The book cost is modest—I paid less than $4.00 for my copy.)

THE LOADING PROCEDURE

The rifle and pistol loader has some flexibility in assembling loads that the shotgunner lacks. When a given table specifies a particular casing, primer, powder, charge, wad column and shot load, the shotshell loader must use all of the components exactly as prescribed. Any substitution of anything other than shot size can lead to serious trouble.

SORT CASES

Separate all empty hulls by make and compare them, externally, so that hulls that look alike are grouped together. When this is done, make up a wooden dowel about five or six inches long with an outsider diameter slightly smaller than the inner-diameter of the casings to be loaded. (Round and smoothen one end.) Lower this into the mouth of the first case and, when it is stopped by the inner base, draw a pencil line on the dowel to correspond with the extended lip at the crimp end. This will serve to tell you the base height of the first shell. Check all the casings to see if they are all the same and remove any that differ. In the same fashion measure, sort, and group all of the casings you wish to reload.

Next, set up your loading press according to the directions furnished by the manufacturer. Anchor it solidly to a heavy bench with "C" clamps or bolts. Be particularly careful if you have to install the dies because these are often adjustable. For our purposes here, I'll assume the new reloader has acquired one of the popular inexpensive lever presses that sell for about fifty dollars.

When the press is set up, and before filling the powder or shot hoppers, take a look at the first casing you want to charge. Often you'll find that the manufacturer has printed its original charge on the outer wall of the tube. If this says, "3–1 ⅛ –8," it indicates that the shell was originally intended to hold 1⅛ ounces of shot. Disregard the "3" because this is a reference to that old dram equivalent bugaboo that we discussed earlier.

While an experienced reloader can often change loads within a given casing, he'd know which set of components to choose. The beginner should stick to a load that is comparable to the original. Using Lyman's "Shotshell Handbook," for example, the beginner should consult the load tables and find the chart that refers to cases of the same gauge and type. Lyman has broken these down by gauge, length, make and description.

That little number "8," incidentally, marked on the side wall of your case in the legend "3–1 ⅛–

#8" refers to the size of the shot. This detail is of little consequence—you can substitute any size of shot for the original as long as the *weight of the shot charge is unchanged*. In other words, loads calling for 1½ oz. of shot must be interpreted to mean 1½ ounces of any shot size you elect to use. The only problem you can run into here is with charge bars designed for heavy waterfowl loads. These are proportioned for large sizes of shot, and, if you substitute much smaller sizes, you could inadvertantly increase the weight of the load and your breech pressures as well.

With the press mounted and ready to go, cases selected, and a suitable loading table at hand, your next step will be to determine if you have all of the components called for.

The loading table, under the heading "powder," offers a model number *together* with a specific weight for the powder charge. For example: the notation "Red Dot 17.5 grs." is interpreted to mean that you need a canister of Hercules Red Dot powder and a charge bar for your loading press that will throw this weight of this specific powder. (Press manufacturers number their bars to indicate powder and shot capacities—check the charge bar table that came with your press or consult your local firearms dealer.)

With the proper charge bar installed in the press, you next check to see if you have the required wads and primers. The specs on these are very carefully spelled out in the loading table— *under no circumstances should you attempt any substitutions for the components listed*.

With cases, press and appropriate components at hand, you'll next fill your powder and shot hoppers and install the bar measure. Line this up carefully so that the powder reservoir is under the powder hopper. Lock the hoppers in the vertical position and you're ready to go on.

As you select the first shell for loading examine it carefully for any structural flaws, inside and out. Unusual bulges in the side walls or case head,

frayed crimp ends, holes at the juncture of the tube and head, or a distorted internal base wad— any one of these—will require that the case be discarded. Don't take chances with malformed or damaged hulls. If nothing else, they'll tend to come apart in the chamber, after firing, and will interrupt your shooting.

One of the dies in the press will have a rather sturdy pin-like protrusion at the bottom. This is the first stage called decapping for removal of the existing, spent primer. Slide the empty case over the body of the decapping die and operate the lever. The old primer should drop out quickly and easily.

Place a new primer in the re-capping die, center the case over it and gently, but firmly, operate the lever again to seat the new primer. Make sure the primer is fully seated so that it does not protrude from the case head.

Now, position the reprimed case under the hollow drop tube and hold it there while you slide the bar measure from one side to the other. This should charge the case with powder. Check, visually, to be sure you have powder in the case.

A die equipped with spring-like fingers is used to seat the wad or wads; slide the case inside this die, drop the wads in from the opposite end, and hold the case while you press the wads into position. Presses differ considerably in this area, so you may have to return to the manufacturer's instruction sheet to determine how your tool operates.

Years ago, when loading paper cases, a heavy cardboard (nitro) wad was required over the powder charge. This was followed by a fiber filler wad. These required some seating pressure. Present-day one-piece plastic wads are generally placed with only enough pressure to seat them firmly against the powder charge. Don't use pressure on these unless you run into trouble at the crimping end. A slight bulging of the finished crimp can

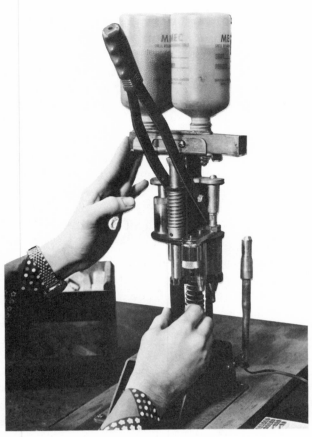

Loading shot with a MEC 250 Shotshell Press.

necessary seal to the powder charge and gas pressures fell off at the expense of velocity. Filler (fiber) wads also had to be thick enough to cushion the shot charge and protect it from the heat and gases of the propellant. The skirted plastic wad very effectively replaces cardboard and fiber but still must be selected to provide proper spacing between these two primary portions of the charge. The skirt, incidentally, is designed to flare under pressure, providing a very effective gas seal.

The wide variety of plastic wads offered today will spare the reloader the task of working out columns on his own; every load offered in the Lyman "Shotshell Handbook" has a specific wad recommendation that has been tested and proven.

With the wad seated, return the casing to the drop tube and slide the bar measure in the opposite direction to drop the shot charge.

Your first case is now ready for the final step—crimping—the most troublesome phase of the whole operation.

Take a peek inside the mouth of that case—do you have about ⅜ inch of wall material left over for the crimp? If not, you've selected the wrong charge for that particular casing and you'd do best to pull it apart without further ado. *Just don't attempt to remove the live primer!* After dumping the powder and shot, fire the primed casing in your shotgun to dispose of it.

Assuming that you have adequate material remaining above the shot charge, let's go on to examine the crimping phase: there are four different crimps employed in shotshell manufacturing and you'll have to determine which one is suited to your particular shell.

Paper cases were "roll" crimped or "star" crimped. The roll crimp is rarely encountered today, requiring a thin over-shot cardboard wad and very little (about a ¼ inch) of tube length. It also requires the employment of a special roll-crimping tool. I don't think today's reloader would have any interest in it.

sometimes be corrected by compressing the wad column.

Modern plastic one-piece wads have greatly simplified this phase of the loading operation. Realizing that shotshell components must be tailored to the *length* of the casing, to result in the availability of precisely the right amount of crimping matter at the closure, the reloader uses the wad column to balance the spacing between the powder and shot charges. The significance of this operation was more apparent to loaders of paper cases who found that a short wad column was as detrimental as one that was too long; that an inadequate nitro (card) wad did not provide the

CRIMP STARTERS

Six and eight point crimp starters are ball bearing lined and have automatic pick-up to assure perfect crimp alignment every time.

SPECIAL PAPER CRIMP ASSEMBLY

This paper crimp conversion kit is intended for shooters who reload paper shells predominately. The crimp assembly which is standard on all Ponsness-Warren tools is designed primarily for plastic shells, and while paper shells can be loaded adequately, this special paper crimp assembly provides the same optimum appearance for paper shells. Installation can be accomplished easily in just a few minutes.

Ponsness-Warren crimp starters for plastic and paper cases.

The folded or "star" crimp for paper cases is done with a two segment die—an outer collar having a tapered inside diameter and a small, flat-headed plunger. Some makers separate the two by placing the tapered collar at the end of their full length sizing die. Crimping is accomplished by placing the shell in the full length sizer, pressuring the topmost edge of the die slightly to fold the mouth of the entire unit under the crimping plunger. A strong steady pressure on the lever

should close the crimp tightly.

Remove the case from the die and examine the crimp, comparing it to a factory new shell. The folded surface should be perfectly flat. If it is bulged a bit, you'll have to pressure the wad on the next shell. If slightly sunken in the center don't worry about it unless the condition is severe. Crimps that are badly sunken or bulged indicate that you've used the wrong load or the wrong wad for that particular casing. Double check all components.

Plastic shells are also crimped in a star pattern but they have either six or eight segments. With these you must use an appropriate crimp starter for the best result. Count the original crease lines in the crimp end and orient the appropriate starter by scribing a line on the outer wall of the die body, in line with one ridge of crimping head. Then, when feeding a case to the starter, align one of the original crease marks with the scribed line on your die. In this way you'll be able to restore the original factory folds.

Your first shell is now ready to go. In spite of the fact that it has taken considerable time to describe the process, it's really quite fast. In a short time production will be running at approximately a shell a minute.

PROBLEM AREAS

At times, reloads can pose a problem when used in automatic shotguns, especially in recoil-operated models. These chamber the shell so forcefully that the crimp can be opened, trickling shot into the bore. When this occurs, the shooter will invariably hear the pellets rolling down in there and he should immediately point the muzzle down to clear the bore and empty the chamber. Loose pellets in the bore will bulge the barrel walls if the shell is subsequently fired.

Sizing can also be a problem to automatic users; swollen cases will stick in the chamber and jam the action. Try chambering empty cases before

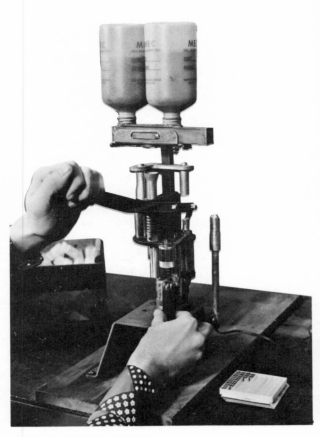

Starting the crimp with a MEC press.

loading and, if the problem persists, write to the press manufacturer.

SHOTSHELL IRONING

Some years ago, when paper cases were still in vogue, someone came up with a little accessory gadget called a "shell ironer." This was made with an internal heating element and served to restore the crimp ends of abused cases, *if used properly.* Trouble started when reloaders would let the ironer get too hot, or permit a case to linger too long over the heat. Excess heat dissolves the adhesives and protective coatings in paper cases. Obviously, heat can also damage plastic cases.

Shotshell ironing can get you into trouble if the ironer gets too hot or if the case remains in contact with the ironer too long. Unplug the ironer as soon as it gets too warm to the touch and treat cases quickly.

To restore cases with an ironer, never let the tool get hot—shut it off when it gets beyond the warm stage and quickly treat your cases before it has a chance to cool. Treat only the mouth of each case.

ROLL CRIMPS

Roll crimping should be done with a drill press, for the best result, although Lyman makes a hand-tool roll crimper which is confusingly named the "Star Roll Crimper." The roll crimp should be avoided, if at all possible, because the over-shot wad it necessitates has a way of blowing patterns into doughnut shapes.

When in hot water over the state of the family budget, some scattergunners will salvage star crimped cases by cutting them down (removing most of the softened crimp ends) and loading them with a roll crimp.

MAGNUM PRIMERS

These are relatively new to shotshell loading. Because they're designed for special purpose loads they should only be used when specifically called for in a given table of loads. These are *hot*, and *cannot* be matched with just any powder or charge.

WADDING CAN CHANGE PATTERNS

If, when using the one-piece shot-encircling plastic wad, you find your patterns are too small and tight, try some of the older loads calling for a plastic over-powder wad in combination with a fiber filler wad—in other words, eliminate the shot reservoir or shot cup. This will usually open the patterns.

LOADING BRUSH LOADS

Dividing your shot load by means of one or two thin over-shot wads has the effect of spreading the pattern. To do this properly, dump your measured shot in a small receptacle, transfer about a third of it to the case you're loading, lay a thin card over the top of that portion of the shot and load another third of the shot. Insert a second thin card wad, load the balance of the shot and crimp. *Don't attempt this with maximum loads.* These card wads have some weight, as small as they are, and they can only be used in standard velocity field loads.

LOADING BUCKSHOT

Here, the handloader is working with large, heavy shot sizes, and since one pellet, more or less,

can greatly affect the finished load (perhaps, even prove dangerous) I prefer to count the number of pellets that make up the desired weight. Thereafter, I'll load pellets *by count;* it's slower, of course, but safer this way.

LOADING SLUGS

These are tricky; don't attempt to load slugs unless you have specific instructions for a specific slug. Roll crimps are the rule. Slugs must be contained snugly against that portion of the load that lays underneath and the roll crimp must be made to contain the slug in that position. If the slug has a chance to move forward—as they tend to do in automatic shotguns—the powder chamber is enlarged and pressures drop off greatly. Often, the slug will lodge in the bore and when this occurs, a subsequent shot would then burst the barrel.

Some slugs, like the Brenneke, have a central cone-shaped protuberance that complicates matters. These have to be loaded so that the entire nose cone is contained within the casing. A special, split, over-slug plastic retainer was developed for this purpose (permitting star crimping).

Finally, and most important, follow slug loading directions *EXACTLY*! There's no tolerance for deviation with these shells!

MATCHING FACTORY LOADS—IMPORTANT

Frankly, this is impossible; attempts in this direction are the primary cause of handloading accidents.

For example: the reloader likes the performance of a specific factory shell, so he takes one apart, carefully cutting it open with a razor. Inside, to his surprise, he finds a powder with telltale red flakes. "Aha," he says, "they use Red Dot powder in these!" Thereupon he weighs the powder from the factory shell and tries to duplicate the load with his tools, cases and components.

He just may blow his head off! What he doesn't

know, is that there are about seven or eight *different* types of Red Dot powder currently manufactured. Each has red flakes and *its own peculiar burning characteristics*. Only *one* type of Red Dot powder is sold to the handloading market. The rest are restricted to industrial use and sold *only* to commercial loading plants.

ONE CANNOT IDENTIFY A POWDER BY VISUAL MEANS.

With handloading, it pays to work cautiously, with deliberation, and to pay careful attention to loading data furnished by reputable sources. Don't *assume* anything—and don't draw conclusions from other's experiments.

LOADING BRASS CASES

For many years shotshell loaders used brass (full length) shotshell cases. While these can be re-used many times they have a number of other advantages with some disadvantages.

The solid brass case requires the employment of an over-shot wad which, as I pointed out earlier, doesn't help patterning. Also, some means must be found for anchoring the over-shot wad firmly within the case since brass is not crimped. Years ago, when loading these for use in a double barrel duck gun, I used a product called "waterglass" for the wad cement. Waterglass is a sodium silicate that serves many purposes—one of which has to do with its adhesive qualities. The local pharmacy usually supplies this.

Since the crimp is eliminated, one does not have to fill the brass case to any specific height. Simply charge cases with the desired load and insert the over-shot wad at the top. This may be recessed considerably within the mouth of the case. Holding the wad firmly against the shot with a toothpick, one can sparingly apply the waterglass with an eye dropper around the wad's perimeter.

Brass cases are ideally used in double guns, but I would hesitate to try them in a pump or automatic because I believe the chambering action would dislodge the all-important over-shot wad.

A few commercial plants still produce full-length brass shotshell cases. If your local dealer is unable to supply them, write the the Alcan Company whose address may be found at the back of this book.

Handloading is safe and it's fun! Besides that, it can save you a lot of money; and the more you shoot, the more you'll save!

CHAPTER 7

Buying a Used Shotgun

Many fine shotguns are found in used gun racks across the country. The variety is virtually unlimited and bargains are readily available to the buyer who knows what to look for!

Those who regularly deal in fine collector's items like Parkers, L. C. Smiths, A. H. Foxs, etc., generally know what they're doing so there's little need to discuss the sophisticated arena of gun swapping. Instead, we'll direct this chapter to the man of limited finances who would like to own a new shotgun but who needs the savings that a used gun buy should provide.

"First things first," we arrive at the not so obvious question of "who" to buy from; the individual gun-owner-seller may appear to be the best bet for a substantial cost savings but, more often than not, he's the riskiest. First, to avoid conflict with existing gun laws, the transfer of any firearm should be recorded with a federally licensed firearms dealer. When both the buyer and the seller are residents

Some old shotguns, like this Colt double barrel, are now collector's items commanding some impressive four-digit values. (Photo courtesy of Richard Horlacher.)

A legal shotgun must *have a barrel (or barrels) that exceed eighteen inches in length* and *an overall gun length of at least twenty-six inches.*

of the same state, it is permissible for them to transfer a rifle or shotgun (not a handgun) without going through the formality of registering the sale, however, both parties would have to be legally responsible and otherwise untarnished in the eyes of the law. Federal law prohibits the loan or sale of any firearm to a mental incompetent, accused or convicted felon, juvenile, or drug addict. Also, the firearm, itself, would have to meet the standards established for a legally acceptable gun. Finally, the seller who fails to record the transfer of ownership runs the risk of subsequent legal responsibility if the firearm is mis-used by the new owner.

In view of the foregoing, a transaction with a federally licensed firearms dealer is, by far, the most desirable route, whether one is buying *or* selling! If this particular suggestion doesn't appeal to you, consider these fringe benefits: the licensed dealer *knows* the requirements for a legally acceptable firearm so he eliminates that particular danger. Also, he'll frequently give the used gun buyer some assurance that the gun is safe and functional together with a return privilege (usually 30 days) if it should fail to perform as expected. Obviously, a firearms transfer by him is duly recorded and residual legal liability is limited to dangerous defects in the gun itself.

It simply doesn't make any sense to trade with anyone other than a licensed firearms dealer. The few dollars one might save cannot begin to offset possible losses if the transaction goes awry.

MAKING THE SELECTION

While it doesn't hurt to decide, beforehand, what kind of shotgun one would like to buy, available funds may strongly influence this decision. Two hundred dollar shotguns don't sell for fifty dollars when used. Unlike used cars, high quality firearms tend to hold their values stubbornly. Some finer pieces even go *up* in value, exceeding their original cost, years after being discontinued. The best used buys are generally found among common field guns that were originally sold in the popular price range. Single shots, bolt actions, pump guns, and some automatics are most typical of these. High quality double guns hold their values better so they provide fewer bargains. Cheaply made foreign doubles plummet in cost and they're usually so beat by the time they reach the used gun rack they provide little attraction.

Offhandedly, I'd say that the pump gun is the most likely type to be found at a bargain. These are manufactured in large numbers, are very popular among American shooters, and, because of their purely mechanical operation, are exceptionally durable and reliable. The Remington 870, Winchester 1200 and Ithaca 37 are three of the most popular models one could choose from. Years ago I would have added the Winchester 12 to this list but these have skyrocketed since being discontinued. Winchester has reintroduced the Model 12 this year, but I know prices will be in

Shotguns like this Ithaca-Perazzi Light Game Model will hold their values stubbornly, often becoming more valuable as the years go by.

the deluxe gun range and bargains will be slow in finding their way to the used gun rack.

Best bets for the ultra tight budget would probably be found in pump guns by Savage, Stevens, High-Standard, Mossberg, Springfield or Montgomery-Ward.

Those who are bent on owning an automatic have to be prepared to spend a little more, at least fifty dollars more, for the cheaper grades. In this area look for; the Winchester 1400 or Model 50; Remington's 11-48, Sportsman 58 or 1100; or one of Browning's assorted models. At somewhat less expense one can look for a Savage, Stevens, High-Standard or Springfield auto.

With side-by-side or over and under double guns, one has to be careful. There are some excellent buys around but the shooter would have to know something about the maker and the model. Beware of strange names.

In over and unders, the Browning, Remington 3200, Winchester 101 and Daly are the most

likely candidates for good used status, but one can't expect to realize any great savings here. These guns hold their value. Of these, only the Remington is American made; the others are well-known imports of established quality.

In side-by-sides prices range from $50.00 to $5,000—(yes, five-thousand!). In fact, some well-known British doubles made by Purdey, Holland & Holland and Greener frequently bring prices closer to *ten thousand*. These, and famous American collector's pieces by Parker, L. C. Smith, Ithaca, A. H. Fox, etc., are obviously not for the limited pocketbook. Instead, look for a well-known foreign make and model or a popularly priced Savage-Stevens. The latter firm has been making good, rugged doubles in the models 530, 311 and Fox B (ST or DE) for quite a number of years and there should be a considerable number available on used racks.

Bolt action and single shot models are, of

Higher grades of popular models, like this custom Remington 870, are also likely to appreciate rather than depreciate in cost; that's why they're such a good investment when new.

English doubles, like this Churchill Ejector Model, usually command "carriage-trade" prices. (Photo by Richard Horlacher.)

course, the least costly. Look for those offered by Iver Johnson, Harrington & Richardson, Savage, Stevens, Springfield, Mossberg, Marlin, High-Standard, Montgomery-Ward or Sears-Roebuck.

Once you've narrowed down the field somewhat, pay visits to a few local gun shops to determine what price ranges your choices fall into. You may have to revise your thinking or prepare yourself for a more extensive hunt.

Publishers of books on used gun values are plagued by the regional appeal of some models—an appeal that is manifested in unusual differences in used gun values. For example, a particular model may be exceptionally popular in Pennsylvania: dealers can sell them off as fast as they come in for one hundred dollars a copy. The same model in Colorado is considered a clunk on the market—in the best condition it will move slowly at an even fifty bucks. The buyer who opts for a regional favorite can expect to pay top dollar for such a model. Those interested in saving money would do best to avoid such pieces.

About twenty years ago, while visiting assorted firearms dealers in the hinterlands, I came across a very nice L. C. Smith trap gun in a rather remote shop. The proprietor complained that he had had the thing "for years" and couldn't move it at any price. When he told me how much has was asking for it I had to comment that it was worth

at least twice the price he asked. He couldn't care less—he just wanted to "get rid of the darn thing" and get his investment back. I bought it on the spot, took it home, and tried it at the local trap club that weekend. It worked beautifully but I couldn't hit anything with it and then, much to my chagrin, I discovered that it was made for a left-hand shooter. Upon subsequently offering it to the southpaw members of our club, I almost started a riot. In five minutes I could have sold a half dozen just like it! It's surprising what a little geography can do to used gun values.

Having settled on a particular type of gun, the used gun buyer should be careful to avoid some of the traps: First, determine if the model being considered is currently in production. If not, are replacement parts still readily available from the manufacturer? This can make a substantial difference in that "bargain" if it should malfunction later.

Next, is the prospective piece in the desired gauge? Does the safety work? How is the trigger pull? Does the magazine operate smoothly? Is it missing any parts?

Stocks are sometimes expensive to replace, so check this one out carefully. Most important, here, is whether or not the existing stock fits you. If it's too short, or made for a left-hander (and you're right handed) it could prove a costly investment. Be wary of any stock that evidences customizing. If the previous owner couldn't tolerate a standard shape the odds are high that his modifications will prove about as useful as three-legged trousers to you! Finally, examine the stock carefully, looking for cracks, checks, etc. If running deep into the wood, these can cause major splits upon firing.

The barrel, of course, requires special scrutiny. If you've read our chapter on the shotgun barrel you'll have a pretty good idea of what to look for here. View exterior barrel surfaces as well as the bore. Look for irregularities in the exterior finish and suspicious bore shadows. If equipped with a rib, make sure it is straight and securely anchored to each post. When an adjustable choke device adorns the muzzle, it, too, should be checked to see if it is securely fastened and operable.

Assuming that you've found an interesting used gun in the proper gauge, having an appropriate barrel and choke, at the right price, and that it has passed your initial visual inspection—where do you go from there?

The next question you should ask yourself is, "Is it safe?" If the gun shop has a shooting facility, ask the dealer to fire a couple of *express* loads in the gun and examine the spent cases carefully, comparing them with a factory-new unfired round. Look for a punctured, bulged or loose primer, unusual swelling of the case head, distortion of the base of the shell, separation of the case sleeve from the head section or a torn or tattered sleeve in the area of the crimp. Visually match the fired casing with the unfired factory round by holding them up side by side. The outer walls of the fired shell should be straight and smooth, check for unusual bulges or tapers. Finally, check the rim of the fired shell to see that it hasn't been torn or damaged by the extractor or ejector.

Satisfied with the case comparison, look the shotgun over again, by examining the barrel inside and out. If nothing has changed in this area, you can go on to the final step: ironing out the details of the transaction with the dealer.

If you are unhappy with the gun after using it in the field, how much time will he allow you to return it for an adjustment? What form of adjustment will he be willing to make . . . a refund? . . . exchange? . . . credit? Ask him to spell out the conditions of the sale on the invoice; this, then, becomes a legally recognized sales contract.

What you'll have to guard against here is the timing. If hunting season is six months off, and you're allowed only thirty days to finalize your decision, you'll have to take special pains to check field performance by other means. Can you visit a

Dummy shells come in handy when checking out a used model. They'll quickly tell the tester how magazines, extractors and ejectors function.

local skeet or trap club in the time allotted? Can you buy, borrow or rent a target thrower (trap) that will enable you to do some informal target shooting on your own.

Patterning the gun, too, would prove helpful but, please, don't go out with a forty-inch-square piece of paper and fire one shot at a distance of forty yards. Read the patterning chapter of this book and do the job properly.

Let's suppose you've found a shotgun that interests you but there's some small feature of the piece that displeases you: what do you do then? Often, the dealer will be happy to make small changes in the gun (at cost) in order to make the sale. Negotiate for these changes at the time of purchase. For example, you may be able to have a recoil pad installed to your specifications for length of pull and pitch. Perhaps the stock finish needs a little touching up, or there are a few bright spots in the bluing that could stand a little patching. Maybe you'd prefer an adjustable choke device on the barrel; what would the dealer charge for that?

For the best trade-in deal, trade "up" to a higher grade of shotgun. This is a Remington 1100 D Tournament Grade Trap Gun.

While it would be unreasonable to expect the dealer to throw in these extras without charge, he'll often give the buyer a good "break" on them when making a sale.

THE TRADE-IN

The value of a trade-in is determined by a number of factors so it is next to impossible to come up with a formula that would apply in any given situation.

Probably the greatest variable to be encountered here applies to what you'd like to trade for? Trade-in's draw better allowances when trading up to more expensive models. They're worth least when trading down, on the same level, or when trading for another used piece.

Most new shotguns, originally priced at two hundred dollars or less, will depreciate close to 30% in value the moment they leave the store if subsequently traded for firearms of similar value. However, when trading up, substantially, the dealer may allow as much as 80% of the original price.

Bear in mind, with any trade transaction, that the dealer has to make *two* sales to show a profit. He wouldn't stay in business very long if his trading policy was overly liberal.

Two other factors may likewise influence the dealer's thinking: one is the regional popularity of a given model (as we discussed earlier), and the second is the general condition of the model you want to turn in. If it is obviously well used and showing signs of general abuse or neglect, it's bound to bring allowances down another 20 to 25%. Obviously, it pays to maintain firearms in good condition. Finally, if the turn-in is a discontinued model for which replacement parts are hard to come by, it will have as much "trade appeal" as a fifteen-year-old hound dog with the mange.

Every firearm, however, is not subject to negative values; many bring prices today that are

Maintain your firearms in good condition and they'll bring higher trade-in values.

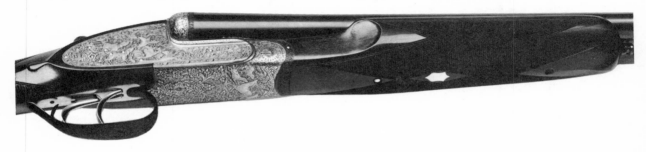

higher than they were originally. Almost without exception, these examples were guns that originally sold for a bit more than popular prices. In some instances values have increased as much as 400 to 500%. You might keep that in the back of your mind when shopping for a new gun. Those slightly more expensive custom models frequently turn out to be the best bargains simply because they tend to escalate in value over the years. When the "little woman" objects to your extravagance you can tell her about your "investment" and ask her if any of her recent purchases can be expected to appreciate in value.

FIREARMS TRANSACTION RECORD

PART I — INTRA-STATE OVER-THE-COUNTER

	TRANSFEROR'S TRANS-ACTION NO.

NOTE: Please read and carefully follow instructions on reverse. Prepare an original only.

SECTION A — TO BE COMPLETED BY TRANSFEREE OR BUYER

1. TRANSFEREE'S *(Buyer's)* NAME *(Last, First, Middle) (Mr., Mrs., Miss.)*	2. HEIGHT	3. WEIGHT	4. RACE
5. RESIDENCE ADDRESS *(No., Street, City, State, Zip Code)*	6. DATE OF BIRTH		7. PLACE OF BIRTH

8. CERTIFICATION OF TRANSFEREE *(Buyer)* — An untruthful answer may subject you to criminal prosecution. Each question must be answered with a "yes or a "no" inserted in the box at the right of the question:

a. Are you under indictment or information in any court for a crime punishable by imprisonment for a term exceeding one year?	d. Are you an unlawful user of, or addicted to, marihuana, or a depressant, stimulant, or narcotic drug?
	e. Have you ever been adjudicated mentally defective or have you ever been committed to a mental institution?
b. Have you been convicted in any court of a crime punishable by imprisonment for a term exceeding one year? (Note: The actual sentence given by the judge does not matter—a yes answer is necessary if the judge could have given a sentence of more than one year.)	f. Have you been discharged from the Armed Forces under dishonorable conditions?
	g. Are you an alien illegally in the United States?
a. Are you a fugitive from justice?	h. Are you a person who, having been a citizen of the United States, has renounced his citizenship?

I hereby certify that the answers to the above are true and correct. I understand that a person who answers any of the above questions in the affirmative is prohibited by Federal law from purchasing and/or possessing a firearm. I also understand that the making of any false oral or written statement or the exhibiting of any false or misrepresented identification with respect to this transaction is a crime punishable as a felony.

TRANSFEREE'S *(Buyer's)* SIGNATURE	DATE

SECTION B — TO BE COMPLETED BY TRANSFEROR OR SELLER

THE PERSON DESCRIBED IN SECTION A:
☐ IS KNOWN TO ME
☐ HAS IDENTIFIED HIMSELF TO ME IN THE FOLLOWING MANNER

9. TYPE OF IDENTIFICATION *(Driver's License, etc.)*	10. NUMBER ON IDENTIFICATION

On the basis of: (1) the statements in Section A; (2) the verification of identity noted in Section B; and (3) the information in the current list of Published Ordinances, it is my belief that it is not unlawful for me to sell, deliver or otherwise dispose of the firearm described below to the person identified in Section A.

11. TYPE *(Pistol, rifle, etc.)*	12. MODEL	13. CALIBER OR GAUGE	14. SERIAL NO.

15. MANUFACTURER *(and importer, if any)*

16. TRADE/CORPORATE NAME AND ADDRESS OF TRANSFEROR *(Seller) (Hand stamp may be used)*	17. FEDERAL FIREARMS LICENSE NO.

18. TRANSFEROR'S *(Seller's)* SIGNATURE	19. TRANSFEROR'S TITLE	20. TRANSAC-TION DATE

ATF FORM **4473** - PT I (9-73)   EDITION OF 6/70 MAY BE USED

Form 4473 Part II
(Rev. June 1970)

Department of the Treasury
Internal Revenue Service
Alcohol, Tobacco and
    Firearms Division

Firearms Transaction Record

Contiguous-State or Non-Over-the-Counter

NOTE: Please read and carefully follow the instructions on the back

Transferor transaction number

Section A—Statement of Transferee or Buyer

1. Transferee's (buyer's) name (last, first, middle) (Mr., Mrs., Miss)	2. Height	3. Weight	4. Race

5. Address (number, street, city, State, ZIP code)	6. Date of birth	7. Place of birth

8. **Certification of Transferee (Buyer)—an untruthful answer may subject you to criminal prosecution. Each question must be answered with a yes or no.**
   a. Are you under indictment in any court for a crime punishable by imprisonment for a term exceeding one year? _____
   b. Have you been convicted in any court of a crime punishable by imprisonment for a term exceeding one year? (Note: The actual sentence given by the judge does not matter—a yes answer is necessary if the judge **could have** given a sentence of more than one year.) _____

   c. Are you a fugitive from justice? _____
   d. Are you an unlawful user of, or addicted to marihuana or a depressant, stimulant, or narcotic drug? _____
   e. Have you been adjudicated mentally defective or have you ever been committed to a mental institution? _____
   f. Have you been discharged from the Armed Forces under dishonorable conditions? _____
   g. Are you an alien illegally in the United States? _____
   h. Are you a person who, having been a citizen of the United States, has renounced his citizenship? _____

Subject to penalties provided by law, I swear that, in the case of any firearm other than a shotgun or a rifle, I am 21 years or more of age, or that, in the case of a shotgun or a rifle, I am 18 years or more of age; that I am not prohibited by the provisions of Chapter 44 of Title 18, United States Code, from receiving a firearm in interstate or foreign commerce, and that my receipt of this firearm will not be in violation of any statute of the State and published ordinance applicable to the locality in which I reside. Further, the true title, name, and address of the principal law enforcement officer of the locality to which the firearm will be delivered are:

Title	Name

Address

I also hereby certify that the answers to the above questions are true and correct. I understand that a person who answers any of the above questions in the affirmative is prohibited by Federal law from purchasing and/or possessing a firearm. I also understand that the making of any false oral or written statement or the exhibiting of any false or misrepresented identification with respect to this transaction is a crime punishable as a felony.

Transferee's (buyer's) signature	Date

Section B—Statement of Transferor or Seller

On the basis of (1) the statements in Section A; (2) my notification of the chief law enforcement officer designated above; and (3) the information in the current list of Published Ordinances, it is my belief that it is not unlawful for me to sell, deliver, transport, or otherwise dispose of the firearm described below to the person identified in Section A.

9. Type (pistol, rifle, etc.)	10. Model	11. Caliber or gauge	12. Serial number

13. Manufacturer (and importer, if any)

14. Business name of transferor (seller)	15. Transferor's (seller's) business address

16. Signature (seller or agent)	17. Title	18. Date

CHAPTER 8

The Youngster's First Shotgun

Having reached the decision that it's time to buy junior his first shotgun, Dad is faced with the process of selecting a suitable beginner's model.

First, has the youngster had previous firearms training? Has he undergone a state-sponsored hunter training program or something comparable conducted by a recognized organization operating under NRA guidance? If so, Dad has a bit more latitude in choosing an appropriate model. On the other hand, if training is to be accomplished with the new shotgun, certain safety precautions limit the field.

Formal firearms training by a recognized instructor is highly recommended over the usual system of informal instruction in the field. No matter how skilled Dad is as a hunter and shooter, a trained firearms *teacher* is something else again.

THE TRAINING SHOTGUN

The very first firearm handled by the new shooter should be as simple, safe and as foolproof as possible. With that criterion, the selection immediately shrinks down to models that can be made to perform as single shots. These would be single-shot break-open types or bolt action models having clip magazines that are easily detached. (With the clip removed, bolt-action shotguns can be single loaded by placing the shell directly into the chamber.)

Break-open type shotguns having external hammers should be avoided because a hard-cocking

Single-shot, break-open or folding models, like this Beretta Companion gun, are ideal for early training purposes, particularly in the smaller gauges.

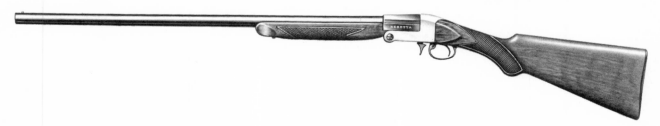

Beretta's Companion Gun, folded open.

hammer may cause a youngster's thumb to slip resulting in a premature discharge.

Tubular magazine guns—pumps, automatics, and some bolts—are definitely not for young trainees. The only exception to this rule would apply to those fortunate youngsters who are to be introduced to shotgunning on the skeet field under expert coaching.

Appropriate single-shot models are best represented by shotguns such as Galef's "Companion Folding Models." H & R and Iver Johnson both make single barrel guns but they're equipped with external hammers. Ithaca has an external hammer model called the "66 Supersingle," however they claim it is designed with a hammer-blocking device that prevents accidental discharge during the cocking operation. Mossberg has three bolt action models: the 183K, 385K and 390K. Savage, Stevens and Springfield likewise have a number of appropriate pieces available.

In addition to the question of adequate firearms training, one must consider the age and maturity of the youth in question. Older, more mature youngsters in their early teens may qualify for a more sophisticated piece of equipment like a double or slide action, but only if they've been properly trained. Again, nix the automatic unless he or she will be doing skeet shooting *exclusively*.

WHAT GAUGE?

Most fathers start their young offspring with a .410 bore, as I did. However, the size of the youngster may be a more valid determining factor. The .410 is a fine little gauge, no doubt about it, but only a real pro can use it effectively. Too often it proves frustrating to the new shooter. Thus, unless recoil and report are prime considerations, give some thought to the 28 and 20 gauges. Feminine shooters, and males of small stature (and tender years) are the only likely candidates for the .410

Once, when attending a new store opening, I was approached by a father who wanted some advice on a shotgun for his son for waterfowl hunting. He had in mind a .410 although he was reluctantly considering a twenty. Much to my sur-

A Montgomery-Ward 20-gauge bolt action repeater can be made to handle as a single shot by simple removal of the clip magazine.

prise, the tall, 180 lb. boy next to him turned out to be the lad in question. While the boy was only fourteen years old, in a relatively short time he would have been dissatisfied with anything smaller than a twelve. I tried, in vain, to explain this to the father and in the end, convinced him to compromise on a twenty gauge *magnum*. With this, the boy could use the lightest standard 2¾″ twenty gauge loads for a time and then, when Dad was ready, the boy could use 3-inch magnum shells which pack about the same amount of lead as standard twelves.

A .410 can be just as lethal as a twelve so that is not a factor to be considered once you have determined that junior is mature enough to own a gun. Furthermore, it's not the size of the gauge that is so awesome, it's what you put in it! Twelve gauge loads containing one ounce of shot offer virtually the same performance as twenty-gauge shells having a one-ounce shot load in spite of the fact that the latter contains a slightly smaller powder charge. When you feel you must restrict the youngster, limit his ammo to standard velocity field loads.

Shotshells for the twelve gauge are made in a very broad assortment of loadings, that's why the 12 bore is so versatile. Try to determine how the youngster reacts to noise and recoil and then consider next year when choosing the gauge. The "sprouting years" are the most difficult to cope

with: when a boy is from ten to twelve years old, it's logical to choose a single shot or bolt action, but anything larger than a standard twenty bore is hard to justify.

PRECAUTIONS

The young shooter is naturally fascinated with his (or her) new shotgun and is anxious to show it off to friends. Parents, therefore, must take certain precautions to eliminate the possibility of accidents. When possible, render the gun inoperable by removing the bolt (from a bolt action model) and locking it away out of the youngster's reach. Do this, too, with *all* the ammunition you may have available.

With some models, like break-open type single shots, it's very difficult to remove any portion of the firing assembly. Here, Dad has to lock the complete gun away.

I have a large gun case with sliding glass doors equipped with a showcase-type lock. Years ago, when my son wanted to show his rifle or shotgun to one of his friends, they had to view them through the heavy glass. Ammo was locked in a separate cabinet and junior was expected to account for every shell that he was given in the field.

Before buying his first firearm, I laid out the ground rules and declared that any violation of the rules would result in the sudden termination of his shooting career.

FITTING THE GUN

With few exceptions firearms are made to adult proportions and these, understandably, are diffi-

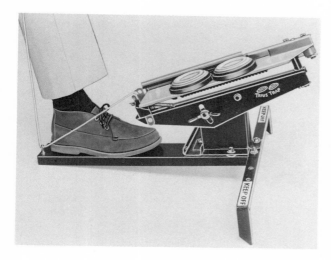

The Trius Trap is an inexpensive mechanical target throwing machine having a spring-powered throwing arm.

cult for the small shooter to handle. Little enjoyment can be derived from clay-target shooting, for example, if one is unable to break at least a token number of birds and with an awkward, oversized shotgun, the attempt is often less than satisfying.

After acquiring a shotgun for the new, small, shooter some attempt should be made to tailor it for size. An appropriate length of pull is of primary concern here; the growing youngster changes dimensions so rapidly it's really a waste of effort to attempt changing pitch, drop or cast. When selecting a new gun bear in mind that the effects of recoil are best minimized by a stock that traces a fairly straight comb line from the receiver; appreciable drop stimulates muzzle jump and this can cause some discomfort. Also, if the stock has a full, well-rounded comb it will be considerably more comfortable than one that is narrow. Another point to consider is that of changing seasons —when wearing heavy winter clothing one requires a slightly shorter stock. To get around this problem, I'd cut the stock to winter length and employ a slip-on removable rubber butt pad during the summer months.

Replacement stocks for inexpensive single-shot and bolt action shotguns are generally easy to come by at modest cost so this shouldn't pose a barrier to the fitting question. Some fathers even save the cut-off section with a view toward reattaching it (with glue and dowels) when the youngster outgrows the shortened version.

TEACH SAFETY

Whether or not expert instruction has been sought, Dad must work at the task of impressing the new shooter with the importance of firearms safety. The "Ten Commandments"— as they're commonly referred to—may be found elsewhere in this volume and should be used as a starting point with little tolerance displayed toward any infraction.

While the ever-present supervision of range officials (and other qualified target shooters) tends to minimize dangers on the target field, special precautionary measures are a must for the beginner's initial hunting excursions. Most of these are quite obvious so there's no need to dwell

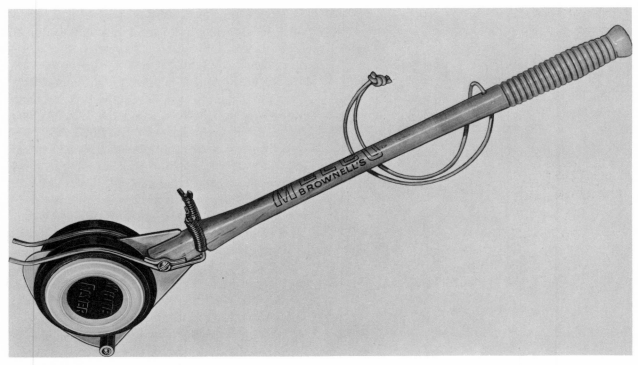

Bob Brownell's Hand Trap will throw either single or double targets. It is a very useful, and inexpensive, training aid.

on them in detail here—a brief summarization should suffice:

1. Plan early trips for secluded sections, away from populated areas, houses, livestock, or other hunting parties.
2. Do not try to take groups of beginners into the field. Each beginner should have one adult guide and the smaller the group, the better—preferably two experienced adults and one beginner.
3. Make sure the shotgun is carried with the breech open, and unloaded, from the car to the hunting site.
4. Regardless of action type and magazine capacity, the beginner's shotgun should be made to function as a single shot.
5. Upon loading the chamber, make sure the safety is immediately placed in the "on" position.
6. The supervising adult must always maintain a position close to the novice—preferably about an arm's length behind.
7. Never transport loaded weapons in a motor vehicle. If forced to drive from one hunting site to another, unload all firearms before embarking and don't permit reloading until you've arrived at the new location.
8. Hunt only the designated game; do not permit shooting at non-game targets.
9. Look for signs of over-eagerness and strive to keep the hunt slow, calm and deliberate.
10. Respect the property of others. Ask the permission of landowners before venturing onto their property, and obey all shooting and hunting laws.

When planning that first field trip pay a visit to

your local firearms dealer and get a run-down on the licensing requirements and hunting laws. Most state conservation departments publish an annual hunter's manual that details the rules and regulations: be sure to ask for a copy.

Game bagged should be properly field dressed and subsequently *cooked and eaten*. No real sportsman will hunt game that isn't destined for the dinner table, so don't give the new hunter the impression that the sport of hunting is limited to the hunt itself. The small percentage of pseudo-sportsmen who violate this code inadvertantly provide ammunition for that bunch of crackpots who would like to see all hunting banned. (Varmints, of course, are another matter.)

In conclusion, since most shotgun targets are of the flying variety, it's a good idea to teach the novice some wingshooting skills before venturing afield. Skeet and trap fields are the ideal training grounds, however, an inexpensive hand trap, a box of clays and a remote open area will serve just as well. Consult the wingshooting chapter of this volume.

CHAPTER 9

The Fundamentals of Wingshooting

There are those who would have you believe that wingshooting is an art.

Believe me, it's a science, every little facet of it! But when all its phases are put together properly a fine exhibition of wingshooting is so smooth, so effortless, that it appears to be an art.

The science starts with the shotgun and the shell—each of which is designed and manufactured to help the shooter hit whatever it is he's aiming at. The next step is to fit the shotgun to the man and the shell to the particular firearm and quarry sought.

Let's start with the shotgun:

While a rifleman can quickly adapt to most any size and shape of rifle, the shotgunner is hard-pressed to do the same with the scattergun. A rifleman concentrates on his sighting equipment, working to keep them aligned on a distant, often blurred target. Frequently, when a rifle is mismatched to the shooter, he won't even be aware of it because he'll compensate for any awkwardness by moving his face about the stock until he achieves the desired sight picture.

The shotgunner, on the other hand, is interested primarily in flying targets. His shooting has a spontaneous quality to it that cannot be duplicated by any of the other shooting sports. Except-

ing the target-shooting areas of scattergunning, the shotgunner can rarely anticipate the speed of his target or the direction it will take. Obviously, he can't predetermine range either.

Once the target comes into view, the shooter must note its direction and speed, at the same time estimating the range or point at which he expects to intercept it with his shot column. The brain is a marvelous computer—all of this data is fed through it in the time it takes to simply shoulder the gun. About the time he gets into an aiming attitude the answers start spewing forth and with relatively little effort, the shooter tracks, leads and fires. Training and practice have taught him how to coordinate these various functions so that they are accomplished almost instinctively. And there, in a nutshell, is the big difference between scattergunning and riflery; the rifleman takes the time to aim carefully and deliberately, concentrating on his sights—the shotgunner doesn't *have* the time to perform the same fashion and he must keep his attention riveted on his target.

Did you ever wonder why a shotgun never has a rear sight, except on slug-guns? Since the shotgunner shoots with both eyes open, concentrating on his target—he's rarely ever conscious of the sights! Thus, the shape of the stock is designed to

After making sure the gun is empty, the shooting instructor will often ask the student to shoulder the gun and point it directly at eye level. In this fashion, the instructor will be able to check the head, hand and arm positions as well as apparent gun fit. (Richard Horlacher poses for this photo.)

place the face in one unvarying position behind the front sight, in a sense, eliminating the need for any sighting appartus at the rear. *Therefore the fit of the gun to the shooter is of vital importance.*

(Gunstock fitting is described, in detail, in the chapter entitled, "The Shotgun Stock." Those who haven't already done so, should read that chapter carefully before proceeding here.)

When the shooter is satisfied that he's working with the right shotgun he should next scrutinize the selection of shotshells that are available to him. We all tend to pay too little attention to this detail and yet, it is every bit as important to our performance as the gun itself! In our chapters on

the shotgun barrel and patterning, we've pointed out the differences that can result from a simple change in shot size, wad or load. And in the shotshell chapter we've included a table of recommended shot sizes and loads for the various shotgun targets. Look these over, select the shells recommended for your anticipated target and *test them in your shotgun!* You'll soon learn which combinations work best for you.

Now that we've stressed the importance of gun fit and selecting the right shotshell, we can get on with the process of shooting.

Certain fundamentals are common to all forms of wingshooting. If one listens to a skeet shooter or trap shooter long enough, one will start to get the impression that each has his own special shooting style. That's very misleading. The target shooter has simply refined some details to better cope with the flight characteristics of a *known target.* The fundamentals of wingshooting, however, remain unchanged. We'll go over the basics first and then go to discuss target-shooting refinements for those interested in claybird busting!

MOUNTING THE GUN

Considerable care must be exercised when shouldering the gun. All the time, care, effort (and money) one has spent to achieve a perfect stock fit will go for naught if one doesn't learn to shoulder the gun in exactly the same manner consistently. I start training the new shooter by having him tuck the butt of the stock under his armpit. Then, by sliding it out, up and back, the butt will automatically fall into the hollow or cup formed at the shoulder. When properly mounted the butt should be bearing flat against the large shoulder muscle—*not* on the upper arm. A slight forward movement of the head should subsequently create the perfect sight picture.

Ask someone to check your mounted position to determine if the entire butt of the gun is bearing against the shoulder. When a portion of the butt is

He who absent-mindedly braces his thumb against the rear surface of a top lever upon firing will get a painfully bruised thumb.

sticking up in the air above shoulder level, something's wrong, try again.

The importance of this seemingly insignificant detail cannot be overemphasized; do it right—consistently—and you'll find your wingshooting skills developing dramatically. In time, you'll even cultivate a form of muscle-memory that will prevent you from doing this any other way.

Assuming that the student is working with a fitted shotgun, and that he has shouldered it correctly, we transfer our attention to hand positions.

The trigger hand is expected to support a part of the gun's weight while holding the butt section in firm contact with the shoulder. This is best ac-

The first crease in the trigger finger should engage the leading corner of the trigger, as shown here.

complished by holding the right elbow rather high, almost at shoulder level. Also, when the elbow is so positioned it will help to form that shoulder pocket that we talked of earlier. When the elbow is held too low or too high (over shoulder height) it tends to distort the pocket, disturbing the butt and creating a condition that will make the shooter acutely aware of recoil.

Many shooters who lapse into the overly high elbow position, especially when getting weary towards the end of a long competition, invariably lament that they're "getting kicked to hell and back."

Considering that the forefinger of the same hand is expected to operate the trigger, one should avoid any strains or stresses. Don't squeeze the pistol grip or otherwise strain to keep the piece shouldered. Relax, stay loose, and do your best to support the gun as effortlessly as possible.

The thumb position varies only slightly accord-

The author exaggerates the shooting position slightly to demonstrate that body weight should be on the forward leg, feet fairly close together, and left knee slightly bent. Note height of right elbow and slight "break" to left arm.

ing to the type of gun being used. Stock designs are intended to permit crossing the thumb over the small of the stock, between the action and the comb. When too little clearance is provided in this area, there exists a good possibility that the thumb will strike the shooter's nose upon firing. Check this; an incorrectly fitted stock could be the cause of the trouble. Sometimes, however, the novice shooter will be found "crawling the stock" (stretching the neck *and* forcing the head forward in an unnatural way).

Strange as it may sound, the position of the trigger finger warrants some special attention. If the trigger should bear against a fleshy part of the finger it is almost impossible to determine when let-off is going to be achieved, or wrap too much of the finger around the trigger and sensitivity is lost. There is only one good bearing area in the trigger finger and this is adjacent to the first crease found back from the tip. Place the forward corner of the trigger directly in the crease. Do not make the common mistake of engaging the trigger with the fleshiest portion of the fingertip.

The forward hand, or forearm-supporting hand, has always been a subject of controversy. Even the experts can't agree on how this should be placed. Some maintain that it should be held as far forward as possible when shooting trap and as far rearward as possible when shooting skeet. Others say it should always be held toward the back of the forearm. Great! But forearms come in many assorted shapes, sizes and *lengths;* so do receivers, or frames, or actions, or what have you!

Forward hand position is really dictated by the length and weight of the gun and, in my opinion, the hands should comfortably bracket the balance point of the individual firearm. The left elbow should be carried fairly high and it should have a modest "break" to it. Under no circumstances should the leading arm be straight. On the other hand, if it is bent severely it will encourage the

shooter to overswing, swing too fast or move spasmodically.

(With some modern gas-operated shotguns painful powder burns inevitably result when the shooter absent-mindedly places his forward hand over the gas-escape ports in the fore-end cap.)

The accompanying photos illustrate good positioning—study these and use a large mirror to compare them with your own position.

Now that we have the gun mounted properly it's time to spring the big secret—the one trick or trait that separates a good wingshooter from an "also-ran." Once the gun is mounted, in an aiming *attitude,* the upper torso, arms, hands, neck, shoulders, head, etc. are locked in that position. *All subsequent motion is limited to those segments of the body from the chest down.* Any independent movement of the hands, arms or head will simply destroy the alignment between the shooting eye and the axis of the bore.

Realizing that we're dealing with an unlimited variety of lateral angles and deviations, you won't need a crystal ball to tell you that this is a hell of a lot easier said than done! For starters, foot positioning is highly critical. The only way a shooter can develop the required flexible body motion is to use a stance that places the feet fairly close together, heels must be no more than six to eight inches apart. Toes can only be spread slightly. The left knee should be slightly broken and the right leg—which often appears to be straight—is not rigidly locked in that position. There must be some "give" to the right knee. Yet, with all of this, the body must be maintained in an erect position, one shouldn't go into the crab-like squatting stance that this description tends to illustrate. Take a

Richard Horlacher, a well-known international competitor, uses the European stance which really doesn't differ too much from ours. Body weight, arms, hands and feet are similarly positioned. Only the leading leg appears to be held straighter.

Author imposed upon fellow trapshooter, Bob Barr, to demonstrate the "no, no's" of shooting stances:
The Crab—legs, here, are so loose the shooter will tend to have difficulty maintaining a smooth swing.

The Flying Eagle—wide spread of the legs restricts the swing and makes shooter painfully aware of recoil.

good long look at the assortment of photographs that we've used to illustrate the matter of stance.

Care to test the concept?

Shoulder the shotgun, assume the described stance, and using only your waist, hips and legs, swivel as far as you can right and left. You shouldn't be surprised to find that you can swing through an arc exceeding 180° without disturbing the upper torso shotgun alignment.

That takes care of the lateral angles, but what happens when a bird or target heads straight for the moon?

Those targets are just as easy: the shooter simply bends his knees, casting the right knee forward a bit while simultaneously arching his body. It's even possible to swing beyond the vertical line with this stance—taking birds that are passing directly overhead.

The point I'm trying to make here is the single most important facet of wingshooting: once the eye is aligned properly behind the sighting plane of the gun, *no subsequent motion can be permitted to disturb that alignment.* No matter how the shooter turns or swings, the cheek must remain in firm contact with the stock and the relationship

The Leaning Tower—the shooter using this stance is completely off balance and his swing (and scores) will show it.

The Crawler—climbs the stock by positioning the face too close to the receiver. Left hand is also positioned too far rearward where it will encourage a jerky swing.

of master eye to sighting plane MUST be unvarying.

POINTING, TRACKING, LEADING

From a ballistic point of view, a column of shot is relatively slow moving and the shooter must make allowances for the time it takes to reach a fast-moving target. If all the techniques practiced to accomplish this were boiled down to their roots, you'd come up with three basic alternatives; the point 'n shoot system which is just that—the shooter simply picks a spot where he thinks he can intercept the target, points the gun at that spot

and lets fly (and generally misses). This is the technique adopted by most amateur shotgunners and one that has many built-in faults; often the target doesn't fly where expected; the lead has to be uncommonly long to allow for all the mental gymnastics of eye, brain and trigger coordination; and, finally, the shooter has to take into consideration the time required for the shot charge to reach the selected destination.

Most of us start our scattergunning careers with the point system and those of us who fail to abandon it quickly are soon left behind. 'Nuff said,

The Totem—a much too stiff-legged stance. Shooter's head is canted far over the comb, beyond the axis of the bore.

let's not waste any more time with the topic.

SUSTAINED LEAD

With this technique, the shooter quickly determines the lead required, points the gun muzzle that far ahead of the bird and tries to "track" the target by coordinating the speed of the muzzle with that of the bird. When the sight picture looks right, he simply touches 'er off *without interrupting the swing of the muzzle.*

That last little phrase is the killer; we all instinctively tend to stop the gun as we fire the shot and that split second's hesitation is what causes us to miss. The "follow-through" in wingshooting is essential and when using the sustained lead technique there seems to be an inborn compulsion to freeze as we fire.

I generally practice the quick-swing method (for a number of reasons that I'll go into a bit further on). However, when pass-shooting at ducks or geese I'll frequently use the sustained lead on distant fast-moving targets. The sustained lead works fine when one is working on *predictable* targets and one has plenty of open space and good visibility. The important thing to remember here, is that one must be sure to lead *enough,* keeping the muzzle in motion throughout the shot.

THE QUICK SWING

In my opinion, this is the only technique that will yield consistently good results but it takes an awful lot of training and practice to develop the skill.

With the quick swing the muzzle comes from behind the target, passes it rapidly, and the shot is released when sufficient lead is gained. Shooting in this fashion, leads appear to shrink—the muzzle is moving so rapidly that relatively little lead is apparent to the eye. Actually, of course, it's simply an illusion, similar leads are required regardless of the technique employed. It's simply a case of saving time; the fast-swinger is committed to a quick shot and wastes no time thinking about it. The real beauty of the fast swing is that follow-through is almost automatic. In fact, it would be downright difficult to stop the swing abruptly. At ranges below thirty-five yards I'm convinced this is the only technique to employ.

Another advantage of the quick swing is that it serves to compensate for any slight flight angles that are not readily recognized by the shooter. By coming up behind the bird and swinging through in one fast smooth motion, the shooter will trace the path of the target, unconsciously moving the muzzle at the proper angle.

This is difficult to describe with words, so I'd better use an example: imagine that you're sitting in a duck boat and a lone, fast-moving duck comes up behind you, comparatively low. His flight is going to take him *almost* directly over your head. While it appears that he's going to be moving straight away, he's really quartering slightly from port to starboard. You spot him overhead, raise the gun and, swinging from behind him, move the muzzle through the bird, out in front, touching one off. Bull's-eye! Without realizing it, you'd be inclined to say this was a straight-away shot. On the other hand, your fast swing *quartered slightly,* left to right and forced you to *shoot low,* under the bird—*the proper lead for an overhead going-away target.* Ask any skeet shooter about a high house station one target.

The quick-swing technique is one that must be diligently practiced but, if your reflexes and co-ordination are up to snuff, it works beautifully. Stick with it, don't let one bad day discourage you.

LEADING THE TARGET

The serious shotgun student will have to concede that the sciences of scattergunning are intricate and fascinating. Did you ever stop to think how wingshooting skills would be affected if shells were loaded to provide a wide range of velocities? The shooter would never know how much to lead a given target! Some believe that magnum loads are much faster than standard or high velocity shells. Not so! They are a *bit* faster, but, not much. The real difference from standard to high-velocity to magnum is found in the *amount* of lead they pack not the speed with which they throw it.

For all practical purposes, theoretical shotshell velocities range from about 1100 f.p.s. to 1575 f.p.s. Actual velocities, measured by chronograph, indicate that they really range from about 1200 to 1400 f.p.s. It's this little detail that saves all of us wingshooters from total disgrace as we switch from the trap field to the duck blind.

English shotgunners are fussier about shot loads than their American cousins: the Englishman often adopts one standard load for all of his shooting—changing only shot sizes. He believes, and perhaps rightly so, that it's easier to perform consistently if one gets accustomed to the velocity and performance of one specific shell. Upon learning their secret, I experimented one season by using only standard velocity loads for all of my shooting. In all honesty, I had a pretty good season that year—even in the duck blind; Nevertheless, I don't think a spread of 200 f.p.s. is going to do too much to throw us off, so I've gone back to the bigger loads for waterfowl hunting.

When teaching wingshooting I bore my suffering students with one pet axiom: *"You'll rarely miss a bird by leading it too much but you'll never touch the bird that you don't lead enough!"* It's been my experience that all newcomers insist upon shooting directly at the target. Getting them to shoot in front of it is sometimes quite difficult.

Leads, of course, vary greatly, depending upon target speeds, flight angles, distances involved and shooters' reaction times. Don't try to fill your head with a lot of numbers because it's a waste of effort. If you practice enough, that built-in computer of yours will soak up the required data and you'll learn how much to lead instinctively. While that sounds like a fairly raunchy bit of expertise, let me hasten to add a little ballistic detail that absorbs the tolerances—*the average shot column measures about fifteen feet in length over normal shotgun ranges.* This gives you considerable leeway—as long as you place that column *out in front of the target.* This explains why one skeet shooter will claim he's leading #4 high house targets by three feet while another states that the same target requires a lead of 4½ feet. Since they're both hitting those targets consistently, who do you believe? In reality they're both right. One may have a faster swing, a better follow-through, or quicker reaction time than the other but, more than likely, one is catching the target with the leading edge of his shot column while the other is snaring birds with the center or tail of the string.

The shot column (or shot-string) stretches in length as it gains distance from the muzzle. Close up, it measures no more than two or three feet in length. Out at twenty-five to thirty yards, it's closer to fifteen feet and beyond that, of course, it's even longer.

The trick to wingshooting is to hold close to targets that *are close*; give them more lead as distances increase. Be especially careful with right angle crossing targets because these require the longest leads. Fast moving ducks, riding a tailwind out around forty yards, often require leads of fifteen to eighteen feet if they're flying at right angles to the muzzle. A 55-MPH right angle target at twenty-two yards needs a lead of about four feet. Leads lengthen dramatically as range increases simply because the shot column is decelerating rapidly; at a distance of only thirty yards it has lost about 500 f.p.s. in velocity, depending upon shot size. (This is the primary reason why big magnum loads are not overly effective beyond fifty yards—the shot has lost so much velocity that it lacks the impact energy needed to penetrate a bird.)

The two most common mistakes the amateur wingshooter makes are: failing to allow for slight angles in flight and failing to shoot *under* overhead going-away targets. Those dead-away targets are rarely moving away in a perfectly straight line—look for the slight angle and lead to that side. (Even the highly skilled trapshooter gets fooled on occasion by that little angle.) Shooting under a low going-away bird feels unnatural.

On one occasion, while hunting ducks with a number of men that I had instructed, three beautiful blacks soared past me, low overhead, and I missed them completely. Immediately, there was a chorus from the surrounding pits, "Shoot UNDER the going-away bird!"

TRIGGER ACTION

Rifle instructors badger and bedevil their students with the phrase, "Squeeze that shot off!" Shotgunners can't do the same and the conversion from rifle to shotgun is often perplexing. The shotgunner has to know exactly when the piece is going to fire so his trigger action is quick and harsh. The problem crops up when the shotgunner pulls too hard, thereby jerking the gun out of alignment. Some practice time should be devoted to this (place an empty spent shell or a snap cap in the chamber.) Train yourself to pull the trigger smoothly but surely, without disturbing your swing or your sight picture. It should be just a smooth swing and—click!

When I suspect that a student is jerking the trigger violently I try to slip an empty shell in his chamber so that I can watch the antics of his muzzle when he attempts to fire on the next target.

TIPS FOR THE HUNTER

To attain any reasonable skill with wingshooting, the hunter must practice. And, since hunting seasons are all too brief, there are only two off-season alternatives: crows or clay targets. The clays are undoubtedly the most convenient.

Gun shops generally offer a device known as a hand trap. It is relatively inexpensive. Add a case of clay targets and the whole package will come to about ten dollars. For those who want a more elaborate set up there are a number of mechanical practice traps marketed by Remington, Winchester and Trius. These will run upwards of thirty dollars.

When using the hand trap it is important that the shooter stand to the left of the thrower and a step or two ahead. Hand traps, when improperly handled, will sometimes release birds prematurely and the shooter who stands to the right of the thrower can often wind up wearing targets. When practicing crossing shots or incoming targets, it is important that some precautionary measures be taken to protect the thrower; a large mound of earth or heavy natural barricade are most desireable. The thrower should be completely hidden from view and screened by an impenetrable shield.

One of the finest practice rigs I've ever seen is a layout called "Crazy Quail." This consists of a pit about six feet deep and about eight feet square, in the center of which is vertically anchored a heavy iron pipe. The pipe has a diameter of four to six inches and is capped with a rotating collar. The top of the collar is fitted with the base plate of the practice trap and a couple of lengths of angle-iron are added to angle downward and support a seat for the operator. With this arrangement it's possible to throw birds at any angle with small changes in elevation (targets have to clear the walls of the pit). The shooter stands from sixteen to twenty yards away so there's no danger to the operator. Needless to say, the operator should arrange some kind of flag or signal to indicate when he wants to leave the pit.

The ammunition used for clay target practice should consist of standard velocity target shells loaded with #7½ or #8 shot.

TIPS FOR TRAP SHOOTERS

At one time I was given the task of organizing a new trap club. While a few of the fledgling members were skilled field shooters, none had ever tried target shooting before, and they had to be schooled, as a group, from ground zero.

While I had considerable experience with large groups of riflemen, wingshooting requires individual coaching and I was in something of a quandry determining how I should go about such large scale tutoring. Finally, I decided that I'd simply give them a brief run-down on the fundamentals of stance, position, gun-fit and range safety, and let them go on from there, doing their own thing. Then, whenever I'd find a shooter having trouble I'd simply work on his most glaring faults. The

technique worked beautifully. Everyone had fun at each weekly outing and no one felt that the coaching was tiresome. Gradually, as they improved, I'd introduce subtle little refinements of the game and they'd pick them up right away. In six months the initial thirty members were shooting like budding pros. Along the way I learned a few tricks myself and developed some interesting simplified training procedures. You might say we taught each other. Briefly, I'll pass on here some of the techniques that proved most successful.

Keep the Gun in Motion—after mounting the shotgun, don't pick a spot at the lip of the trap house and freeze in that position while calling for your bird. Just as pro golfers have learned the importance of the "waggle," shooters will often move smoother and faster if they don't stop their motion to call for a bird. Aim the gun at a higher angle while mounting the butt, then swing down in a "J" pattern. As the muzzle starts to move up to the desired level, call "pull" without interrupting the swing. You'll be amazed by the new speed with which you'll get on target.

Don't Watch Your Competitor's Birds—the only real opponent you have on the target field is *yourself*. No one else can beat you if you refuse to be beaten! So why get up tight watching a competitor run a long string? Concentrate on your own birds and pretend you're standing out there all by your lonesome. Psyche yourself *up* by telling yourself, "I can smoke any damn thing that they care to throw out there—even percolator lids!" *Let the other poor guys do the worrying.*

Don't Rush—Be Graceful—in any sport that you care to name, the stars move in a peculiarly smooth and graceful fashion. They're confident, and their movements reflect that mental attitude. No feathered game or target can outdistance your shotgun, so why rush? *Look* like a pro and you'll tend to *shoot* like one! Make it a point to move smoothly and calmly, going through all the motions in a very deliberate manner.

Don't Second Guess—the instant you achieve that first desired sight picture—shoot! Don't waste time or risk ruining your swing by studying the target. Double-checking loses birds.

Adjust Your Vision—the pupil of the eye functions much like the diaphragm of a camera lens. When light is dim or subdued, the pupil is enlarged, to gather as much light as possible. Under bright lighting conditions, it will shrink noticeably. When shooting against a dark background, keep you eyes attuned to the poor light by looking at the ground while waiting your turn to shoot. When the horizon is bright, look skyward between shots.

Angles and Leads—because I found that the new trap shooter had difficulty determining angles and leads, often overlooking slight angles entirely, I devised a special training procedure for the novice. This worked so well that many of the boys refused to abandon it when they subsequently entered major competitions.

Most trap shooters will draw a bead over the forward left corner of the trap house when calling for a bird from station one; then they'll aim over the center of the trap house from station three and the right forward corner from station five. I taught the novice to set up for the straight-away bird from each position. Thus, birds that angled to the left were easily recognized and led to the left. With this technique the shooter on station one would line up over the forward edge of the trap house slightly right of center. From station three, he'd hold over the center, and left of center from station five. This really helps the newcomer.

Set Your Stance for Your Most Difficult Target —this is always the crossing bird, so on station one the shooter should adjust his stance and position for the extreme left-hand angle. Then he swivels his hips and legs around to the right to draw the desired alignment over the trap house. Anything to the right is virtually a straightaway so the slightly contorted position is no real handicap. From station five, the position should be geared for the extreme right-hand angle. Station three offers the easiest angles—the stance should be directed over the center of the house.

Skeet Shooting Tips—some of the pointers that I outlined earlier for trap shooters would also prove useful to the skeet enthusiast. Please read that portion before continuing.

At one time, skeet rules dictated that the gun had to be held in an unmounted ready position with the butt carried below the level of the right elbow. This was referred to as the "dropped-stock position." Today, many skeet shooters ignore the fact that they're permitted to mount the gun, they continue to use the dropped stock position because they believe it smoothens their swings. This gets back to what I said earlier about freezing in the ready position. Most perform best when the muzzle is in motion when calling for a bird. Try it! The only change I make between trap and skeet is that, with the latter, I trace a pattern that looks like a horizontal fish hook from stations 2, 3, 4, and 6. On stations 1, 7 and 8 I use a vertical motion, like the upright "J" I outlined earlier for the trap shooter.

Stance—this little factor is even more important to the skeet shooter than it is to the trap enthusiast. Angles are more severe and the shooter has to be able to swing widely without hindrance. Keep those feet close together. Don't squat! Stand erect and *stay loose*. Work on your stance and swing diligently by dry-firing at home. It sometimes helps the skeeter if the gun stock is a bit shorter than his measurements dictate. But a "bit" I mean no more than half an inch shorter than normal.

Delayed Shot—this is something I really can't fathom. I've seen many excellent skeet shooters stand and wait until a bird is almost on top of them before firing. It seems to me that they're

The international skeet ready position—butt of gun must be held below elbow when calling for a bird.

taking an unnecessary risk in missing such targets because their patterns at extreme close range are unusually small.

At one time skeet rules required that targets be broken over the center stake. In International Skeet I believe that rule still applies. Actually, as I see it, it's *easier* to break targets over the stake. The pattern has had a chance to expand by the time it reaches stake distance; the swing doesn't have to be so radical; the lead is small when shooting from stations 1 and 7; and, finally, the shooter is far less likely to lift his head off the stock if he goes for the bird out there.

Lifting the Head—this is one of the major bugaboos of skeet shooting—there's a natural compulsion to lift the face off the stock when looking for the second target in doubles shooting. Train yourself to keep your head *down,* on the gun. Do your looking through the natural sighting plane.

Stations Seven and Eight—these are the easiest skeet targets—and the easiest to miss if one gets careless.

The station seven low-house bird is a low, almost level straightaway. Any experienced skeet shooter will tell you that this one accounts for most of his inexplicable misses. Why? Because he mounts his gun low as he calls for the bird, raises it too quickly for the shot, and shoots right over the target. Mount the gun at *eye level* so that very little vertical movement is necessary to get on target. In fact, the bird will often appear over your front sight almost magically and you can touch off the shot with little or no swing. *Point* the gun at such a target, don't swing.

Station eight consists of only two quick and easy trick shots. Shooters miss these because they aim too deliberately and because they take a stance directly facing the trap house opening. Take

Skeet shooter, on station #8, directs his stance and muzzle at the point where he plans to break the target.

a stance facing the point at which you expect to break the bird. Then swivel around toward the trap house. Call pull just as you're reversing your loop and fire as soon as the target is blocked out by the muzzle of the gun. Keep the muzzle in motion and both shots are easily accomplished.

Skeet Leads—each shooter has his own built-in yardstick for computing leads and no two are the same. What appears to be three feet to one shooter may look more like four and a half feet to another. Also, slow swingers will work with longer leads than those who use the quick-swing method. Nevertheless, to give the budding skeet shooter a starting point, we are reproducing a table of the approximate leads required from each skeet station. This is based on the assumption that the shooter will fire when the target is in the vicinity of the center stake.

Station	High House	Low House
#1	6″ below	6″
#2	1 foot	1½ feet
#3	1½ feet	2½ feet
#4	3½ feet	3½ feet
#5	2½ feet	1½ feet
#6	2 feet	1 foot
#7	6 inches	dead-on
#8	dead-on	dead-on

Finally, with skeet shooting, don't hold at the trap house openings when calling for birds—this will force you to swing too fast, too violently. Give yourself eight to ten feet head start, depending upon the station.

Faults to look for when having difficulty:

1. Check to see if you're mounting the gun properly.
2. Stance right, or are your feet spread too far apart?
3. Swinging smoothly, or jerkily?
4. Don't lift your head from the stock.
5. If you slap the trigger too energetically you'll destroy your aim.

The successful hunter carries the gun in both hands, at the "ready," so he can quickly take advantage of any given opportunity. Those who carry the gun over the shoulder or in the crook of the arm are simply out for the airing.

6. Left knee bent, flexible?
7. Don't flinch!
8. Are you stopping the swing as the shot falls? *Follow through*!
9. Keep those elbows up!
10. Shoot in front of your target.
11. Don't count hits or misses. Let the scorekeeper tend to that little detail.
12. Concentrate on the targe that is about to be offered—forget that last miss, nothing can bring that target back.

CANTING THE GUN

To the shotgunner this little detail doesn't have the significance that it does to the rifleman; however, there are times when it can influence scattergun performance. With any form of shooting, whether it involves the handgun, rifle, or shotgun, accuracy is largely dependent upon the shooter's ability to keep the sights aligned directly over the axis of the bore. When one cants the gun, even slightly, it simply will not shoot where it's aimed. Fortunately, the shotgun provides considerable margin for error in this respect. Nevertheless, it pays to beware of the canting tendency—especially when using an over and under or side-by-side double.

PREPAREDNESS COUNTS

One fault that is commonly found among hunters is that they're not always ready when an opportunity presents itself. The hunter who carries his shotgun over his shoulder or draped through the crook of his arm, is going to pass up many golden chances or, at best, he'll get off some very poorly directed shots.

The shotgun should always be carried with the trigger hand in the grip position and one finger resting lightly on the safety. If the muzzle is pointed skyward, the butt can be rested on the hip or belt line. The left hand is positioned just ahead of the action so that it can be slid forward, into the forearm position, as the gun is mounted to eye level.

A skilled old hunter taught me this when I was just a boy and it's served me very well over the years. I can't possibly count the number of times I've filled my bag because I was the only one in the party that was ready for each shot.

CHAPTER 10

Transporting the Shotgun

When a shooter plans a trip for hunting or target shooting, he must give some careful thought to the problems he may encounter, especially in light of the stiffening regulations covering interstate and international travel with firearms. Damage prevention is not the sole objective, as it once was!

Today, the shooter has to work out the details of a trip beforehand—as soon as he decides where and when he plans to hunt or shoot. Then he'll have to determine how he's going to get there, and how he expects to return. This chapter can be important to the traveling shotgunner and we strongly recommend that the reader study it in its entirety.

PREVENTING DAMAGE TO THE SHOTGUN

Most hunting and shooting excursions are taken within a few hours of home base and a car is the principal means of transportation. Since the shooter will usually be the only one handling the shotgun, there's little need for anything heavier than the traditional padded, soft gun case to prevent nicks and gouges to wood and metal. On long trips, however, when a considerable volume of other hard gear is to share the trunk compartment with the shotgun, a rigid, foam-lined case will probably prove more desireable.

When a cased firearm is to occupy a nearly empty trunk compartment something has to be done to prevent its movement within the trunk. Sharp turns may cause it to slide from one side to the other and cause damage to the muzzle or butt. It's best to tie down cased guns or wedge them in place with soft luggage.

Whenever public transportation is to be used, exceptional care must be taken to avoid gear damage. Baggage handlers, unfortunately, are not renowned for the gentle loving care they give luggage. Only rigid gun cases will do when traveling by bus, boat, rail or air. Takedown cases are easiest to handle because they are somewhat smaller in size but, with these it is essential that components are well separated and cushioned from any possible contact with each other: a shotgun barrel, for example, can pound a fancy wood stock to a pulp if not carefully separated. Protective dividers are important.

The famous English style "Leg o' mutton" case is ideally designed for long hauls with take-down shotguns like the side-by-side or over and under. These are made on a durable frame, heavily cushioned internally and covered, externally, with a heavy grade of leather.

For non-takedown shotguns one will need a

Soft, full-length cases, like these are well suited to auto travel.

The rigid case is more desirable for travel by any means of public transportation.

full-length hard case which is generally offered with a foam rubber lining. A number of manufacturers are turning these out at reasonable prices. I use one even with take-down models because it spares me the trouble of disassembling the gun.

When full-length hard cases were first introduced I obtained one in hopes of avoiding the curiosity of fellow travelers and baggage handlers who were too often attracted to my obviously cased guns. I thought the luggage appearance would disguise the firearms contained therein but, upon my first trip to an airport, a baggage handler came along to help me in with my gear, took one look at the hard case and said, "Goin' huntin', eh?"

Regardless of what type of case one selects it is important that ammunition is never packed in the same case with the firearm. Damage, of course, is a consideration here but, more importantly, there are laws against such practices, particularly insofar as air travel is concerned. Then, too, it is unwise to provide a sneak thief with both the firearm and its appropriate ammo. Pack ammo with your clothing or toilet articles, in seperate luggage. On hunting trips I generally use an old G.I. type duffel bag and wrap my shells in heavy outerwear which is stored midway in the bag.

SHOTGUNS AND THE LAW

Ever since Earl Warren's Supreme Court pulled the teeth of our criminal laws we've had a startling increase in firearms crimes which has resulted in a hue and cry for more firearms laws. Politicians, who make the laws, seemingly cannot accept the clear-headed logic that it's our system of justice that is to blame. At any rate, since 1968 we've had a tidal wave of gun laws (mostly bad) from all levels of government. The long and short of it is that the law-abiding sportsman must now tread on eggshells to avoid conflict with the law.

For example, some of our cities and states now have poorly drafted laws on the books that are prone to broad interpretation by law-enforcement officers. In other words, a given question can go either way—depending upon whim or fancy, or the state of your beard at the moment. New York City, for instance, has a sweeping "city-license" regulation that is designed to register all resident gun owners (for a nice fee, of course) and this can trap the unwary transient. In New York, get in—and get out—as fast as you can. Don't linger for more than twenty-four hours with your shotgun because it can deposit you neatly in the local hoosegow. Chicago has something similar. New Jersey has a statewide identification card system and this, too, can bring grief if you plan to stay in the state for any length of time, say for an extended skeet or trap tournament.

Actually, there are far too many of these nuisance laws on the books for us to report on them all here. Worse yet, there are changes and additions coming through every day. To avoid headaches, check the laws of the area you intend visiting. Then, assuming that you can comply with them, travel directly to your destination without stop overs or lay overs en route. Return home the same way—in a non-dallying straight line!

Travel by auto can be particularly hazardous, even in a shooter's home state. Many states have laws prohibiting the transport of loaded firearms in vehicles on public roads. It makes no difference if the chamber is empty—one shell in the magazine can put the owner behind bars. Just moving from one bird field to another, across a public road, constitutes a violation if the magazine is charged. From a safety standpoint, of course, one should never take a loaded shotgun into any moving vehicle, but the shooter is now faced with double jeopardy! Make it a point to empty the shotgun completely before moving it anywhere, and then store it well out of reach (in the trunk?) before driving off.

CROSSING INTERNATIONAL BORDERS

The Gun Control Act of 1968 prohibits the importation of firearms by non-licensed individuals. It specifically provides that only federally licensed importers or manufacturers can import them. This won't cause the hunter any problem when traveling *from* Texas *to* Mexico, for example, but it can give him a heap of aggravation when he attempts to return. This law has to consider smuggling possibilities since even the sporting shotgun can now be viewed as contraband. Thus, any shotgun, regardless of where it was made, is considered an import at our borders *unless the traveler registered its American ownership with United States Customs prior to departure.* The fact that a given model bears the stamped imprint of an American firearms firm *does not* exempt it from this restriction simply because smugglers would quickly seize upon the stamping gimmick to circumvent the law.

To prevent trouble, register *all* of your firearms with U.S. Customs before leaving the country. It makes no difference where the guns were produced.

Assuming that you are planning a hunting trip into Mexico, call or visit your nearest U.S. Customs office before embarking on your journey. They'll furnish the necessary forms. Then, if driving across the border, make it a point to stop at the U.S. Customs office on the *American side* to show them the firearms and get the registration validated. Upon your return you'll have to present this to the customs officer on the U.S. side of the border, again, to effect re-importation. Obviously, you must take pains to avoid losing the registration certificate while out of the country. Travel by boat would necessitate a similar routine. International air travel is a bit more complicated because only our large international airports can be expected to house customs offices. When traveling from a small town to a foreign destination, airlines will most often attempt to check your luggage all the way through to your destination. If you have to register a firearm how are you going to regain possession of it long enough to show it to a U.S. customs officer? Not all airline clerks are aware of these requirements so you can't rely on any advice they give you. The best thing to do is to arrange registration by mail long before your anticipated departure. Under such circumstances U. S. Customs will probably accept the authentication of a local official.

Importation of Firearms by Non-licensed Civilians

The Alcohol, Tobacco and Firearms Division of the Internal Revenue Service presents the following information on the importation of firearms by persons other than firearms licensees and members of the Armed Forces on active duty overseas.

Department of the Treasury

Internal Revenue Service

Alcohol, Tobacco and Firearms Division

Publication 672 (9-69)

Section 922(a)(3) of Title I of the Gun Control Act became effective on December 16, 1968. Section 922(a)(3) makes it unlawful for any person other than a licensee under the act to transport into or receive in the state where he resides any firearm purchased or otherwise obtained by him outside that state, except for shotguns and rifles purchased in a contiguous state as provided for in Section 922(b)(3) of Title I.

In view of the restriction contained in Section 922(a)(3), it would be unlawful for you as an individual to import a firearm on and after December 16, 1968. However, an importer or dealer located in your state of residence and holding a valid license under Title I of the Gun Control Act of 1968, could submit an application to this office to import the firearm you ordered, under the provisions contained in Section 925(d)(3) of Title I. Enclosed are four copies of Form 6 (Firearms) for the possible use of any licensee that might handle the importation of a firearm for you.

If you choose to have a licensee handle an importation for you, the licensee should file an application to import with this office, showing himself as the importer in Item 5 and you as the consumer in Item 7, on Form 6 (Firearms). The foreign shipper should be instructed to ship the firearm(s) to the licensee. The delivery of the firearm(s) would then be consummated between yourself and the licensee in your state of residence and he will record the receipt and disposition in his records.

A permit must be obtained for each firearm to be imported, regardless of the date purchased.

No permit or authorization from this office is required to bring into the United States a firearm previously taken out of the United States by the person bringing it in. The Bureau of Customs is authorized to release a firearm without a permit from the Director, Alcohol, Tobacco and Firearms Division, upon a proper showing of proof that the firearm was taken out of the Country by the person bringing it in.

If the firearm(s) has not already been taken out of the Country, you should register it or them with the Bureau of Customs on Customs Form 4457 at the point and time of your departure. (Reference: Section 178.115(a), Part 178 of Title 26, Code of Federal Regulations)

No permit from the Director, Alcohol, Tobacco and Firearms Division is required for a nonresident of the United States, or a resident of the Panama Canal Zone, to bring into the Country firearms for legitimate hunting or lawful sporting purposes. However, such firearms and such ammunition as remains following such shooting activity are to be taken back out of the territorial limits of the United States by such person upon conclusion of the shooting activity. (Reference: Section 178.115(d)(1), Part 178 of Title 26, Code of Federal Regulations)

Department of the Treasury
Bureau of Alcohol, Tobacco and Firearms

Affidavit Concerning Importation of Firearms or Ammunition Previously Taken Out of the United States

STATE OF _____)
) SS
COUNTY OF _____)

_____ , being first duly sworn, deposes and

says that his present address is _____

and that he departed from the United States (including possessions thereof) at _____ ,
                                                                          (Place of exit)

on or about _____ , taking with him on his person or with his baggage or effects, whether ac-
                  (Date)

companied or unaccompanied, out of the United States or its possession the following firearm(s) and ammunition:

Firearms

Manufacturer	Country of Manufacture	Caliber, Size or Gauge	Model	Serial No.
1.				
2.				
3.				

Ammunition

Type	Quantity	Caliber
1.		
2.		
3.		

Affiant further swears and affirms that the aforementioned firearms and ammunition are being returned to the United States for his personal use.

_____
Signature

WITNESSES:

Subscribed and sworn to before me
this _____ day of _____ , 19____.

_____

_____

_____
U.S. Consular or Visa Officer,
Notary Public or any Federal officer
authorized to administer oaths.

ATF F 4568 (1-75)   EDITION OF 8-72 MAY BE USED

Mexico offers the bird hunter some fine opportunities. Shooter in this photo has set up in a grain field for white-wing dove. (Photo, courtesy of R.A. Steindler.)

TRIPS TO MEXICO

Last year, when writing my "Book of the Rifle" I reported on Canadian regulations applying to the American visiting Canada with a rifle for the purpose of hunting. Hunters traveling to Mexico are more apt to be carrying a shotgun because they have some excellent bird hunting south of the border. So, I thought, I'd offer Mexico's regulations in this volume.

Stan Slaten, a friend of mine, happens to be the Outdoors Editor for the *Houston Post,* one of the Southwest's largest newspaper. Stan regularly hunts and fishes in Mexico and I made it a point to capture some of his time at a recent trade show. Here, in a nutshell, is what Stan advises:

First, decide where you want to hunt and line up your guide or outfitter. This can often be done by mail. (Guides will run from $60.00 to $100.00 per day and will furnish just about everything you'll need except clothing, firearms, ammunition, cigarettes and alcoholic beverages.)

With that squared away, you'll next have to ar-

THE DEPARTMENT OF THE TREASURY
CERTIFICATE OF REGISTRATION
BUREAU OF CUSTOMS

Form Approved
O.M.B. 48-R0394

Number

Name of Owner

Address of Owner

Description of Articles

I certify that the information shown hereon is true and correct to the best of my knowledge and belief.

Signature of Owner

Port

Date

Signature of Customs Official

Customs Form 4457 (3/71)

range to get about six passport-type photos of yourself. These are necessary for identification purposes, licensing, etc.

Having accomplished these preliminaries, pay a visit to your local sheriff or chief of police to request a statement attesting to your good character. You'll have to rely on your guide to handle the licensing details for you. Just make sure you're doing business with an established and reputable organization because you'll now have to pay him some sizeable funds in advance. He'll want a minimum of $10.00 to arrange for the license and an additional $100.00 for the small game license fee. Send him a check or money order for the appropriate amount together with your photos and character reference. Be sure to specify *where* you want to hunt because a hunting license is good only for one specific state. On a separate piece of paper provide the guide with a description of the gun or

guns you plan to bring with you, just in case he might need this information. Ask him to mail the license back to you so you'll have it in your possession when you cross the border.

Do not try to take your bird dog into Mexico with you: you'll have no trouble bringing him in, but it's next to impossible to bring him back!

Cigarettes and alcoholic beverages are cheaper in Mexico than they are here, so buy them there! Shotshell ammunition is *not* cheaper in Mexico and they have only paper-case loads, no plastics. Ask your outfitter what types and quantities you should bring with you.

If you plan to bring firearms with you into Mexico, don't forget to register them with U. S. Customs before crossing the border.

Coming back across the border with game birds can be troublesome; American laws are tough on this point. For one thing, you can't bring any

Mexican quail into the U. S. unless the birds are actually cooked. You can bring back geese, doves and ducks but you'll have to be careful to observe the limits, and quantities vary *according to the day of the week*. Check on these regulations when you first cross the border because they are subject to change from time to time. Incidentally, all ducks, geese and dove must be dressed and plucked except for one wing which is to remain feathered. (Guides will invariably arrange for this according to U. S. requirements.)

If at all possible, try to have your birds frozen and packed in dry ice. Exposure to heat over a prolonged period of time could easily spoil them.

Hunting excursions into Canada are somewhat less exasperating, nevertheless one should arrange licenses, guides, etc., well in advance and, again, be careful to pre-register all the firearms that are going to make the trip. It should also be noted here, that passports are not required for travel into either Canada or Mexico. In place of a passport one should carry adequate proof of their U. S. citizenship, i.e., voter's registration certificate, birth certificate, naturalization papers, etc. Carry as much proof of U. S. residency as possible, one document may not suffice if it is tattered or marred.

Hunters visiting Africa are almost invariably after big game and frequently neglect to bring along a shotgun. That's a mistake because Africa has some fine bird shooting. Hunting the perimeters of their campsites, shotgunners are often able to bag an assortment of delicious game birds that native cooks delight in preparing for the table.

Concluding this chapter on traveling with the shotgun, emphasis must be placed on the importance of preventing theft. Larcenous individuals have a ready market for firearms; to thwart them you'll have to be ever vigilant—in short, don't let your gun cases out of your sight for a minute! When you must turn them over to baggage handlers, at an airport, for example, try to stay with them right up until the time they're loaded on the plane. Watch the baggage wagons from a window in the passenger compartment to make sure they're actually loaded. The easiest way for a thief to make off with your pet blunderbuss is to see to it that it misses your flight! Be particularly wary when traveling through large cities! Follow the same procedure with buses and trains.

CHAPTER 11

Hunting Dogs for the Shotgunner

Books on hunting dogs are written by dog experts and I must confess at the outset that this author can't qualify in that department. However, as an ardent shotgun hunter who has had considerable experience hunting over dogs the insight I've gained may prove helpful to the reader simply because the gunner's viewpoints are rarely expressed by dog authorities.

Gather any group of shotgunners over a hot toddy and it's just a question of time before they exhaust the topics of wine, women and song, electing instead to discuss game, guns and dogs. Invariably, in these discussions it will be found that each shooter has some particular species of canine that he favors over all of the rest and that the most eloquent speaker of the group will invariably succeed in selling his ideas to the novice hunter who quietly sits in the background, unobstrusively soaking up all of that fascinating dog lore.

However the chips may fall, experience has taught that there is no such thing as a "super dog" and that in any given breed there will be found a number of jewels along with a goodly number of jugheads upon which one wouldn't be inclined to waste the price of a milk bone!

Then too, it is found that each breed has some distinctive characteristics of its own and that these can often make them more desireable than others for a specific form of hunting. Experience has also indicated that many hunters unintentionally or ignorantly ruin their dogs through lack of training or by training improperly. This usually happens when families get into the act (after dad has selected that new bird dog pup) by refusing to go along with recommended training procedures: youngsters want to teach the pup to do parlor tricks, or pull a sleigh; mom forbids housing the dog outside because, one, he'll freeze to death, and two, he'll disturb the whole neighborhood with his barking. It's the smart (and rare) ol' bird hunter who will simply threaten to carry his dog back where it come from at this point, but that's what he should do!

A good working dog can have only one master —his teacher and handler. No second party should be invited to participate in his schooling beyond fulfilling the role of silent assistant. Dogs are easily confused and slight variations in commands (even to varying tonal qualities in the same commands) will serve only to disrupt their think tanks. Hunting dogs are working dogs—they must be treated as such and taught to respond properly to every command with little tolerance on the trainer's part for behavior that departs from the norm. Only in this fashion can one hope to develop a superior performer.

SELECTING THE BREED AND PUP

For all practical purposes each species of hunting canine can be broken down into one of three possible sub-categories: show dog, field-trial dog and field dog. The hunter is interested only in the last category. Show dogs are bred for their beauty —not their noses, stamina, courage or brains. Field-trial dogs are light years ahead but they are chosen and groomed to fulfill the peculiar requirements of field-trial competitions. They're usually slightly smaller specimens of their breeds, lightning fast, but lacking the rough and ready temperments required for rugged day-long hunting in mixed terrain.

This is not to imply that any animal can be expected to hunt hard for hours on end but rather to convey the idea that larger field-dog specimens, while not so sophisticated, are more flexible examples of their breeds.

Because of the differences in types within a given species, and because hunters have acknowledged the validity of some field-trial thinking—particularly as it serves to upgrade the breed—a special form of field test is popularly practiced under rules and conditions closely resembling those of the usual field trial. This is called the "Versatile Hunting Dog Trial." Hunters, perhaps, have been a bit too single-minded in selecting dogs for field use. They've been concerned only that that new "eating, sleeping and you-know-what machine" will hunt anything when called upon to do so. Field trialers go about things in a more scientific fashion. Consequently, there has been a tenuous linking of field-trial people with hunters on the Versatile Trial field.

Former hunting breeds that were bred to the point of uselessness by those little old ladies with their benches, brushes and ribbons may start making their way back to an honest day's work via the versatile dog people and I look for good things to come from this; wouldn't it be nice to think of the Irish setter as a hunting dog again?

To intelligently select a particular species of dog, the hunter must first answer the questions: "What am I most interested in hunting and how do I plan to hunt it?"

The man who wants to hunt quail in October and ducks in December, with the same dog, is probably asking for more than any one dog can deliver. Also, because some dogs are characteristically more rangy than others, the foot hunter has to be careful to get a dog that favors working in close. It's pure hell to spend a day chasing a fast, far-ranging animal!

For all practical purposes we can say that any dog selected by a shotgun hunter will be a hound, retriever, pointer, setter or flushing dog. So, if we discuss these five types, fundamentally, we will narrow down the field somewhat.

HOUNDS

There are many species of hounds but the shotgunner is interested only in the two that are suited to rabbit hunting—the beagle and basset.

The problem here is to find a beagle that can be trained to hunt; too many of this species have been indiscriminately bred to fulfill roles as house pets and prove to be jugheads in the field.

When discussing beagles I never fail to think of a good hunting friend who dearly loved to hunt and eat rabbits. Late one January afternoon he called me to relate how he had bought a brace of "fully-trained, first-class beagles" and that he planned to hunt them (for the first time) the following day. When he told me what he paid for them I whistled, never realizing that beagles could be worth so much.

I picked up my proud beagle-owning buddy the next morning at 5:00 A.M. for the two-hour drive to one of our favorite bunny fields. The dogs, I had to admit, looked impressive as he loaded them (and all of their paraphernalia) into the car. They sported collars with bells attached and ol' buddy had a shiny new whistle that the dogs would respond to without hesitation—or so he claimed!

We arrived at the first snow-covered field about 7:00 A.M. With the hounds straining at their leashes, we locked the car, worked our way over a barbed wire fence and loaded our guns. Then, in a field that was literally crawling with bunnies, my buddy unsnapped the leashes and turned those two magnificent beagles loose. Yipping and barking, they ran side by side, straight up the slight knoll in front of us. Smilingly, we stood and watched as the tips of their tails disappeared over the rise—and that's the last we ever saw of 'em!

We scoured the area, blowing on that danged whistle, until well after dark but heard nary the tinkle of a single bell. By late afternoon my companion was mad enough to shoot both those hounds—if he could've found them!

Advice? Hunt over those trained rabbit hounds at least once before plunking down any hard cash for 'em. Don't buy pups if you can possibly avoid it. If you can't find *trained* beagles, get your pups from a breeder that handles *only* hunting dogs. Finally, and this is where my old friend made his biggest mistake, don't turn any new animal loose in the field until he's come to regard you as "family."

Basset hounds, I believe, are a better bet simply because they haven't been doted over by the pet shop breeders the way the beagle has.

One problem common to the beagle is that you'll find some lean young animals are too fast—they'll overrun the rabbit or run so close behind him that you're always courting the danger of shooting the dog. It's fare more desireable to have a slower dog that maintains a fifteen or twenty foot gap behind his quarry. Also with exceptionally fast dogs rabbits will often run "to ground," denning up where they can't be reached, or flushed; they'll stay above ground more with slower hounds, almost as is they enjoy leading a merry chase.

On the other hand, as beagles and bassets mature they tend to put on a lot of weight, particularly if they're also family pets who beg secretive under-the-table handouts. Guard against this; work to keep your dog a bit on the lean side. Overweight dogs don't last very long in the field.

Some years ago, one of my basset-owning friends would take his dog with us on bird hunts. This old hound had a wonderful nose and we found he'd flush pheasant and quail for us if we simply let him hunt at his own pace. I've seen some bird dogs that couldn't do as well.

FLUSHING DOGS

Spaniels, with the exception of the Brittany and two water-dog varieties, are flushing dogs and we are concerned, here, with the cocker spaniel and the English springer spaniel.

The Brittany is more properly classified as a pointer. The American and Irish water spaniels are water retrievers.

Flushing dogs don't point. Instead, they rush at squatting or running birds, forcing them to take wing. They do retrieve, however, and they can be used on a wide variety of game.

Considered an excellent hunting dog at one time, especially for woodcock shooting in heavy thickets (from whence he gained his name) the cocker spaniel has fallen into disrepute because he was just too darned attractive and affectionate to those seeking house pets. Today a hardy group of cocker fanciers are doing their level best to bring him back to the field. For those who are primarily interested in woodcock hunting, the cocker would be a good bet if one can find a *hunting-cocker breeder, and if he can find a pup with good potential.*

The English springer is something else again. He's a natural hunter who loves to romp in the field; he'll flush anything that flies or runs (includ-

ing rabbits—to the disdain of some springer experts) and he'll retrieve from water too! He's a very versatile animal.

Of all the hunting breeds, the possibility of coming up with a "really bad" springer specimen is rather remote. As long as the dog has a halfway decent nose, he'll hunt—even as an untrained pup! They tend to work close and they'll push a running pheasant into the air quickly.

Running pheasants, incidentally, often leave pointing dogs with empty points, occurrences that are highly frustrating to both dogs and hunters. It is for this reason that springers are considered ideal for ringnecks. Some trainers I've run into refuse to use their pointers on pheasant for fear that their dogs will start to break points. Much time and effort is devoted to this training so it does seem rather foolhardy to take chances on compromising that discipline.

Most springers are natural retrievers so this ability is easily developed. Insofar as water retrieving is concerned, one must be careful not to urge the dog into water that is too cold. On chilly days, when the animal does venture in for a bird, a good toweling and a warm blanket are required upon his return. Cold weather retrieving is better left to heavier-coated dogs like the Labrador.

Springers can be used for grouse, pheasant, quail and woodcock. In a pinch, they'll help the duck hunter by retrieving when the weather (and water) is tolerable.

RETRIEVERS

There's a large assortment of dogs to choose from in this category. Most are heavy full-bodied animals with short necks and short legs. They're rugged breeds too, able to take most any kind

A springer spaniel pushing a cock bird into flight. Let the bird out for a ways; shot at this close range, you'll ruin a good dinner with shot. Some field-trialers would frown on the way this dog has leaped after the bird. (Photo, courtesy of R. A. Steindler.)

of terrain or weather that they're urged into.

While not ideally suited to dry land hunting, most can be used as flushing dogs on pheasant. Some, on occasion, will even take on some of the characteristics of a pointer when marking a 'possum-playing bird—though the "points" (if you can call them that) are often ludicrous.

Essentially, these are water dogs and, more specifically, cold-weather water dogs so they will suffer in a pheasant field on a warm day, requiring more frequent breaks and more water than a pointer or spaniel.

For the ardent duck or goose hunter, however, no other type is to be considered. It is suggested only that one examine several species before making a decision. Look for breeders of Labradors, Chesapeakes, goldens, curly-coated and flat-coated retrievers. Then take a peek at the Irish water spaniel and the American water spaniel.

Some water retrievers who are expected to live as house pets often bring down the wrath of the housekeeper simply because they have very oily coats and they're not too fussy where they spread the surplus. Carefully examine the coat of a contemplated animal if this is a criterion.

POINTERS AND SETTERS

Since these are all pointing dogs I'm at a loss to explain the origin and current need for the term "setter." At this late date we'll simply have to bow to tradition.

With the setter-suffix we can choose from the English, Irish and Gordon. "Pointers" are: English, German shorthaired, German wire-haired and wire-haired Griffon. A few other breeds also qualify for pointer status and these are the Brittany spaniel, Weimaraner, and Vizsla.

Early in my bird-hunting career I had several opportunities to hunt over German shorthairs and Weimaraners. Frankly, I soon wearied of them. Too many of these were too high strung or they were too independent and uncomfortably aggressive. I often thought that I wouldn't want my children exposed to them. Worst of all, they ranged so far and wide that I was forced to hunt at a trot, and that's no way to spend what should be a pleasant day in the field. According to their breeders, these are supposed to be close working dogs but they'd never prove it by me.

I've never had a chance to work with a Griffon or Vizsla so I wouldn't know what to expect from them. One Griffon-owning hunter I chatted with raved about his dog but that would have to be discounted because most dog owners tend to overlook faults when talking about their animals (and this writer is as guilty of that as the next guy!).

The Brittany and Gordon are two breeds that leave me puzzled. Some of my best experiences in the field have been with these species. On the other hand, they've also contributed to some of my worst. I once suspected that one Brittany I stumbled after had a nose like a rubber duck. I kicked birds out behind her all day long. Then the clincher came when she almost stepped on a pheasant and continued on her way without interruption. This wasn't an old dog, mind you, just a totally disinterested one.

Another Brittany, some years later, went through bird fields like a vacuum cleaner. Again, it's the dog, not the breed.

Hunting in Illinois over English pointers, I was impressed with the way they'd find birds and hold points. On those occasions though, I was hunting from a jeep and their wide ranging tactics were not out of place. Some time later I hunted quail over the same breed of dog, in New York State, and these specimens worked closer. Being on foot, I was concerned before the hunt that I was about to spend another day at the races. It seems that Western breeders want dogs to range broadly because they have such wide open spaces to cover—dogs are trained to hunt in that fashion. Eastern breeders appear to train a closer-working dog.

There may be no validity at all to this observation, but I feel that Western and Eastern pointers are distinctly different strains of the same breed. Perhaps it's just the training that makes the difference, nevertheless, can anyone tell me how long would it take to cultivate a genetic difference?

In speaking of hounds, flushing dogs, pointers and retrievers generally, it can safely be said that most are very gentle animals around the home. Even most big and rugged Labradors are well behaved around children. My springer will sit like a statue while a two year old is poking fingers into his eyes or ears (but he'll slip off and hide as soon as the toddler's attention is diverted). Except for an occasional poorly-bred beagle that may be inclined to snap, only the German short-hair and Weimaraner have shown me cause for concern on this score; but in all fairness to these breeds, the specimens I relate to may have been poor examples—too closely inbred or too vigourously handled in training.

One can minimize the risk of coming up with a bad dog if he follows a few simple rules:

1. Select a pup only when the complete litter is in company with the bitch—not when most of the pups have already been removed. (As I stated earlier, hunting qualities of beagles are so "iffy" I can't recommend the practice of buying beagle pups. Only trained hounds.)

2. Do your utmost to select the pup when it is between six and seven weeks old. Their personalities develop rapidly after the seventh week and by waiting longer you'll be running the risk of exposing pup to unfavorable influences.

3. Never, never choose the pitiful little creature that sulks at the back of the pen while his litter mates are poking their noses through the fencing to get at you. That little pup is often the most appealing because he arouses so much sympathy—but he already has a personality problem and, by hanging back, he's demonstrating that he *doesn't like people!* Invariably, if you choose him you'll be taking on a peck of trouble.

Point! A classic stance in typical bird cover. Note, also, that some breeds of dogs will hunt close and, for pheasants, that is desirable since the birds will hold well for the dog. If they do take flight they won't be too far away from the gun. (Photo, courtesy of Winchester.)

4. If at all possible, get an impartial expert (on that particular breed) to make the selection for you. By the same token, it's not a good idea to take children with you to the selection ceremony.

Having outlined the types let's compare their qualifications to hunting needs and see if we can't arrive at some common denominators that will serve to help us select the proper breed.

The Southern quail hunter who occasionally hunts ducks would be making a mistake if he were to look for a dual purpose dog; especially if 90% of his hunting time is spent in pursuit of quail. To him, only a pointer or setter would prove satisfactory. In short, select your primary target first, then try to find the dog that best fills the bill. Don't let secondary hunting pursuits weigh too heavily in this decision.

Northern duck enthusiasts should really look for a heavier water retriever like the Labrador, Chesapeake or Golden. In a pinch these can also

Only the dog's owner or handler should attempt to take retrieved birds. Guests must never interfere with the handling of someone else's animal. (Photo, courtesy of Illinois Department of Conservation.)

be used on some upland birds, particularly ringnecks, but they won't shine in that area.

The ardent woodcock hunter has a problem because many bird dogs simply refuse to retrieve woodcocks. There's something about the bird (the odor?) that turns them off. Also, woodcock hunting is often best conducted in heavily thicketed terrain. The hunter needs a dog with the gumption to plow through briars and tangles without hesitation. The springer would do well here; or a good hunting cocker—if he can be found, and some like setters for this work.

Mid-western pheasant shooting is best done with a dog like the springer. However, there's so much excellent duck hunting in that flyway that it wouldn't be unreasonable to choose a retriever instead, using him for both.

The ruffed grouse is an unpredictable bird that can thoroughly frustrate the best of dogs. While he can be hunted with most any breed, both the dog and his handler will have to train together diligently before any impressive field work can be expected.

Grouse appear to be smarter or spookier than most birds because they won't permit a dog to get close. Pointers have to execute their points from a distance and flushing dogs have to learn to work slower and closer to the gun.

Most of the dove hunting I've attempted was comparable to pass shooting. I simply set-up in an improvised blind and waited for the feeding flights to come to me. Under these conditions any retrieving specimen would do the job. Occasionally, while hunting quail in Arkansas, I found that dove would co-mingle with coveys of quail and that a pointer would make no distinction between the two.

In summation, a good bird dog is the sum total of all his phases: i.e., his in-bred potential and your expertise in selecting the right breed, the right pup and the right trainer. Get a good start and you'll need learn only how to bring out his best traits in the field.

HUNTING WITH THE DOG

It's one thing to slog through bird fields on your own and quite another to hunt with companions close at hand. Hunting with a dog likewise requires some adjustments on the hunter's part, particularly if the dog or dogs are owned by someone else. Until you've field-handled your own dog some of the rules of conduct, and the reasons for them, may not be readily apparent.

The guest hunter working over a strange dog has to be careful to let the dog owner (or handler) conduct the hunt. The handler knows how fast to work his dog, how he wants him worked, when he should be pushed or corrected and when he is misbehaving. The guest must never interfere. At the very outset, the guest should take a position to one side of the handler and a step or two rearward so that he can watch the handler's moves without difficulty. The gun should be carried with the muzzle pointing skyward and slightly facing the off side. The guest must adjust his pace to the handler's; moving only when the handler moves and stopping when the handler stops. This is most important! At no time during the hunt should the guest offer commands to the dog, nor should he expect the retrieving animal to bring birds to him. These are the cardinal sins—intruding upon functions that are the handler's exclusive domain.

It's a good idea, before the start of the hunt, to make friends with a strange dog, just so he'll become familiar with your scent and understand that you belong in the picture. Kneel down in front of him and extend your hand, palm up, in a close-to-the ground fashion. Never approach a strange dog from above to pat him on top of the head; they sometimes misinterpret this action. After you've scratched his neck or ears a bit, let it end right there. Now he's expected to go to work and he'll work best if you remain unobtrusive.

With pointing dogs, determine who is going to do the shooting before moving in to flush the birds, and then let the handler do the flushing. It goes without saying that one must be careful to avoid getting the handler trapped between the rising birds and the gun.

All hunting species are called upon to work hard when in the field and they must be given frequent rests and water, especially on warm days. Don't push dogs too energetically or they'll simply decide that it's not worth all the effort.

When you're running your own dog, it won't

Give the hard-working dog frequent rest periods, water and an occasional small treat to keep his interest. It's also a good idea to check him frequently for ticks, burrs and cuts.

take long to determine the work pattern that he naturally wants to follow. Some need a ten-minute break ever forty to forty-five minutes; others will go at high speed for well over an hour and then require a twenty-minute rest. If you let the dog decide how hard and how fast he wants to work, he'll perform better over the long haul.

Some animals have to have light snacks to maintain energy (and interest) over long periods, so it's a good idea to carry some of the dog's favorite dry treats in the pocket of your hunting jacket. After he's rested and watered, offer him a *small* tidbit.

At least once or twice during the course of a day-long outing, the handler should examine the dog to see if he's picked up any painful burrs, or ticks. I carry a small wire brush in my pocket to remove burrs because my dog has a talent for sweeping them up with his shaggy ears. Paw pads, too, must be checked for cuts or to see if they've picked up any foreign matter that could develop into later trouble.

On one memorable mid-winter Northern Adirondack grouse hunt I absent-mindedly crossed a fast running icy stream, expecting my Springer to wade across behind me. He dipped one paw in the frigid water, sat down on the bank, and howled with indignation. I had to re-cross the stream to carry the dog over on my shoulders—to the great amusement of my hunting companions. While being carried ol' Max let me know just what he thought of me by barking in my ear! Be considerate of your dog and make allowances for difficult terrain.

DOG ILLNESSES

The first thing one should do upon acquiring a new pup is to take him to a good vet. Ask the doctor to go over him carefully. Assuming the dog passes this examination, let the doctor know what shots (and worming) the dog was given by the breeder and continue on from there. Most vets will subsequently send you notices when booster shots are called for.

On the first visit, also ask the doctor to give you the drops required for control of ear mites. Mite infestation are inevitable among dogs that work in the field so, the first time you find the animal scratching his ears you should start treatment to spare him unnecessary suffering.

As I mentioned earlier, ticks are also a constant threat. They're easily removed if you get to them fast enough: use a pair of tweezers and gently lift the body of the tick so that it can be extracted, gently, without tearing off the head under the skin. Deeply imbedded ticks are more of a problem; I've used the heat of a cigarette, drops of alcohol and about anything else I could find to aggravate the darned things and get them moving in the right direction, with varying success.

After getting wet, dogs with long, shaggy ears are highly susceptible to ear infections. I've had to depart from recommended grooming practices by clipping my springer's ears closer to minimize this problem. One vet even suggested that I tie or tape his ears up, over his head, to facilitate a natural flow or air after a dunking. This, and a general wiping of the outer ear canals with a clean tuft of cotton does much to prevent the problem.

Look out for the robust dog that suddenly starts acting sluggish. He may need another worming. An overly large appetite together with a skinny frame and a bloated stomach are pretty good indicators of worms.

Heart worms are the current major threat to canines. These are spread via mosquitoes and once planted in the bloodstream of a dog, it's just a question of time before they kill the animal. Shortness of breath and lack of vitality are the usual symptoms. Treatment is very tricky once the disease is contracted so take the dog to a vet; don't try to treat him yourself because there is a good chance that you'll kill the animal. Fourteen dogs have expired from heart worms in my own little town in the past year so I can't over-emphasize the seriousness of this threat. If you already have a dog that hasn't been checked for this take him to a vet without further delay and have the dog tested. The vet will instruct you on the required procedures for administering preventative medicine as a matter of routine thereafter.

There's no question that a good dog can make a hunt more fruitful and enjoyable; until you've hunted with one you won't know what you've been missings!

CHAPTER 12

Shotguns for Waterfowl

Mention a shotgun for ducks or geese to any group of shotgunners and you'll immediately conjure up images of 10- and 12-gauge magnums equipped with long barrels and extra full chokes. By popular definition, these are the real waterfowl guns.

Yet, more ducks and geese are shot annually with the plain old garden-variety 2¾-inch twelve gauge than anything else!

The fact is, long barreled magnums (with tight shooting chokes) are perfectly suited to pass shooting where the hunter rarely gets an opportunity at a bird closer than forty yards. On the other hand, more ducks and geese are shot over decoyed layouts, in grain fields, or in small marshes and ponds where the standard twelve bore will turn in a very satisfactory performance, if fed the proper ammo. One doesn't *have* to shoot a magnum to bag his limit. Nevertheless, let's start at the top, with the largest bores shooting the heaviest shells.

THE TEN-GAUGE MAGNUM

For a time following WW II ten-gauge guns were as scarce as a ham at kosher luncheon—they simply weren't being produced! Used gun prices on pre-war models literally sky-rocketed and dealers who traded in used specimens moved them out as fast as they came in. Then, little by little, a few imports started trickling into the country, usually in the form of side-by-side doubles. Foreign manufacturers were really reluctant to go into 10 gauge production because they have virtually no home market for it. The few pieces that did pop up here came from small producers having very limited productions.

Today, it appears that the ten gauge is about to return in interesting numbers. Some better side-by-side specimens are already offered by larger importers and Ithaca has kicked the door open with their new 10-gauge autoloading Magnum. Word trickling down through the grapevine hints that other American firms will soon unleash some ten gauge surprises of their own.

The biggest problem one will run into with older specimens, is that many were made with chambers shorter than 3½ inches. Because modern 10-gauge shells are made in lengths of 2⅞ and 3½ inches—one must be careful not to load a 3½-inch shell into a gun having a shorter chamber. By

Magnum shotguns are the choice of those who specialize in waterfowl hunting. Most ducks and geese, however, are shot with the standard 12 gauge.

Ithaca's new Mag-10 gas-operated auto is sure to excite the interest of ardent goose hunters.

all means, have a gunsmith check out that old relic before putting it to use.

Oddly enough, the only advantage to the ten gauge is that it will put *an eighth of an ounce* more shot into the air than a 12-gauge 3-inch magnum. The ten gauge is no faster, velocity-wise, than the twelve. (The heaviest ten-gauge load packs 2 ounces of shot and the three-inch twelve— 1⅞ ounces.) Anyone who feels he must have that edge is probably laboring under the opinion that the ten gauge is deadly at 100 yards! Frankly, it isn't! Seventy-five yards is the extreme range for both the twelve and ten simply because no one has found a way to significantly increase the muzzle-velocity of the shot load. Those heavy-shot loads, incidentally, in both the big magnums, provide some pretty hefty recoil at the butt end. Those who feel they must have a magnum ten should make sure the gun is packing at least 9½ to 10 pounds in weight.

For shots up to seventy yards, however, there can be little doubt that the Magnum 10 is more effective than anything else. My comments are intended only to deter the would-be buyer from adopting the popular notion that the ten gauge brings those 100-yard geese into range.

THE TWELVE-GAUGE, 3-INCH MAGNUM

If I felt I had to have a magnum for waterfowl, this is the one I'd choose—simply because it would enable me to use other twelve-gauge shells as well.

I like versatility! Autoloading models, of course, will inevitably malfunction when you try to run 2¾-inch shells though them but, even so, they'll function as single shots with the lighter loads. With a double, pump or over and under there's no problem.

Another advantage of the twelve mag is that 3-factory shells can be had in a broad variety of loadings. The ten gauge, by comparison is generally loaded only with 1⅝ ozs. of #4 shot or 2 ozs. of #2 shot. This is rather restrictive.

In non-auto models, the 3-inch twelve will accept all 2¾-inch magnum shells as well as all conventional 2¾-inch twelve-gauge loads. Thus, one can run the full range of shot sizes.

THE SIXTEEN GAUGE

While there is no true 16-gauge magnum (today), ammo plants have been loading a 2¾-dram shell with a 1¼-oz. shot load and labelling this "16 Magnum." This is a heavy load for a sixteen, but one that can safely be used in all sixteen-gauge models that are relatively current manufacture and in good shooting condition. Shot sizes, for the "Mag" load are #2, #4 and #6.

If some readers have puzzled over my little reference to "today," above, it is because there was a 3-inch sixteen gauge made at one time. Few firearms people are aware of the fact and I, too, laughed when I first heard the claim. Then my old friend, Bill Amestoy, pulled out a 16-gauge Parker stamped to indicate three-inch chambers. At that point one would be inclined to think that some custom gunsmith had simply bored out the chambers, that is, until Amestroy pulled out a half a

Remington makes their Model 1100 in a 3-inch twelve-gauge version for those who want something a bit heavier for those hard-to-decoy species.

case of 3-inch 16-gauge shells loaded by a now defunct commercial plant.

The sixteen gauge has been heading downhill since WW II because the increased variety of twelve gauge shells have encroached upon it in one direction while the souped up twenty—specifically the 3-inch version—has pressed it from the other. Between the 12 and the 20, the 16 gauge is now so completely overlapped it really doesn't make much sense to buy one. Either one of the other two gauges will give you all the loads handled by the 16 with a few added for good measure.

THE TWENTY-GAUGE MAGNUM

The hottest load made for the Magnum twenty consists of a 1¼-ounce shot load, equal to the heaviest 16. Also, since the 3-inch twenty can be had with 1 and 1⅛ ounces of shot as well, it matches a good number of the light 12-gauge loads.

The twenty magnum is an ideal choice for the new waterfowl enthusiast, particularly the budding teenager. It is also a good choice for the women's libbers who hanker to share a frigid duck blind on a frosty morning. These comments, however, shouldn't scare off the adult male—many grizzled old veterans have switched to the hot twenty because they feel it is a bit more challenging.

CONVENTIONAL 12, 16 and 20

As we stated at the outset, more waterfowl is bagged with a standard 2¾ - inch twelve than anything else. The important thing to remember when going with the traditional 12, 16 or 20, is to match the ammo to shooting conditions and don't get carried away with the nearby magnums that are folding birds seventy yards up. With the standard gauges, limit your attempts to birds that are *under* sixty yards off.

Favor the larger shot sizes in express loadings.

Remington's Model 870 pump gun can also be had in 20-gauge, 3-inch magnum—a shell that is very popular with those who favor the lighter gauges.

With the 12 bore, one can go to the 2¾-inch magnum shell which pushes 1½ ounces of shot into the air. That's an effective load, one I've used in an old clunk of a recoil action auto for more than ten years with considerable success. I must confess, though, that recoil from this shell in a 6½-lb. field gun gets progressively more punishing as a good duck day wears on. Eventually I was beaten into submission and installed a tougher recoil spring. weighting the stock at the same time. Now the durn thing is tolerable. (Perhaps I should add that I use this on salt-water divers in Long Island Sound—birds for which there are large daily limits.)

BARREL LENGTHS AND CHOKE

The waterfowler's natural tendency is to opt for a long barrel with an extra full choke. Such a selection is fine if one plans only pass shooting. In a duck blind, with a large raft of decoys, or with a good bird caller, such a barrel combination may not be necessary. Whenever the birds can be coaxed into ranges under forty yards with any real consistency a modified or improved-modified choke may be more desirable. Some special magnums are made with tightly choked thirty-two inch barrels. The longer barrel length does nothing to help performance ballistically, it simply provides a longer sighting plane that, some feel, will help sight alignment on distant targets. With double-barrel guns, side-by-side or over and under, a combination of modified and full chokes are usually offered in barrels measuring twenty-eight or thirty inches. Twin tubes of greater length can be awkward. Obviously, a choice of chokes is highly desireable, especially in light of my earier comments on the modified choke.

OVERALL WEIGHT

Heavy magnum loads can be punishing if fired in comparatively light field guns. When choosing a shotgun specifically for magnum shooting, favor heavier models. Recoil can be minimized, too, by a gas-operated autoloading action. Weight, in a waterfowl gun, is not as detrimental as it would be in a gun intended for upland game because the shooting generally lacks the uplander's spontaneity.

Duck and goose hunters often go for the heavier buttstocks with full pistol grips and beavertail fore-ends.

SOME TIPS ON BOATS, DECOYS AND CALLS

Waterfowl hunting is usually done in the late fall or early winter when most waterways are pretty danged cold and the hunter burdened with heavy clothing and gear.

The selection of a duck boat therefore depends entirely on the type of water upon which it is to be used. A low riding rig with little freeboard can be downright dangerous in choppy waters.

For years I used a low silhouette double-ended twelve footer in Long Island Sound and I had more close calls than I'd care to count. In Northern waters look for stability, safety and comfort first; then set about rigging camouflage material if you feel it necessary to disguise a conspicuous freeboard.

In warmer climates, or on protected waterways, the low silhouette is much preferred! Some hunters have even made good use of small inflatable craft under such conditions.

Regardless of how big the duck boat is, it should never contain more than two hunters. Any more than that is decidedly dangerous. Two men in one boat should sit at opposite ends, facing each other. Preferably, both should be right-handed or both left-handed so that only one man will be shooting at given flight. Stringent safety precautions are essential in such tight quarters.

Incidentally, the duck boat is no place for a gun equipped with an adjustable choke device having a ventilated sleeve. I once made the mistake of sharing a boat with a hunter so equipped and my ears rang for a week thereafter!

Camouflaging is another important factor that will influence the hunter's chances. One doesn't wear brightly-colored caps or clothing when waterfowling. Lightly-colored boats should either be repainted olive green or marsh brown and/or draped with burlap and marsh grass.

THE DUCK BLIND

Blinds vary greatly in size, shape and description, depending upon whether they are temporary improvisations or semi-permanent installations that are intended for season-long use.

The shallow pit blind is widely used in grainfield country from Texas to Saskatchewan. Hunters usually visit the shooting site the day before the hunt to observe the flyways and dig their blinds.

In marsh country, the hunters brings a machete, some fishing line and something to sit on. Then, selecting an appropriate site, he'll cut and tie bundles of marsh grass, arranging them to screen his shooting stand.

Sophisticated blinds, such as those leased on a seasonal basis in the Chesapeake Bay area, are permanent structures. Some are quite elaborate, with hinged doors, space heaters, shelves, benches and gun racks. Many are built on stilts over shallow water areas so that a duck boat can be hidden underneath. The portable folding blind of camouflage-painted material, over a wire or aluminum-tubing frame, is also very practical because it can be set up so quickly, and moved with little difficulty.

DECOYS

Ducks and geese have been lured by everything from crumpled bits of newspaper and pieces of bedsheet to exquisitely carved and painted realistic reproductions. The fact of the matter is that some species of waterfowl are easier to decoy than others. Also, the finest and most expensive decoys

Camouflage outfits, such as this one by Ten-X, enhance the waterfowler's opportunities. Specialized shooting clothing is generally found in better gun shops.

will go for naught if they're not used properly.

When hunting scoter off Long Island a simple string of silhouette decoys made from black-painted masonite will do the job nicely, but one can't expect to coax a mallard or pintail into gunning range with such a decoy. The wary breeds require considerably more subtlety. For this reason, one will find considerable variety in the types of commercial decoys offered:

Inflatable Decoys—"DEEKS" is a comparatively inexpensive line of decoys made from a light rubber, designed with an O-ring base extension.

When dropped on *calm* water these will trap enough air to inflate. Their biggest advantage is that one hunter can handily carry a large number of decoys with ease. Don't try these in choppy waters.

Papier Mache Decoys—offered by a number of firms. Large, light, and lifelike, these are well within the reach of the thinnest wallets. For calm water layouts, the only significant problem one will have with papier-mache is that of maintenance—they must be handled carefully and repaired and reconditioned periodically.

Cork Decoys—rank among the best because they're light and durable though they can't be as elaborately carved or painted as wooden models.

Wood Decoys—highly durable though somewhat heavy and bulky. The primary advantage one will find with wood decoys is that they are often carved and painted very realistically—details that make them most desireable for those "hard-to-decoy" species.

Some decoys are made life-size while others are obviously oversize. The oversize decoy can be much more effective simply because they can be seen from a greater distance.

More important then the size and realism of a decoy, however, is the way it is used. Large rafts are preferred but, if they are poorly arranged they can't be expected to lure anything into gunning range. One must keep certain fundamentals in mind when arranging decoys: ducks, like planes, prefer to land into the wind, so, set the point of the layout upwind of the blind position. Next, neither ducks nor geese will set down towards the head of a settled flock—they'll invariably land some distance besind the spread and swim into position at the tail end. Therefore the blind should be positioned some distance to the rear of the layout, in the landing area. Decoys are generally laid out in rough patterns such as an inverted "U" or "V" with gaps in one of the tail-end extensions to form an invitation for cruising flocks. Avoid nice, neat

P.S. Olt makes a variety of game calls; this is their L-22 Regular Goose Call. This game call can be very effective, if the hunter learns to use them properly.

Olt's DR-115 Double Reed Duck Call is one of the author's favorites.

straight lines: arrange the decoys in clusters, small groups of three or four, irregularly spaced.

How many decoys does it take to do the job?

On large bodies of water, Long Island Sound or Chesapeake Bay, for example, stools of 100 to 200 decoys are not unusual. With large bodies of water it takes a lot of decoys to attract the attention of the high flying formations.

Stools for smaller lakes, and narrow rivers can be considerably smaller—three or four dozen should do the job. I've often had good luck with twelve to eighteen decoys on small ponds. In open grain fields the spreads can range from a dozen or so to sixty or seventy. A good caller can get by with fewer decoys.

DUCK AND GOOSE CALLS

One frosty December morning, some years back, I was hunting blacks in a marsh on Long Island's north shore. My companion and I had just finished setting out about three dozen deeks (the inflatable rubber decoy) when another group

Be prepared when you head for the duck boat or blind because no one will show much sympathy if you're unable to cope with the weather. Cold weather outfits, like these from Ten-X, are a must!

of hunters came into the far side of our marshy inlet to set up their blind some distance from us.

As the sun crept over the horizon we could see the first small flights take wing in the distance but some time elapsed before any headed our way. And then, suddenly, a small flock appeared low over the water, heading through about mid-way between our blind and our neighbor's. Since they were obviously out of range of both blinds, someone across the marsh grabbed a game call and cut loose with the most god-awful blasts I've ever heard. Instead of calling the birds in, the call had just the opposite effect—it seemed to chase them away! About ten minutes later, another flock appeared and headed in our direction, obviously decoying into our layout. Again, the novice across the marsh cut loose and the entire flock picked up and lit out before we had a chance to get off a shot.

That was too much for my companion. He stood up in the blind, cupped his hands in front of his mouth and yelled across the marsh (expletives deleted) ". . . one of you guys—drown that danged nut with the game call!"

Thereafter, all was silent across the way and the shooting improved. Luckily, birds would get past us would often circle over the other blind while making their getaway, so our quiet neighbors had some good shooting too.

That's the game call story in a nutshell; if you don't know how to use it, you're better off without it. The average novice tends to blow too loud, too long and too often. Not only that, but unless he's studied bird calling he doesn't know what calls to use.

Ducks and geese have excellent hearing, soft tones on a call are quite effective over considerable distances. The experienced caller will only use the call to attract attention to his rig and the closer the birds, the softer he'll call. As long as the flight is heading in his direction he won't call at all. If it starts to veer away, the hunter may make a soft feeding gabble on the call just to get them back on line. If new to the calling business, one should get a recording of duck and goose calls from his local dealer and practice them at home. Then he should carefully study the reactions of the birds in flight. In this way he'll quickly learn what not to do.

Concluding this chapter on waterfowl guns and hunting I have to add a few words on the subject of clothing: waterfowling is a cold-weather sport and the hunter has to be ready for anything. Be sure to take along rain gear and plenty of warm clothing. Once the blind is set up and the decoys rigged, no one wants to call it quits because one member of the party is drenched or freezing. There's little pity in the duck blind for the hunter who is inadequately prepared.

CHAPTER 13

The Upland Game Gun

In this category are included the prime shotgun targets: quail, dove, pheasant, woodcock, and assorted species of grouse.

There's little need to detail guns for rabbit and squirrel because these aren't winged targets and because they're taken with just about anything that throws lead. Other regional favorites, such as the chukar, hun and sharptail are generally hunted in the same manner as pheasant and grouse so that information can be applied to these species; only shot sizes may differ and we'll note those differences as we go along.

QUAIL

These are covey birds that can be "walked up" or, preferably, hunted with the aid of an appropriate bird dog—generally of the pointer variety.

In the South, where the quail flourishes, large coveys of forty to fifty birds are not unusual. In certain mountainous or Northern areas, coveys tend to be much smaller. On Long Island, for example, I rarely found them consisting of more than ten or twelve birds.

Essentially, the bobwhite quail roosts on the ground, in a tight circle with his mates, but he has also been found in trees. Like the pheasant, he'll often run rather than fly at the approach of a

hunter, providing he has adequate ground cover. It's not unusual to find him "sitting tight" either, if he feels the danger is going to pass. His natural coloring would lead one to believe that he'd be easy to spot while playing 'possum, but that's not true; he blends into scrub growth beautifully. Many a time I've gone into a patch, after flushing a covey, to find one lone bird tunneling into the ground cover.

There's a thrill to the flush of a covey of quail that never fails to excite even the oldest and most experienced hunter. The birds seemingly erupt from the ground, scattering in all directions, and since they're fast and noisy they can startle the hunter who is unaware of their presence.

Gauge is not important to the quail hunter if he normally hunts with a dog. Anything from .410 to 12 will do; however, the smaller the gauge, the more sporty the shooting. I'd favor a twenty or twenty-eight gauge in a lightweight, fast-handling side-by-side or over and under. To get the most desireable weight and balance, these would likely be quality models at higher than average cost.

When the family budget refuses to stretch that far, I'd look for a lightweight pump or auto, in the same gauges.

Lacking a dog and forced to walk the birds

Rabbits, America's most popular upland game target, can be taken with most any gauge and shot size. Most, however, prefer standard velocity 5's or 6's, regardless of gauge.

up, I might be tempted to use a slightly larger gauge, especially if I had reason to believe the birds would be wary. In a 16 or 12 bore, however, I'd use only the lightest possible loads—brush #8's or skeet #9's. Frankly, the twenty gauge appears to be the best all-around quail gun.

A short, twenty-six inch, barrel is the most desireable, and this should be bored with an improved-cylinder choke. Those who can afford it, should opt for a ventilated rib. Select the fastest handling gun available and be sure it balances well. Then ask your local gunsmith to check the fit of the stock.

Standard velocity shotshells are the rule and shot sizes can range from #7½ to #9. There's no need for anything heavier. When forced to hunt with a larger gauge, or tighter choke, use only brush #8's.

Western varieties of quail can be taken with the same range of shot sizes and generally the same barrel specs, although some Western hunters prefer longer barrels and tighter chokes.

DOVE

There are two basically different strains of these; the mourning dove and the white-winged dove. The mourning dove is found throughout most of the U. S. though he tends to spend his winters in the South. The white-wing is a native of the Southwest.

Many quail "purists" prefer the smaller gauges, like this "28" from Remington. With larger gauges shooters often turn to brush loads.

Depending upon the season and whether or not he is breeding, migrating, or simply planning his next move, the mourning dove can be bold or timid and rarely predictable. He is unquestionably the most elusive of all winged game: in flight he seems to delight in aerial maneuvers, swerving, diving and climbing for no apparent reason. One gets the impression that he doesn't know where he wants to go; yet his flight always seems to follow a pattern that gets him from "here" to "there" in an irregularly straight line. The experienced wingshooter inevitably walks away from his first dove shoot with his chin on his chest because all the rules of tracking and leading have gone for naught. With the dove one learns to snap-shoot!

I was introduced to dove hunting by a good friend from Arkansas who took special pains to prepare me for a humbling experience. When we finally arrived at a newly cut corn field I succeeded in bagging the first four birds that came my way—which led me to give my Arkansas friend the subtle "Yankee needle." *And then I went on to miss the next six!* (Did you ever see a hunter suf-

fering from hoof'n mouth?)

At times dove will be found co-mingled with coveys of quail. Generally, however, they'll travel in pairs, disdaining company even from others of their own kind. Most hunters set up on the perimeter of newly cut grain fields where sporadic incoming and outgoing flights will make for lively pass shooting. Late in the day the dove will habitually head for water before retiring for the night. Some excellent shooting is found in the vicinity of water holes.

The twelve gauge dominates this sport because one needs large patterns and plenty of lead to score with any regularity. Short, open-choked barrels are best when used with standard velocity #7½'s, #8's or #9's. The double gun should be bored with improved cylinder and modified chokes.

As for a dog, any retrieving specimen will do the job.

The white-wing dove of the Southwest is something else again. His flight pattern is not as erratic but he's small, very fast and unusually wary espe-

The English style straight-grip stock and splinter fore-end minimizes gun weight, improves balance and makes for an ideal upland game gun.

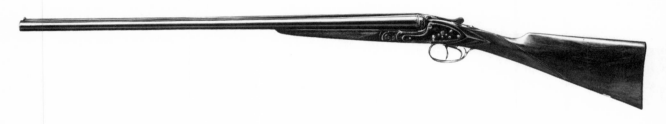

cially when subjected to some hunting pressure.

The best hunting occurs during the migrating flight periods and then in the vicinity of the Mexican border—in Texas, Arizona, New Mexico and Southern California.

Again the twelve gauge is most appropriate though twenty-eight inch barrels with modified or full borings seem to be preferred. Because of the distances involved, slightly larger shot sizes will deliver more game to the platter. Try #6's and #7½'s and don't hesitate to use express loads if the birds are really wary.

Well-fitted light guns will serve best; because of the number of shells expended, recoil can be a factor—gas-operated autos are the most popular for this reason. With doubles, choose modified and full chokes. Retrievers, again, are the dogs to use.

THE PHEASANT

This Chinese import is unusually hardy and has taken to northern areas where the hunter is denied quail, chukar, dove and the like. He does particularly well in the grain fields of the midwest.

Hunters complain only that the pheasant would rather run than fly. That's certainly true, but one can adapt certain hunting techniques that would serve to block the running bird or, one can employ the services of a good bird dog.

When hunting without a dog, you'll need a group of hunters, at least four. Half of these are placed as standers between the bird field and the natural cover forming the escape route. Standers *don't shoot,* they simply prevent birds from leaving the field via the ground route. The balance of the party enters the field from the opposite side, slowly criss-crossing their way through. For safety's sake, it's important that hunters refrain from shooting at running birds. All targets should be high enough to force shots well over the heads of the standers. By the same token standers should sit or kneel as the guns get within range and *all* muzzles must be kept pointed skyward.

With dove hunting one quickly learns to snap-shoot —either that or go home skunked! The mourning dove is undoubtedly the wingshooter's most difficult target. Note the generously-proportioned game bag on this Ten-X hunting jacket.

In the east, when hunting in brush country, or over dogs, a twenty-six inch improved-cylinder barrel will do best in combination with #6's or #7½'s. Most prefer express loads but I've never had cause to complain about the performance of my standard velocity shells with #5's or #6's.

In an automatic I'll place the number six shell in the chamber followed by a five in the first magazine position. With my over and under, I'll put the six in the open choked barrel and the five in the modified.

With the pump gun it's possible to load a standard velocity shell in the chamber and follow it with an express load in the first magazine position. The hunter will thus have a better opportunity with the follow-up shot if he should miss the first.

Considerable controversy stirs the ranks of experienced pheasant hunters and it's really impossible to establish any hard and fast rules. One close friend of mine insists upon a 28-inch modified barrel and #9 shot. A third member of our group insists that "Express-fives" are the thing to use on that "rubber-assedbird." There's little ground for debate because they're both bagging birds with consistency! I guess the question of shot size and load really depends upon what a *particular* gun does by way of patterning and performance.

In the wide open spaces of the Midwest, a longer barrel and a tigher choke are sure to be more desireable—the twenty-eight inch modified digesting "Express fives or sixes." Some even go to the thirty-inch full.

Working without a dog in the open country of Iowa or the Dakotas, the thirty-inch barrel would not be out of place.

The pheasant is not hard to hit if taken "on the rise." Because of his size he appears to need a little extra time to build up steam, so when flushed, he'll invariably struggle up to an altitude of about twelve feet before gaining any real air speed—then he'll level off and be gone. Most hunters try to catch him as he tops his towering climb; at that point he seems to hesitate for a fraction of a second before setting his wings for the getaway flight.

Pointing species of bird dogs are not generally used on pheasant because of the latter's running instinct. Instead, most prefer a retrieving breed like the Lab or Chesapeake. The springer spaniel also does well with this bird.

WOODCOCK

There's something about the woodcock that unglues the most conservative of minds. Men who toil diligently in their chosen occupations all year long will suddenly turn up with glassy eyes and a cold sweat as woodcock season approaches. Then on opening day, they'll come down with all manner of exotic, near-terminal illnesses which last, miraculously, until the day the season closes. One long-suffering employer, losing patience with his prize salesman's annual relapses growled, "Where does he hunt those damn birds? at Lourdes?"

At the risk of contributing to this sophisticated form of adult delinquency, I'll go on to discuss guns for the wily woodcock, but first a little background on the target itself.

The woodcock is one of the few birds that favor nocturnal feeding. A relative of the rail, he'll lay up most of the day in a well camouflaged ground

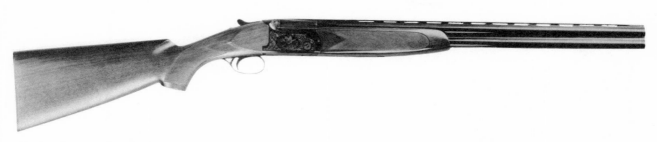

A 20-gauge Falconet Ebony.

nest and then, about twilight time, he'll venture forth to start his rounds. He favors heavily thicketed terrain in swampy lowlands where his long bill can easily penetrate the soft, often muddy, earth to reach worms and other sub-surface dwellers. His remarkable bill functions much like a sonar device: when he drives it deeply into the ground it's so sensitive that it picks up the vibrations of angleworms and the like, enabling the bird to locate his food with unerring accuracy.

Because of his penchant for low swampy grounds, the woodcock is found in heavy brush areas where the density of alders and briars make the going rough for the hunter. Dogs, too, suffer in such terrain. Guns, for hunting in such heavy cover, should be short, light and easily handled. The double gun, whether side-by-side or over and under, is particularly popular among "Timberdoodle" hunters, especially when equipped with slim straight-grip stocks and splinter fore-ends. The .410 and 28 gauge rank highest (with the purists) and the 20 gauge lags close behind. The twelve gauge, however, is not unheard of—even if frowned upon by the more dedicated breed.

While deceptively fast and somewhat erratic in flight, the woodcock is easily killed, if hit, with #7½, 8 or 9 shot. (Most prefer the number 9.) Standard velocity loads are the rule.

Open chokes are favored (in larger gauges) because shooting is generally accomplished at fairly close range. The #8 Brush load is particularly appealing to those who are obliged to hunt with a large gauge and/or a tight choke.

The cocker spaniel was originally developed for this type of hunting but has fallen into such disrepute that few are encountered today. Most hunters tend toward the springer spaniel, the Brittany or a good setter. The important thing is to find a dog that has the gumption to plow through the heaviest clumps of brush without hesitation. Some individual dogs, of assorted breeds, shy away from the woodcock,—often refusing to retrieve— and I've never come up with a satisfactory explanation for this. Does the bird have a scent that disturbs the dog, or is it the long potentially dangerous bill that scares them off? Since downed birds often fall into impossible thickets, a dog's retrieving ability is of paramount importance.

Clothing plays an important role with the woodcock hunter so special mention has to be made of this facet of the sport. Heavy brush pants (preferably with leather or vinyl facings) are a must! Jackets, too, should resist penetration by briars. Boots should be at least knee high and waterproof (many prefer hip boots). Sturdy leather gloves are also desireable.

GROUSE

Rare is the hunter who will buy a gun expressly for grouse shooting. While certain species of the grouse family are considered lordly targets, they are most often pursued with guns better suited to other forms of scattergunning. Perhaps this is because grouse are unceremoniously lumped into this general category commonly titled, "upland game," and few of us would care to spring for a

Heavily faced brush pants are essential for comfort in thorny, brushy terrain. These are by Ten-X.

hunter spends in their pursuit. (I know a couple of Canadian guides that will gladly swap their T-bone steaks for a couple!) If you are inclined to concede these points you'll understand why I feel that the grouse is deserving of a better fate than to be centered in the pattern of a crow hunter's extra full choked 12 bore.

The true grouse purist—that rare breed that dedicates his hunting efforts, and his pocketbook, to this singular goal, has some very definite ideas about the ideal gun for his sport. We'll start at that point and go on to discuss make-do procedures one can adopt to make use of his favorite all-around scattergun.

There are three major factors to consider when selecting a shotgun for *any* form of hunting. First, the hunter should be sure his shotgun fits him: too many hunters assume that any gun coming off the rack will do if it has a trigger, a stock and a barrel. The fact is, very *few* guns really fit their buyers. The average hunter will rarely sense the difference in the store, but the difference is dramatic in the field. Stocks should be tailored for length, drop at comb, drop at heel and pitch.

The second detail to look for is balance. Note the position of your hands after dry-firing the gun. Measure to a point about midway between the palms of both hands. That point should be the balance of that gun. (You can check it by balancing the gun on one finger.) If it is not close, the gun will not handle well under field shooting conditions. When the balance point is too close to the trigger hand, the gun is popularly termed "muzzle light" and the shooter will almost surely overswing his targets. When the balance point is too close to the forward hand, the gun is "muzzle heavy" and the shooter will have trouble catching up to his target. Balance can sometimes be corrected by removing material, or adding weight to the buttstock. But only minor faults can be corrected in this manner.

The third, and last major consideration is over-

separate firearm for each specimen that makes up that broad grouping. Nevertheless, birds like the ruffed grouse provide excellent sport, excellent fare for the table, and are worthy of the time a all weight. Generally, the lighter the gun the faster it will handle. Grouse hunters need all the natural speed they can get, a heavyweight gun is therefore a definite handicap. Almost any gun will feel light and manageable in the store. But what will it feel like after eight hours of tough going in the field? My own rule of thumb for a field gun is 6¼ to 6¾ pounds. Anything heavier is awkward. Really fine English doubles cost as much as they do because they're light and meticulously balanced.

Type of gun is a matter of preference; the hunter should know what he favors—side-by-side double, over and under, automatic, pump, etc.,—before he visits his local gun dealer. The individual's pocketbook has a strong influence on this question. Generally, good quality pump action guns are the least expensive. Automatic types are a bit more expensive and good twin-barreled guns are the most costly. Extras, such as ventilated ribs, engraving, single triggers (on double guns) etc., would add considerably to cost. Good quality guns are a good investment, frequently increasing in value as the years roll by. Cheap, economy guns are often worth 30% less than their sale price as soon as they leave the store and they rarely give any real satisfaction in the field. This is especially true with side-by-side and over and under guns. The shooter who can't afford a quality model would do better with a pump or automatic. On occasion, though, it is possible to find a bargain in a used double or over and under. (See the chapter entitled "Buying a Used Gun!")

Incidentally, shooters with very limited finances should not discard the idea of a bolt action shotgun. A great many grouse are shot with these inexpensive models, in spite of the fact that the shooter rarely gets more than one shot at any given bird.

CHOKES, BARRELS AND AMMUNITION FOR GROUSE

In other chapters we discussed in detail, gauges, barrels, and chokes. Here, we'll learn how to apply the rules to grouse hunting. The important thing to remember is that chokes and ammo are all-important, *not* barrel lengths. Next, decide what species of grouse you'll regularly hunt. Where will they be found? How will you hunt them? What is the average shooting distance under those conditions?

Short-Range Shooting—average shot taken at 20 to 30 yards—typical of Eastern brush country hunting of ruffed grouse, or of hunting over dogs. With pumps and autos the best choice is an improved cylinder choke with a 26-inch barrel. Double guns should be improved-cylinder and modified with 26-inch barrels.

Ammo—in pump guns, use a standard velocity #7½ or #8 in the chamber followed by an express #7½ in the first magazine position. When the first shot misses the target, the second will provide a bit more velocity and shot. This little trick can't be employed when using some automatic shotguns because they must be adjusted for either standard or high-velocity loads and cannot be expected to function reliably when the loads are mixed. With most automatic shotguns, the hunter should use a standard velocity #7½ or #8 shell in the chamber, followed by a standard velocity #6 in the first magazine position.

The hunter using a side-by-side or over and under has the advantage of two chokes—the second barrel (modified) throwing a slightly tighter pattern than the first (improved cylinder) barrel. Consequently, a number of options are available to the double-gunner: the first barrel can be loaded with a standard velocity #7½ or #8 and the same shell can also be used in the tighter-shooting second barrel. Or, he can substitute an express #7½ in the second barrel. When the birds are really holding "close," it would pay to use even smaller shot with the first shell—standard velocity #9's and standard #7½'s for the back-up barrel. Days when the birds are unusually wary call for the combination of high-velocity #7½'s and #6's.

Open Field Shooting—average shot taken at 30 to 40 yards—typical of hunting over flushing dogs. Single barrel guns should be equipped with modified choke barrels (generally 28 inches in length.) Double barrels can be improved-cylinder and modified or modified and full. Again—usually 28 inches in length. AMMO—the standard velocity #7½ is still the best first choice. In a pump gun, back it up with an express #7½. In an auto, use a standard velocity #6 in the magazine for the second shot. On those days when the birds seem to be extra skittish, use express loads exclusively. Double gun hunters can go with the standard velocity #7½ in the first barrel and an express #7½ in the second. They can also go to the express loads exclusively when they're having problems getting up to the birds.

Long-Range, Open Country Shooting—average shot taken at 40 yards or more—typical of Western grouse hunting: this is the sport for full choked barrels in a pump or auto and these are generally offered in a choice of 28 or 30 inches in length. Twin-barreled guns are best selected with a combination of modified and full chokes in similar barrel lengths. AMMO—high velocity shells are in order, preferably in sizes #6 or #7½. The hun, sharptail and chukar can be taken with similar equipment.

However, with some of the larger species like the often unpalatable sage grouse—slightly larger shot sizes may be called for.

For the average hunter there is little doubt that the standard 12 gauge is the best choice for versatility and effectiveness. Experienced shotgunners who enjoy the challenge of a handicap often go with the 20 gauge. Lighter gauges, such as the 28 and .410 really separate the shooters from the strollers. Women, youngsters and shooters of small stature usually handle the 20 gauge better than they would the harder recoiling 12.

THE IMPROVISED GROUSE GUN

Very often the duck or crow shooter will get an invitation to go on a grouse hunt: if he owns only a full choked 12 bore when conditions call for more open chokes, he's got a problem. Besides the obvious trick of waiting until the birds get out to full choke range there area few other options open to the over-gunned shooter. First, he should use only the lightest possible standard velocity loads—shells containing no more than 1⅛ ounces of shot. He can also use a slightly larger shot size —6's instead of #7½'s—to reduce the number of pellets he's going to have in that concentrated pattern. Some ammo makers produce a shell called a Brush Load which is made with a compartmented shot reservoir designed to disburse the shot charge quickly. Generally loaded with #8 shot, this is an ideal bore opener.

High-velocity (express) loads, under these conditions, would yield only feather confetti.

Now, let's reverse the problem—the gunner has an open choked gun when forty-yard shots are the order of the day. High-velocity loads will help, especially when they're selected for maximum shot capacity. More importantly, the gunner should look for shells made with one-piece plastic wads having a complete shot-enclosing compartment. These tend to concentrate the pattern. A smaller shot size (#8's instead of #7½'s) would place more shot in the pattern but there's a point at which the effectiveness of the larger, heavier, shot is advantageous.

The ruffed grouse is a very wary bird, one that tries the best of bird dogs. He's hard to approach, fast, and often seems to have graduated from the "School of Elusive Maneuvers" (since he invariably manages to get a heavy-limbed tree between himself and the hunter as he makes his getaway)! Because he is usually hunted when the leaves are down, the crunching step of the hunter alerts him. For this reason, when hunting without a dog it's often more fruitful to go out after a rain.

Grouse lie up close to food and water (like most game birds) and they prefer heavy stands of spruce. Look for this combination. On sunny days following cold or wet spells, look for them on high hardwood ridges.

THE UPLAND GAME, GENERALLY

There is one feature of the upland game gun that clearly separates it from guns used for waterfowl or target shooting—*the upland gun has to be one that points quickly and naturally.* Upland gunning has a spontaneous quality to it that is unmatched by other scattergun pursuits. To provide the most desireable handling characteristics, the upland gun has to be selected for weight and balance, and then, it must be custom fitted to the individual shooter. After making your selection, pay a visit to your local gunsmith and have him tailor the gun to your particular physical requirements. The cost is generally modest and it often decides whether or not you'll be a "crack shot" or a "chicken shooter."

CHAPTER 14

Shotguns for Big Game

Many years ago someone developed a thing called "Paradox rifling." This consisted of a shotgun barrel that was partially rifled (shallowly) towards the muzzle, supposedly to impart rifle-like rotation to a solid slug for big game hunting purposes. The balance of the barrel was smooth bored. Obviously, the barrel didn't prove too effective, or other simpler and cheaper methods proved just as good, because no one (to my knowledge) is offering a Paradox rifled barrel today.

Another attempt to spin the solid shotgun slug, or "punkin ball"—as some prefer to call it, was made by creating a slug with diagonally slanted ribs or wings. This is still with us today and most shooters still believe that the slug spins like a rifle bullet and will prove accurate at distances of a hundred yards or more. T'ain't so! Modern high speed photography has demonstrated that the rifled slug spins, but ever so slightly, rarely making more than one rotation in thirty or forty feet. Certainly not enough to give the projectile any real stability.

It must be borne in mind, too, that the operating pressures and velocities of a shotgun are considerably lower than those of a big game rifle so, even with so-called high-velocity charges, one can't expect the shotgun to approach the performance of even a mediocre rifle caliber at distances exceeding fifty yards.

True, there is a variety of sophisticated slugs available, but the best of them would not extend the game-bagging range more than thirty yards or so, and even that is probably stretching matters.

The Brenneke and the Benco-Vitt slugs are somewhat similar since they both make use of the wadding by fastening it to the base of the projectile. This adds length to the ballistically inferior slug and somewhat improves flight characteristics by dampening yawing motion. The primary difference between these two is that the Brenneke is offered in a Rottweil factory-loaded round while the Benco-Vitt slug is offered only as a handloader's component. Slug loading is a very tricky operation, factory-produced shells should be preferred.

Another slug that I've had some limited experience with is called the "Stendebach slug." This one looks something like an unbalanced bar bell with a round hole running longitudinally through its center. The inner walls of the hole are spirally ribbed and the outer walls smooth. While traditional slugs, those made by Remington, Winchester, Brenneke, Benco-Vitt, are slightly hollowed at the base, the weight limitations are such that the slug is barely as long as it is wide. The see-through hollowing of the Stendebach projectile results in a considerably longer missile—better from an accuracy standpoint. Whether it is as effective on impact may be something else again. Frankly, I just don't know, never having had an opportunity to test one in the field. I can attest to its accuracy however, because I shot about six rounds at a paper target over a range of approximately eighty yards. The shotgun was equipped with an ordinary shotgun-bead front sight—no rear sight—and you could have covered the group with a teacup.

Speaking of accuracy, my experience with slugs has pointed up one quirk that you might look for: most of the slugs I've tested, in a wide variety of shotguns, tended to shoot high! Since the natural tendency with a shotgun is to hold "over" to allow for the expected drop of a heavy projectile, it behooves the shooter to do some extensive testing with paper targets before going into the field. You may be in for a surprise. See where your particular shotgun places those "punkin balls" by shooting from a rest and determine point-of-impact at assorted distances up to about 80 yards.

In some areas, primarily in our densely populated Eastern states, slugs are prohibited and big game hunters are restricted to the use of buckshot loads. I'll never understand this thinking because to my mind the slug is much more effective at short range while having a maximum range that is not that much more dangerous than that of buckshot. With the slug I'm sure hunters would hit cleaner—and miss cleaner!

When hunting big game, many states now require that you wear outer garments of red or blaze orange.

The Ithaca Model 66 Buckbuster shotgun is a single-shot model equipped with a short barrel and rifle-type sights.

Western Field M170, a 12 gauge bolt action repeater with a 24-inch "Slugster" barrel.

The M-W Model 556 pump action slug gun for big game hunting.

Composition of Big Game Shells

	Powder Charge equivalents	Lead Charge
Slugs		
12 gauge slug	3¾ drams	1 oz. slug
16 gauge slug	3 drams	⅞ oz. slug
20 gauge slug	2¾ drams	⅝ oz slug
410 gauge slug	(maximum)	⅕ oz. slug
Buckshot		
12 gauge	3¾ drams	00 Buck (9 pellets)
12 gauge	3¾ drams	0 Buck (12 pellets)
12 gauge	3¾ drams	1 Buck (16 pellets)
12 gauge	3¾ drams	4 Buck (27 pellets)
16 gauge	3 drams	1 Buck (12 pellets)
20 gauge	2¾ drams	3 Buck (20 pellets)

The twelve gauge is obviously the most effective, and the most popular, when shooting is limited to buckshot loads. Here, the shooter would normally choose 00-Buck or 0-Buck shells. A single "00" pellet weighs approximately 54 grains and the entire load, of nine pellets, about 486 grains. The "0" pellet weighs about 48.2 grains, and the twelve pellet load—578 grains. An ounce is equal to 437.5 grains, therefore the "00" load is equivalent to 1⅛ ounces—the "0" load, about 1⅓ ounces.

Buckshot loadings can be a bit heavier than their slug counterparts simply because they consist of assorted loose pellets. Ballistically, a solid projectile is more difficult to propel, increases pressures, and must be kept a bit lighter than shot loads to compensate.

CHOKES FOR SLUG GUNS

Chokes are intended only for "shot" loads and have little if any effect on the rifled slug. I mention chokes here only to lay to rest an unfounded notion that slugs cannot be used in full choke guns. In any modern shotgun, in reasonably good condition, there is no danger whatsoever in running a slug through the full choke. On the other hand, and for whatever it's worth, I've always obtained

Remington's Model 1100 Deer Gun—a gas-operated autoloader offered in 12 or 20 gauge.

Marlin's Model 120 pump action slug gun, equipped with a long eye-relief top-mounted scope.

the best accuracy, with slugs, when using a 28-inch barrel having a modified choke. Since a number of other experienced shooters have confirmed this to me, reciting similar experiences, I'll pass it on. Just don't write me to ask, "Why?"

Slug guns, ironically, are normally produced with cylinder bore barrels measuring twenty-two to twenty-four inches. In light of what I've said of the 28-inch modified barrel it would appear that makers have overlooked something. Not really! The twenty-eight-inch barrel is a bit awkward in heavy brush country where the slug gun is normally employed. A shorter barrel handles considerably faster and, since accuracy is only slightly compromised, the average shooter is better equipped with the shortened version. Bear in mind, too, that brush country hunting usually requires quick, "pointed" shooting rather than deliberate aiming.

While slug guns are offered in a variety of

gauges I would strongly recommend that the big game hunter limit his thinking to the "twelve." It's a handicap to hunt big game with a shotgun to begin with, why should anyone seek to add to this handicap?

SLUG GUN SIGHTS

If the slug gun is to be employed, as it was intended, it requires only an open rear sight or, at most, a "peep" sight which manufacturers usually offer on slug models. One can get by with the standard shotgun bead but it can be a bit chancy if no rear sight is used with it. Quite a number of these guns are regularly found with scopes, generally of low magnification (1 to 2½X). These would be used by shooters who are faced with patches of brushy terrain rather than solid, heavy woods. In heavy cover the scope may prove self-defeating although some of the newer long eye-relief models would probably not interfere with instinctive "point" shooting.

Whatever sighting instrument one chooses, he should take pains to target the shotgun carefully

Ithaca's Model 37 "Deluxe Deerslayer" may be had with a factory-installed long eye-relief scope.

GUN FIT

Realizing that the slug gun is generally used in heavy brush where opportunities come suddenly —and fleetingly—it is apparent that the hunter rarely has time to take deliberate aim. Bucking the odds, one should take pains to minimize them by custom fitting his shotgun so that it points as naturally as the extended finger. Consult the chapters on "The Shotgun Stock" and "Home Gunsmithing" that we've included in this volume.

Shotguns are rarely equipped with slings but it wouldn't be out of place to mount one on a slug gun. The sling will often prove useful when one has the time to aim deliberately. There's no question that it will relieve arm-strain resulting from long sessions in the field.

WHERE TO HIT BIG GAME

My favorite target when shooting deer *with a rifle* is that pronounced hump projecting upwards from the back in the area over the front shoulders. This is where the spine is most vulnerable and when so hit, the deer falls where he stands, quickly and painlessly. Best of all, meat damage resulting from a bullet so placed is virtually nil. Neverthe-

with the appropriate shell, zeroing the rig the way he would a rifle. Leave nothing to chance because Lady Chance has a talent for poking her finger in the hunter's eye!

less, I'd be reluctant to attempt that shot with a shotgun because it requires pin-point accuracy—something the shotgun can't be counted upon to deliver.

With the slug gun it's best to vary the target area according to the shell being used. With the slug I'd always look for a body shot in the area of the shoulder, about six inches above the lower line of the chest so if you miss a bit rearward, you should take the buck through the heart. A shoulder shot should drop the animal quickly and keep him down. A front end miss may place the slug in the neck or miss cleanly. A deer hit solidly in the neck won't go anywhere—even if the slug misses the spinal cord the concussion of the impact will put the buck down long enough for you to get to him.

With buckshot loads, I'd look for a neck shot, *if the deer were standing still,* otherwise I'd again go for the shoulder.

Fast-moving deer really don't offer much to the hunter by way of alternatives; the trick with these is to get in a good solid body shot in the front shoulder area.

When a downed animal is lost to the shotgunner it's usually caused by the hunter's eagerness to get to him. Don't rush for an animal as soon as he's down; instead, reload immediately and stay put for a minute or two so that you'll be ready for a second shot if he should regain his feet. If, after a short delay, he appears to be remaining motionless, walk towards him slowly and quietly with the gun "at the ready" and the muzzle pointing in his general direction.

The single most important point I can make on

the subject of big game hunting with the shotgun, is that the hunter must realize he's working with a firearm having a very limited effective range. Regardless of whether you're using slugs or buckshot, you must resign yourself to the task of getting *close to the target!* The ideal shot will fall within a range of fifty yards. *If* you know where your shotgun will target it's load, and *if* you're firing at a standing target, with time to aim deliberately, you can stretch the range to 70 yards with buckshot and 80 yards with the slug. It doesn't pay to attempt shots exceeding 85 yards because hitting the target solidly is very "iffy" business—dropping the target even "iffier!"

CHAPTER 15

Special Purpose Shotguns

If we were to attempt to name all of the shotgun types that could be classified as "special purpose guns," we'd have a title for this chapter that would fill the page. Essentially, we are concerned here only with target guns, combination guns, models for "turkey" shoots and guns that would be appropriate for law-enforcement use. Shotguns designed for big-game hunting (slug use) are described elsewhere in this volume.

SKEET AND THE SKEET GUN

It's not enough, in my opinion, to simply list the specs for the average acceptable skeet gun. One should know something about the sport itself so that the reasoning behind the skeet gun will make sense.

Bear with me while I outline the sport for the benefit of the newcomer:

Skeet shooting programs are regulated under the rules of the National Skeet Shooting Association which is headquartered in Dallas, Texas. The national organization registers matches, records scores, and classifies participants with others of comparable skill. Their official organ is a monthly magazine entitled, *The Skeet Shooting Review*.

Skeet matches are separated according to gauge so that someone using a .410 doesn't have to go up against a competitor shooting a twelve gauge. The four divisions, according to gauge, cover the 12, 20, 28 and .410 gauges. There is no competitive format for the 10 or 16.

The skeet field is comprised of two trap houses which face each other across a measured span of 120' 9". The house on the left (behind station one) is a high house where targets are thrown to emerge about ten feet above ground level. On the opposite side of the field, the low house is positioned immediately behind station seven—targets start from the low house at a height of 3½ feet. A straight line drawn between the target openings of the two houses would bisect station eight which lies precisely midway between the two. Eighteen feet in front of station eight is a target stake over which must pass targets thrown from both houses. (This stake is often preferred to as the "target crossing point.")

A field tracing a semi-circle having a 21-yard radius makes up the balance of the range and determines the locations of stations 2, 3, 4, 5 and 6, which are evenly spaced around its perimeter.

The course of fire is called a "round of skeet" and consists of twenty-five shots at a like number of clay targets. To make this more understandable to the reader we'll describe, briefly, the

The gas-operated autoloader, like this Model 1100SA by Remington, has attained great popularity on the American skeet range.

Some skeet shooters still prefer the traditional pump gun. This is Remington's Model 870SA Skeet Grade.

The over and under gun is making strong inroads among skeet shooters. This is Ithaca's Competition I Skeet Grade.

course in sequence. Starting at station one, the shooter will load one shot (a standard velocity skeet load with #9 shot) and take a position facing the target crossing stake. When he calls for his bird, it will fly out of the high house (almost directly over his head) offering a rather high going-away bird. The first bird missed has to be repeated (to make up the 25th shot) so if he misses this one, he'll have to reload and ask for the same bird. Assuming he scores, he'll load a new shell,

aim toward the low house and call "mark" for his second bird. This will emerge from the low house, across the field, and quarter towards him so that it crosses the target stake.

With both birds accounted for, the same shooter will now load two shells, assume the stance he used for the first one, and get both a high house and a low house bird simultaneously. He fires at the high house bird first and follows with the low house bird which he'll break somewhere to his left, shortly after it has crossed mid field. Since both birds cross the stake in close proximity to each other, there is a good possibility that the shooter

COMBINATION SKEET AND TRAP FIELD

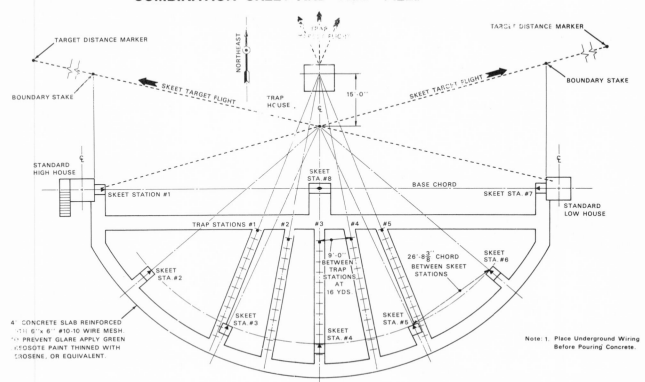

Combination skeet and trap fields are becoming more commonplace because of the rapidly growing interest in both sports.

The target-crossing stake (shown behind the trap house) is only used in skeet and the distance from the stake to the leading edge of the shooting stations measures 21 yards.

Diagram courtesy of the National Rifle Association.

will hit both with the first shot. In strict registered matches, he'd be scored with a hit and a miss. In friendly, informal matches, the shooter would normally be given a chance to repeat the doubles.

This is called a "speed-up" skeet round since singles and doubles are fired in one turn. Some matches stipulate that all singles shooting must be completed first, from all stations, and that shooters return to stations 1, 2, 6 and 7 for the doubles targets to wind up the round.

From station two, the same routine is followed: a high house target, then one from the low house, and then a set of doubles.

From stations 3, 4 and 5 there is only singles shooting—a high house bird first, followed by one from the low house.

On station six, the pattern changes: here the shooter takes the high house single then a low house single but, when he calls for his doubles, he fires at the low house bird first then swings to the right and finishes with his high house target. The same sequence is applied to station 7.

Station eight offers only two singles targets, one from each house. There it is—eight stations with two singles from each accounts for sixteen birds. Add four sets of doubles and we have twenty-four targets. Now, go back and add that first missed bird (that had to be repeated) and you'll have a

Remington's Model 3200 Skeet over and under. This deluxe version is labelled "One of 1000."

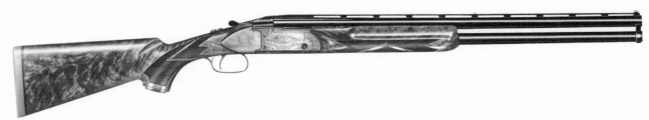

Ithaca Model 51 Skeet Grade gas-operated autoloader.

full round of twenty-five.

Oh—but suppose you didn't miss a shot, you lucky dog!! Now you get your choice of positions for one lonely, single target (I prefer a low house target from station 7.) Just don't miss now!

INTERNATIONAL SKEET

The American skeet shooter generally calls for his targets with the gun shouldered and aimed. When he calls, "pull" or "mark," the targets are released instantly.

With international skeet there are some subtle differences; the butt of the gun must be held below the level of the elbow with the toe of the stock bearing on the hip until the target appears and there can be some delay between the time the shooter calls for the bird and the time it is actually thrown. This delay, while not exceeding three seconds, is just enough to disrupt the shooter's concentration and shooting rhythm: in short —it can be unnerving! International traps (mechanical target-throwing devices) are also ad-

justed to throw the birds a bit faster and a bit farther about 11 yards) than they would ordinarily travel on a conventional American field.

International skeet fields are essentially the same as ours, and guns, too, are comparable. On my last European jaunt, however, I found considerable interest in slightly longer barrels (up to 28 inches) among international shooters. Some also claimed that they were favoring slightly tighter chokes.

As you can see, the skeet gun should provide two quick shots. For this reason double guns or automatics are favored by skeet enthusiasts. There are some, however, who do well with a pump gun, though this type isn't found on the skeet field as often today as it once was.

In any form of target competition "alibis" (second-chances) are few and far between so, if you do succeed in getting a match official to grant you one, he'll do so very grudingly because other competitors may find cause to object. For this reason, any over and under or side-by-side double used for skeet shooting should be made with a non-automatic safety. Failure to disengage a safety device is *not* good grounds for an alibi and I

176 SPECIAL PURPOSE SHOTGUNS

True trap models, like this one, are made with long barrels and tight chokes. They're also invariably ribbed and often fitted with Monte Carlo stocks.

don't think any match official would stick his neck out more than once in the course of a given contest—it simply isn't fair to the other competitors and it tends to disrupt the round.

With single barrel models, the skeet gun should be bored with a skeet choke (minimum muzzle constriction). An improved cylinder choke is a suitable substitute because it often approximates skeet dimensions; nevertheless, as we've explained in the chapter on barrels, manufacturers tend to put more time and effort into creating a barrel for a skeet gun on a true "skeet choke" designation is more desireable.

Ribbed barrels are the rule rather than the exception; shooters want the sighting plane that is provided by a solid or ventilated rib.

The skeet gun stock is generally cut rather straight with little, if any, cast. The average stock has a drop-at-comb of 1½ inches, and a drop-at-heel of 2½ inches. Length of pull approximates 14 inches. These drop dimensions are just a bit greater than the dimensions applying to a standard field gun because the skeet shooter prefers to maintain a slightly more erect head position for better visability.

The international skeet format differs somewhat from the conventional American form of the game: the gun cannot be mounted when calling for a bird; there can be up to a 3-second delay in releasing the bird; targets fly a bit faster and about eleven yards farther. (Photo, courtesy of Ten-X Company.)

Overall gun weight is of prime importance because a long, grueling skeet match can make even the most durable contestant acutely aware of recoil which is best minimized with a gun that is a bit heavier than a conventional field model. Thus, the skeet gun should fall between 7½ and 8 lbs.— some prefer even a bit more weight. Lighter guns are frowned upon.

Double guns should be equipped with a single trigger, though it needn't be selective. Plain extractors or some form of delayed ejection is also desireable because skeet shooters inevitably turn to handloading to cut costs.

To sum up, the skeet shooter needs a fast two-shot repeater with a skeet choke(s) in a model that has substantial weight and good balance. Automatic safety devices are to be avoided like the plague. Ribbed barrels are preferred.

TRAP AND THE TRAP GUN

Trap shoots are conducted under the auspices of the Amateur Trapshooting Association headquartered at Vandalia, Ohio. This national organization registers matches, records scores and handicaps, and classifies shooters according to skill. Their official publication, available to members at a modest fee, is entitled *Trap & Field*. Vandalia, incidentally, is the site of the now famous Grand American Handicap Trap Shoot each August. This event is attended by thousands of trap shooters from all over North America.

Trap, unlike skeet, presents in a random pattern so the shooter never knows exactly which direction a given bird will take. There are some limitations, however, so the shooter can be assured that all birds will fly *away* from him and within a

INTERNATIONAL CLAY PIGEON FIELD-DEFINITIVE DRAWING

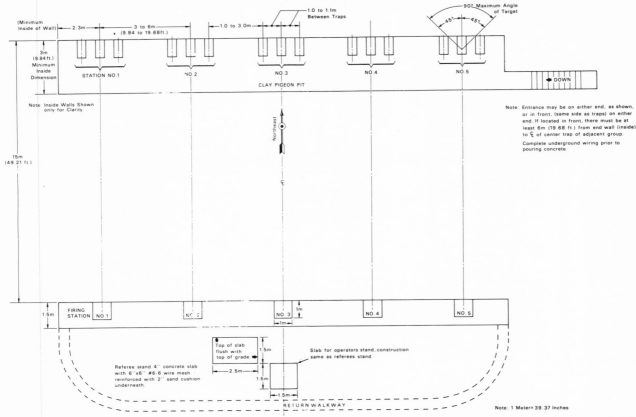

The International Clay Pigeon range—a real challenge! Author much prefers the international form of the sport because there are far fewer perfect scores recorded. Would like to see this range used extensively in the U. S. so American shooters would not be so severely handicapped when entering international competition.

Diagram courtesy of the National Rifle Association.

roughly framed triangle having its apex at the center of the trap house and outer limits that trace angles of about 25° from the center line. Actually the ATA rules that any target within an angle of 47° is legal: most trap clubs, however, adjust their target-throwing machinery to keep birds within 22° of center.

The trap field has only one trap house and this is located in the middle of the range, standing approximately 3 feet above ground level. Sixteen yards behind the trap house, and arranged in a gentle semi-circle, are five shooting stations, numbered one through five—starting from the left as one looks at the trap house. Additional shooting stations are usually provided at one-yard intervals rearward, up to a 27-yard limit to accommodate handicapped events. (See accompanying diagram.)

Trap shooting is a bit more formal and competitive then skeet; shooters don't converse with each other during a round. Instead, each man takes his appropriate starting station, according to the

The pump gun still dominates trap competitions. This is Marlin's Model 120.

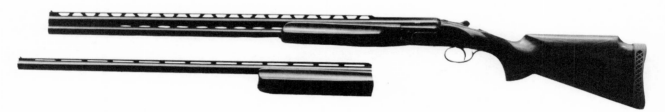

Those who can afford it, will often opt for a deluxe combination trap gun with more than one set of barrels. This Ithaca-Perazzi goes for $1795.00.

sequence in which he was squadded, so that all positions are manned before the first shot is fired. The lead-off man, at station one, then calls for his first bird. As soon as his shot falls—and regardless of whether or not it was hit—the number two man will shoulder his shotgun and prepare for the next bird, calling "pull" when he is ready. Each man fires in turn, until each has had five opportunities at his first station. No one moves until the fifth man has taken his last bird from the fifth position. Then, the entire squad moves up one station—the number five man walking back across the field, behind the line of shooters (with an empty gun) to take up his next position on station one. The man who started on station one now occupies station two—nevertheless he continues to lead by shooting first from the new position. After each five birds, the entire squad advances one station until the man who started on station five shoots his fifth bird from station four. Each competitor has then completed a course of twenty-five targets.

Standing sixteen yards behind the trap house, the average trapshooter will break his birds twenty yards in front of the house—a total distance of thirty-six yards. As he improves, he'll shoot faster so that his birds will be taken at a distance of thirty-three to thirty-four yards.

This is a sport that is limited to twelve-gauge guns and these are usually designed with long barrels and tight chokes. Ribs, again, are the rule rather than exception.

Overall gun weight is also important because trap events can prove lengthy and recoil is a factor to even the hardiest of competitors. Eight pounds is about ideal though weights will range from 7¾ to 8½ lbs.

Most trap matches are "singles events" so single-shot models are not out of place. Nevertheless, because "doubles events" are also conducted by most trap clubs, many competitors favor a double gun (usually an over and under) or an automatic or pump gun. The automatic shotgun should be a true trap model with an empty hull deflector so as not to disturb the shooter on the adjoining station.

Most trap events are conducted from the six-

This is one of Ithaca's famous single-barrel trap guns. Custom-made on a special order basis, models like this can easily exceed $2000.00 in cost.

The Monte Carlo stock is becoming increasingly popular on the trap range.

Trap guns should be fairly heavy, about 8 lbs. or more. Autoloading models, like this one, should be equipped with a shell deflector to avoid having ejected hulls strike the shooter on the adjoining station.

teen-yard line and this is where the beginner can expect to start. In handicap matches, however, skilled competitors are moved back and grouped with others of comparable skill. "Top guns" can expect to compete from twenty-seven yards. Shooters lacking a posted handicap are automatically assigned a twenty-two yard position.

To cope with the variety of shooting conditions, i.e., singles-doubles, 16-yard and handicap events, the ardent trap shooter will often select a gun having interchangeable barrels. Thus, from sixteen yards he'll use a thirty-inch barrel with a modified or improved-modified choke. For doubles events, he'll use a full choke barrel (in a pump or automatic) and a modified and full or improved-modified and full in a double barrel gun. For handicap shooting he'll look for a tighter choke—as "full" as he can get it—and perhaps, even a longer barrel. Some doubles shooters opt for slightly shorter barrels, or chokes that are a bit more open, but it would be unwise for the beginner to experiment in this direction until he's gained some experience.

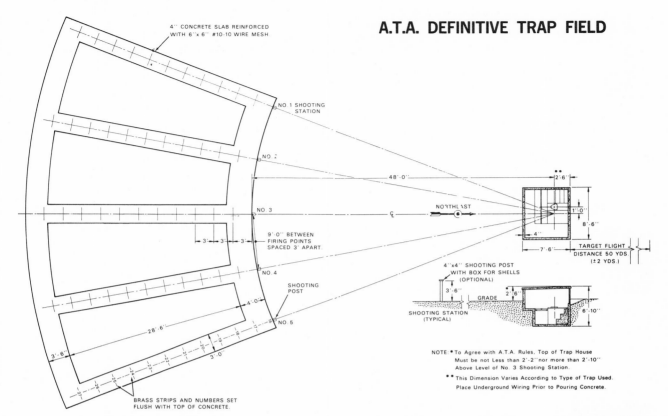

A.T.A. DEFINITIVE TRAP FIELD

4" CONCRETE SLAB REINFORCED
WITH 6" x 6" #10-10 WIRE MESH.

NO. 1 SHOOTING
STATION

NO. 2

48'-0"

NORTHEAST

NO. 3

9'-0" BETWEEN
FIRING POINTS
SPACED 3' APART.

3' 3' 3'

NO. 4

SHOOTING
POST

4'-0"

TARGET FLIGHT
DISTANCE 50 YDS.
(± 2 YDS.)

NO. 5

28'-6"

3'-0"

4"x4" SHOOTING POST
WITH BOX FOR SHELLS
(OPTIONAL)

3'-6"

GRADE

SHOOTING STATION
(TYPICAL)

3'-6"

BRASS STRIPS AND NUMBERS SET
FLUSH WITH TOP OF CONCRETE.

NOTE: * To Agree with A.T.A. Rules, Top of Trap House
Must be not Less than 2'-2" nor more than 2'-10"
Above Level of No. 3 Shooting Station.

** This Dimension Varies According to Type of Trap Used.
Place Underground Wiring Prior to Pouring Concrete.

The traditional American trap field.
Diagram courtesy of the National Rifle Association.

If "alibis" are difficult to come by on the skeet field, they're even further out of reach on the trap range. Trap shooters have little tolerance for anything that interrupts the shooting rhythm of the squad and they fully expect each participant to perform without a hitch. Automatic safety devices will inevitably bring grief!

Incidentally, trap and skeet competitors who handload must be careful to carry an empty-shell container (or large pockets) because most clubs enforce the rule that "empty hulls that hit the ground belong to the club!"

TURKEY SHOOTS AND TURKEY GUNS

We'll have to clarify a few points here because

the term "turkey shoot" has two distinctly different meanings.

When a club runs a "turkey shoot," they are invariably referring to some form of target shooting event in which paper or clay targets are employed and in which oven-ready turkeys are awarded as prizes. Generally, target shooters will compete in their normal manner though some form of scaling may be applied to the standings of the competitors to result in some winners by chance. At other times, a form of "luck" target is used to give everyone an equal opportunity to march home with a bird. There are many forms of "luck target" but the type most popularly employed consists of a large block of small numbered squares having odd values, printed on light target paper. The values of the squares struck by a shot, or shots, are totaled to determine the participant's

Remington is now offering extra interchangeable trap barrels for their Model 1100TB in a 34-inch length. These must be purchased separately.

score. When a shotgun is employed, with this target, the shooter looks for the tightest-patterning model he can find to get as much shot as possible into the target. For this reason, too, he will often insist on a barrel longer than thirty-inches (in spite of the fact that it's the choke and shell that determines pattern concentration—not barrel length).

The other form of "turkey shoot" obviously, is the pursuit of the wild turkey—a sport that has grown considerably in the last two decades through the efforts of our conservation bureaus. Wild turkeys are now stocked in many of our states and subsequently protected until flocks attain huntable size.

The turkey is probably the most wary of our game birds and often frustrates the best efforts of the most experienced hunter. Since he is so difficult to approach, hunters will often shoot at the standing or running bird, a practice that is frowned upon when hunting any other winged species. It follows that such standing shots are often attempted at considerable distance. In areas where turkey hunting is restricted to shotguns, the hunter wants a tightly choked barrel and high-velocity shells loaded with larger than ordinary shot. Rarely will he use shot smaller than #2 and often he'll employ BB shot or small buckshot. Long barrels, again, are the rule. The pump gun and automatic are probably the most popular of turkey guns, followed closely by a side-by-side or

over and under double.

In areas where rifles are permitted, the ideal choice is a combination gun offering an instant choice between shot or bullet.

A few years ago I hunted wild turkey in a rifle area with an over and under combination gun having a .222 caliber rifle barrel mounted under a single 20-gauge magnum shot barrel. While I wasn't successful on this particular hunt, I felt I was equipped with an ideal turkey gun and could have taken advantage of any reasonable opportunity.

Considering meat-spoilage factors and the precision shooting that any substantial distance would require, one is best advised to employ a light, varmit-size, rifle caliber, preferably in the .22, .24, or .25 class. Precison sighting equipment would also be appropriate. Shotgun gauges should be large: 10, 12 (may be magnums) down to 20 gauge magnum, although the ordinary 16 gauge will do the job, if one can get close enough to the target. The turkey is not an easy bird to put down for keeps so heavy gauges, express shells and large shot will help prevent the bird from running off when dropped. The turkey is deceptively fast, once he's had a chance to build up some air speed, and he's also a speedster on the ground. When you get one down, don't waste any time getting to him!

BIG GAME AND BIRDS

Combination guns that would be suitable for game birds and big game are not very popular in the U. S., simply because our seasons rarely overlap and those interested in big game hunting are reluctant to alarm their quarries with sporadic

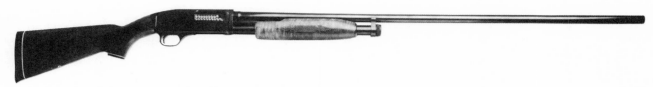

The turkey-shoot competitor will give this model a long, hard look. It's a Marlin Model 120 equipped with a 40" extra full choked "MXR" barrel.

The wild turkey hunter will like this combination gun which is made with a .222 caliber rifle barrel under a standard 12-gauge shot barrel.

Turkey calls are very effective, when used properly.

shots at birds. These guns are far more popular in Europe where hunting is limited to preserves and where furred or feathered game may be pursued simultaneously.

The American interested in a combination deer and grouse gun would do well to study European offerings. One can choose from combo's having one shot and one rifle barrel, two shot and one rifle (a Drilling gun) or two rifle and one shot, or two of each!

The most common of these combination guns will offer one or two 16-gauge barrels with a rimmed 8X57mm rifle barrel. Twelve- or twenty-gauge models are usually offered on a special order basis. As for rifle calibers, it pays to avoid rimless shells because extraction and ejection can become problematical with a break-open type gun. There exists a considerable assortment of European rimmed shells in the 6 and 7mm range so suitable substitutes are easily found.

LAW-ENFORCEMENT SHOTGUNS

Many shotgun producers offer a "riot gun" to police organizations and this is usually a form of pump gun having a short (20-inch) barrel, open choke, and large magazine capacity.

Some years ago, one automatic shotgun maker offered a recoil-operated auto model with an extension magazine tube having a seven-shot capacity. This, I believe, has been discontinued because policing agencies preferred the reliability of the pump action over the sometimes balky automatic. When someone has to put his life on the line in a shoot-out, this thinking is certainly understandable.

The pump gun used for this purpose should be

Experienced turkey hunters know the value of camouflage clothing. This outfit is offered by Ten-X.

adva- ageous. When using a sling, however, the security officer should be trained to carry the gun behind the left shoulder (if right handed) in a muzzle down position with the left hand resting on the fore-end. A simple forward pulling motion, accompanied by a slight twisting action, will place the piece in a firing attitude.

While the riot gun can be a very effective combat weapon, it's usefulness is highly dependent upon the skill of the user. One must learn how to operate the safety device and slide action instinctively. A good working knowledge of effective range and ballistic qualities are likewise important and the best way to develop these abilities is to arrange for regularly scheduled practice sessions.

Riot guns are often carried or stored for long periods so maintenance can be a problem. Rust deposits that impede the action in any way could easily render the piece inoperable. All specimens should be tested periodically and thoroughly cleaned once a month.

Ammo for law-enforcement use would depend upon the conditions facing the officer. Loud blank loads will often discourage a small menacing group. Bird shot loads, directed toward the legs, would provide a bit more discouragement when the situation is difficult. When faced with a dangerous armed adversary 0-buck or double-0 buck loads are the shells to use. Belligerent armed adversaries firing from behind a protective barricade are best countered with heavy rifled slug loads. Chances are the slugs would not penetrate some heavy defenses but they'd tend to unnerve some culprits, inducing them to abandon their defensive positions or, perhaps, even surrender.

The famous German ammo plant of RWS Dynamit-Nobel makes an assortment of special shotgun loads having flares and incendiary applications which are restricted to governmental sales. On occasion, some of these devices could prove helpful.

a hammerless model simply because one can't count on having time to fumble with a cocking action. It should also have a rather large push button safety located on the tang or through the trigger guard. The important thing to remember here, is that left-handed officers would be severely handicapped by a right-hand operated safety.

Guns should be carried loaded, cocked and with the safety on, except if anticipating imminent action.

Since most riot guns are carried by patrolling guards, a sling arrangement would probably prove

The shotgun for police use should be a hammerless pump action model with a short barrel and rifle sights. This is Remington's Model 870, made in 12 gauge only.

The tactical or strategic use of a riot gun really calls for the availability of a broad variety of ammunition. On the other hand, patrolling officers should carry guns loaded only with buckshot loads. A couple of rifled slug shells, carried in the pocket, could be substituted when there exists cause to stop a moving vehicle or flush a felon from hiding.

A division of RWS Dynamit-Nobel makes an assortment of special purpose shotgun shells for governmental use.

CHAPTER 16

Shotgun Cleaning & Gunsmithing

In this chapter we will present the "how-to's" of a number of simpler gunsmithing tasks that can be attempted by the layman together with details on cleaning the shotgun and preparing it for storage. Some tasks will be conspicuous by their absence simply because they are things that are better left to qualified gunsmiths.

On that subject of gunsmiths, the reader should realize that, like doctors and lawyers, gunsmiths have areas of specialization. Thus, when shopping for gunsmithing work, look for the man who specializes in the area that interests you. While all smiths will replace parts, there's a world of difference in the custom stock made by a specialist and the one turned out by a "general practioner." Many gunsmiths, too, specialize in *types* of guns: you'll find pistolsmiths, riflesmiths and experts in shotguns. Only large specialty shops, like Griffin & Howe in New York (a division of Abercrombie & Fitch) and Pachmayr's in Los Angeles staff experts in all fields.

Considering the lengthy apprenticeship generally required, and the broad knowledge to be acquired in many different and highly technical areas, the gunsmith ranks as one of the most underpaid professionals in the country; gunsmithing prices are bargain prices! Consider, too, that the gunsmith invariably provides an information service for which he is *not* compensated, i.e., he keeps an eye on proposed firearms laws, hunting seasons, the rules and regulations of competitive events, etc., etc., information that he dispenses without charge to his customers.

CLEANING THE SHOTGUN

The shotgun has to be cleaned more frequently and more thoroughly than either the rifle or the pistol. In the barrel, for example, lead deposits will build up quickly in the forcing cone and choke, necessitating periodic removal. Furthermore, the shotshell itself, because of its rather complex construction combining a variety of components, contributes to maintenance problems through the volume of residual matter that it spreads through the bore and action areas, particularly in repeating models. Deposits of this nature will eventually and inevitably impair performance if permitted to accumulate.

To effect proper cleaning, one should start by field-stripping the gun, separating the barrel from the receiver if at all possible. A solvent, such as Hoppe's #9, applied to the bore and vigorously brushed, will loosen and remove lead and powder deposits. Bear in mind, however, that solvents are

Bob Brownell's "GUNSMITH" patch.

corrosive and that they must be removed from all metal surfaces immediately after use. Solvent-treated surfaces should be subsequently dried and carefully oiled.

Restrict the use of bore cleaners and solvents to the bore only—don't use them elsewhere! To clean breech and magazine surfaces plain old kerosene is much preferred because liberal applications will flush away residues while leaving a thin oily film. I generally use a small stiff brush to work the kerosene into hard to reach areas. When satisfied that the breech is clean, I'll rinse the brush in kerosene and use it to apply a light coating of gun oil. Wooden components should be treated with linseed oil or paste wax; keep solvents away from wooden surfaces.

When storage is planned for an indefinite period, all metal surfaces should be lightly greased; just take care to remove it before subsequent use —particularly from the bore.

Shooters often encourage rusting of metal surfaces, unwittingly, by simply handling the firearms they display. The perspiration that one transmits to metal from his hands is highly acid. Wipe guns down with an oily cloth before replacing them in the cabinet or rack.

Finally, when storing any firearm, do your best to relieve tension on the assorted springs the gun contains. Place a snap cap or an empty, fired shell in the chamber and pull the trigger. With recoil operated autoloading models, remove the fore-end cap to decompress the recoil spring.

THE PRE-SEASON CHECK

It's a good idea to go over your battery of shotguns at least a month before the start of the season. This way if you find a part that needs replacing you'll have time to obtain and install the replacement.

Degrease the stored gun carefully, paying special attention to the bore. Examine the stock and fore-end to see if they still fit tightly. Any swelling or shrinking of wooden components can cause splitting if left uncorrected. If the buttstock, for example, on a pump or auto, is loose, remove the butt plate or recoil pad and tighten the stock bolt, *by hand only,* using a large screwdriver.

The stocks on side-by-side and over and under guns are considerably more difficult to adjust; with these, a visit to your gunsmith is in order when you find fault with the way they fit. Above all, don't attempt to shoot a gun equipped with a loose or badly swollen stock because it is almost certain to crack or split.

INSTALLING A RECOIL PAD

To do this job properly, one should simultaneously attempt to custom fit the stock to the shooter. Length of pull and pitch can both be adjusted during the pad fitting process. (Refer to the chapter entitled "The Shotgun Stock" for information on taking these dimensions.)

MEASURING
STOCK PULL

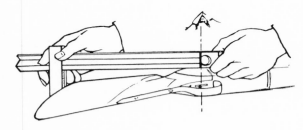

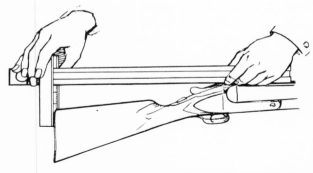

Measuring length of pull and drop at heel with Bob Brownell's "Pull & Drop Gauge."

First, you must determine what style and size of pad you require and the best way to come up with these answers is to visit your gun shop. Take the butt end of your shotgun with you. A good shop will be able to show you a broad variety of pads for skeet, trap and hunting, in assorted colors. When you've settled on one, make sure the pad you've picked is *long enough* to enable you to continue the natural stock lines when shaping it to

size. Every stock differs in size and shape so it is not possible to buy a pad that will perfectly fit any given stock. For this reason, pads are made considerably oversize, allowing material for individual shaping.

Assuming that you've determined length of pull and pitch, your first task is to relocate the butt line to allow for the thickness of the pad. When this is done, you should have a pencil line on the stock which traces the desired angle of pitch and which represents the length required when pad thickness is to be added. The next step is to extend this line completely around the stock with a soft pencil (one that won't scratch the existing finish if it requires subsequent correction). Use a soft plastic flexible rule for this purpose. If the line doesn't return to its starting point, it's not straight.

Closely fitted to the line, but on the side of the stock opposite the portion that is to be removed, run a strip of masking tape so that it completely encircles the stock. This should help prevent scratches in the stock finish near the work area. If you're much concerned with protecting your stock finish, wrap the entire stock in heavy paper or cloth, leaving only the work area exposed.

Sawing must be accomplished slowly and carefully—you cannot simply saw through the stock the way you would an ordinarily piece of wood. In fact, you can't saw directly through at all—this would cause splintering of the lower wood surfaces.

Saw about $\frac{1}{16}$ of an inch short of the line to leave yourself some material for final sanding. Draw the saw blade lightly and gently on a back stroke and cut a line through the finish, completely around the stock. Extend the line in a rearward direction, never forward. Slowly deepen the cut, by degrees, and by systematically turning the stock so that you're always cutting towards the middle, or core.

When cutting is finished, you must true up the base for the pad. Line it up very carefully against a disc or belt bed; use fine sandpaper and light touch against the sanding surface. You want a perfectly flat, smooth surface.

Next, decide whether you want to glue the pad on or if you want it to be removable. Of course, if you have an anchoring bolt running through your stock, you haven't much choice—you have to keep it removable.

To assure a good tight fit of pad to wood, it's a good idea to hollow the center of the butt panel a bit so that only a quarter of an inch of wood, around the perimeter, is in heavy contact with the base of the pad. An electric grinding tool or small, half-round chisels can be used for this purpose.

After hollowing, scribe a vertical line through the center of the butt. This is to indicate the position of your mounting screws.

Take the screws (they come with the pad) and insert them the wrong way through the base place of the pad. When the screw points protrude slightly through the rubber of the finished side, take your razor and make one simple cut through the rubber, over each screw point. This will permit the screw heads to penetrate the pad without roughing up the finished surface.

Insert the screws from the right side so that their points protrude slightly through the base. Hold the pad against the butt and position it carefully so that there is plenty of surplus material extending below the toe of the butt where the sharply angled lower line of the stock is to be continued through the pad.

With a pencil, mark the positions of the screws on the vertical pencil line previously drawn on the butt. Check to see that neither of the two screws is located too close to the edge. Be especially careful with the toe screw because this is most often the culprit that splits a chunk of wood out of the stock. If the natural grain of the stock forms a small triangular block at the toe, you'll have to be very, very careful.

Now, if you have tapered speed bits of screw contour, use them; otherwise select a drill bit of about half the diameter of your wood screws. Drill the upper, heel hole, first. Put some wax in the screw threads and try it in the hole. Stop the head about ⅜ of an inch short of seating. If it seems to be an overly tight and difficult fit, you may need a slightly larger drill for the lower hole.

Drill the toe hole, wax the screw threads, and try seating the screw to within ⅜ " of the butt. If you think you're getting too much resistance, stop —remove the screw and very carefully enlarge the hole. Try the screw again; when it moves smoothly, you're ready to continue.

Thin a small measure of shellac with a little alcohol, mix it, and paint this on the exposed grain of the butt. Seal the wood well, with two or three coats, and allow it to dry for at least an hour between coats.

If you plan to glue the pad in place, use the equivalent of Elmer's glue; treat both the base of the pad and the butt face to a light application, and screw the pad solidly in place. Wipe any surplus glue off exterior surfaces without delay.

The finishing steps of this operation will show the world what kind of a craftsman you are; get careless or impatient, and you'll blow the whole job.

Set up the disc sander with a medium grit paper on one side and a fine grit on the other. Do not use coarse papers—or you'll never get a smooth professional finish. Another thing—you must use a very light touch while sanding the pad to size. Don't bear down on the work.

Before starting, study the stock carefully, sight the planes as you slowly resolve it between both hands. Notice how the flat sides flare outward towards the butt, how they narrow towards the grip? Do you see how the lines change around the toe and the heel as they move towards the sides? You must strive to maintain these contours so that the finished pad appears to be a natural extension of the wood.

B-Square Company makes a recoil pad jig that greatly simplifies pad installations.

Start with the most severe angle first, around the toe. Line up the bottom line of the stock so that it is parallel to the surface of the sanding disc. Sand a flat in the toe—work the base of the pad close to the edge of the disc so that there's no danger of the disc running through the masking tape that's protecting the stock finish. Don't try to get it down all the way, settle for "close" and leave a little bit of material for hand finishing. Follow the same procedure with the top of the pad—again,

being careful to continue the natural line of the stock.

Next, do both sides by rolling the butt gently against the disc to pick up the gently sloping top to bottom curl.

When you've completed this step, you should have four fairly flat surfaces that trace the four basic lines of the stock. Go back and take the corners off, carefully; stock lines change rapidly in the corners so you'll have to do this by cutting a series of small flats, changing the feeding angle for each.

Jigs are essential for proper sight adjustment. This is B-Square's "Barrel Sight Jig."

When you find the disc getting uncomfortably close to the masking tape, blend the flats together with a gentle rolling motion and go on to the next corner.

Final finishing is accomplished by placing the stock in a padded vise or gun cradle and by filing the base plate of the pad to size. Use a fine file and work slowly, with a pushing motion—don't draw the file rearward. Get the black base plate down to size and ignore the rubber portion of the pad for the time being. When it appears that you've arrived at a perfect fit, wrap some fine sandpaper around the flat file and polish the edge of the base and spacer.

If the rubber portion has a good shape, simply dress it with a sandpaper-covered file. Otherwise, go back to the disc sander—use the fine side—and lightly sand it without letting the disc touch the base plate.

Remove the masking tape and check your finished job by feel!

Work out any little ridges or bumps that remain.

Wax the stock and you're finished!

FRONT SIGHTS AND MIDDLE BEADS

Shotgun sights are either screw-thread fitted or press-fitted. With screw threads there's no prob-

This special B-Square jig is used to find the center of rib for installation of a middle bead.

lem to changing a front sight. Press-fits are something else again—you'll have to find a suitable replacement sight that comes close to the pin size you need; this should be ever so slightly oversize so that it has to be forced into the sight base hole in the rib. Pressing is a problem simply because it requires a delicate touch; any crudely applied force will deform the bead.

The best way to accomplish this task is to make up a couple of soft wood blocks for your bench vise. Place these between the jaws so that the barrel and sight can be inserted between them. Now,

with some help to turn the vise handle, hold the barrel and bead in position while your helper gently closes the vise.

I generally apply a drop of epoxy cement to the sight hole before inserting the new sight, and I do this even with threaded sights.

Middle beads, common to ribbed barrels—especially those employed in target shooting—are considerably more difficult. Here, the big problem is to locate the base hole dead-center in the rib. A jig of some sort is a *must!*

(B-Square Company makes a small and efficient jig for this purpose.)

The middle bead is considerably smaller than the front bead so when mounted some distance

Most firearms dealers carry shotgun-sight assortments, like this one from Bob Brownell, which makes it easy for the shooter to find a suitable replacement.

from the muzzle it should blend into the front sight when the gun is properly sighted. Any visual separation between the two sights points up faulty gun mounting. To locate the middle bead position on the rib measure fourteen to sixteen inches *from the breech end* of the barrel. With short barrels, favor the fourteen inch dimension; sixteen inches would be more appropriate on barrels exceeding thirty inches in length.

When the barrel is equipped with a ventilated rib you may have to shift the bead position a bit to center it over a vertical supporting post. Do not mount the bead in an unsupported area of the rib.

TOUCH-UP BLUING

It would serve no useful purpose to discuss full scale bluing operations here because books can be written on this subject alone. Whenever the layman attempts to reblue an entire shotgun, he's simply asking for trouble. Such work requires a considerable amount of equipment, a wealth of knowledge and a heck of a lot of skill. Even the so-called "cold blue" method is beyond the realm of the average hobbyist. Anyone contemplating such major work would be far wiser to ship the shotgun off to a good gunsmith.

To those who have more than a hobbyist's inter-est in the subject, I recommend Roy Dunlap's book, "Gunsmithing." Mr. Dunlap covers the subject thoroughly.

Touch-up bluing should only be attempted on a small scale. Any effort to re-do the entire side of a receiver, for example, is invariably wasted. Two problems are universal—covering the worn area uniformly and matching the surrounding color of the original finish. Gun blues come in a wide variety of color ranges from deep blue to black. It may be necessary to experiment with more than one commercial touch-up blue to get a satisfactory result. All of the commercial preparations, how-ever, will invariably call for the use of sterilized cotton, rubber gloves and a cleaning agent (alcohol or Oakite). To this list I usually add some Q-tips, an artist's brush (that has been cleaned thoroughly in Oakite) and a propane torch.

With small screws and bolts old German gun-smiths simply polish the heads and heat them with a high flame, quickly, before quenching them in oil. No commercial bluer is needed and the re-sulting color is pretty good. Be careful with this process; don't heat the screw or bolt too long or make it too hot. The oil quench should be in a very small container, one that will just contain the part that you're bluing. Use a rather heavy ma-chine oil. Don't attempt this process on anything other than screws or bolts.

With any form of bluing, it is important that the surface of the metal is polished carefully and cleaned in a degreasing agent. Once cleaned, the metal should not be handled with bare hands be-cause natural oils, so transmitted, will cause re-sistance to the bluing action.

Read the directions that come with commercial bluers carefully. These vary greatly and each has to be handled in its own unique fashion. Use only thoroughly clean applicators and be sure to pre-pare the surface properly.

Often it will be found that a fairly good color

match can be achieved by the application of several light coats of the bluing preparation. Also, when having difficulty, try heating the surface with a propane torch before applying the bluer. When doing this, especially on barrels or receivers, be careful to heat only the surface of the metal—apply a high flame, quickly and immediately follow it with the bluer.

STOCK REPAIRS

The most perplexing problems with stock repairs are found with stocks that have high gloss epoxy finishes. The easiest stocks to work on are oil finished. While most repairs can be accomplished with little effort, restoration of finishes can prove very frustrating.

Cracks and Splits—These should be caught and fixed as soon as possible. Neglect a hairline crack today and you can be faced with a major split tomorrow.

Almost any popular wood adhesive will do the job; however, a fast-drying type (like Elmer's) is probably easiest to work with.

Simply cushion a clamp in front of the split area so that the split will not enlarge when you spread it to apply the adhesive. With small tang splits and the like, I use round wooden toothpicks to open the fault. Then I carefully pack the crevice with the adhesive, making sure that the glue penetrates deeply. A flat toothpick—or the moistened and hammered end of a round pick—will help to push the glue down into the crack. Then, re-set the clamp over the work area to close the split tightly. Be sure you employ adequate cushioning material to avoid new damage to the stock or its finish. Also, wipe off any overflow immediately.

Let the repair dry overnight before removing the clamp. Buff off any resultant roughness with a fine grade of steel wool, restore the finish (if necessary) or wax.

With larger cracks or splits, an epoxy adhesive would probably prove more desirable. I use Micro-Bed or Bob Brownell's Acraglas Kit.

Before applying either of these, it pays to wax the stock carefully in the vicinity of the repair. Thus, if you get some overflow it will be easy to remove.

Open the crack, install the adhesive, apply a cushioned clamp and gently wipe off any overflow.

Major breaks can also be repaired with Bob Brownell's Acraglass and, if carefully done, the joint will be almost as strong as the stock was originally.

When repairing a butt section that has broken off completely through the small area of the pistol grip, a *hardwood dowel* (3⁄8″ or 1⁄2″) is required. Place both pieces together carefully—mark a pencil line across the break (along the side) to indicate its length. A second guide line should then be drawn through the center of the tang, along the top surface.

Find a drill having the same outside diameter as the dowel.

Now, because you can't expect to drill into a ragged end grain and maintain drill position you must prepare the hole site with a hand grinder or chisel. Find the exact location for the start of the hole by crossing the two reference lines. Prepare the spot and, with an assistant to sight against one line (you'll guide against the other), drill into the end grain to the required depth. Do both halves in the same manner. Cut your dowel to length (perhaps 1⁄8″ shorter than the length of the hole) and score it in a spiral pattern with a V-shaped coarse file. Round the ends slightly.

Assemble the stock, with the dowel, dry—to test the accuracy of your joint. Make any required corrections and, if you are forced to enlarge one hole to get the two halves aligned, you should employ some hardwood slivers as shims to strengthen the joint.

Test it again. Disassemble the unit, mix the glass in accordance with the manufacturer's instructions, and pack it into the holes carefully. Coat one end of the dowel and firmly seat it in one hole. Glue the bare end and force the remaining portion of the stock around it.

To keep everything in line until the glass hardens, you can tie some heavy cord through the trigger guard and around the center of the butt. Wrap the break with a single sheet of waxed paper and clamp it from the side.

Let it dry for at least forty-eight hours before removing the clamp and cord. Dress exterior surfaces with files and/or sandpaper and restore the finish.

When it is possible to drill through the break area from an internal plane, say through the action area, it is better to glass the two halves together first. Wait until the glass has hardened (24 to 48 hours) and drill after joining the two pieces. This eliminates alignment problems.

When the hole is completed to the proper depth, score a ⅜ or ½ inch hardwood dowel, apply a liberal coating of glass to the hole and the dowel, and tap it into position. Again, let it harden before cutting the protruding end of the dowel.

For the strongest possible union, some would drill small diagonal holes through the break from the outer surfaces of the pistol grip. This practice would necessitate some rather professional finishing.

Lifting Dents—With oil-finished stocks, this repair is comparatively easy. Simply remove the finish from the dent area, apply a wet cloth over the spot and heat it with an iron. Let it dry and keep repeating the process until the fibers of the wood have raised to fill the depression.

If it is a stubborn dent, one that is rather deep, mask the area around it and repeat the steaming process until the fibers refuse to come up any further. Then, heat some thinned linseed oil, to just below boiling, steam the dent and drop the heated linseed oil into it.

You'll rarely be able to get it up to the point where the surface if fully restored, but you should be able to raise it enough so that a light sanding will even it with surrounding surfaces.

REPAIRING STOCK FINISHES

Oil Finishes—The biggest problem here is matching the color of the original finish. Tubes of artist's oil paints in burnt umber and yellow ochre colors often prove useful, if used sparingly.

When the repair has been made, it should be sanded with a very fine grit of paper. Thin some shellac or varnish and seal any raw wood that remains in the repaired area. Buff it down with the fine paper, or steel wool, again.

If confronted with an abundance of open pores in the wood surface you'll have to fill them before applying the oil. Commercial fillers are best for this purpose.

Sand again, and try a light coating of boiled linseed oil. Rub it in thoroughly and check it for color. Realizing that it will darken under successive coats, stick to applications of unadulterated linseed oil if you feel it will eventually bring the desired result.

When it appears that you'll have difficulty matching the color of the original finish, you'll have to experiment with the oil color additives. Thin a *small amount* with a little turpentine and mix it with the linseed oil. You'll soon discover that a little color goes a long way. Add it very, very sparingly to a much larger measure of oil. I usually start with only enough color to coat the tip of an artist's brush and paint it on the bottom of a mixing cup. Oil is added slowly, while stirring, until the desired tone is reached. Test it on a hidden stock surface before applying it to the exterior of the stock.

When the color match meets with your approval, use only plain boiled linseed oil over it to bring up the finish. Apply several coats, slowly, over a period of a week or ten days and permit each coat to dry between applications.

Epoxy Finishes—Most polyurethane resins are two-part liquids—resin and activator (catalyst). Such preparations are better suited to complete stock refinishing jobs. For small repairs I prefer a product called Flecto Varathane.

Since all of these products are sold with complete instructions for application, simply select what you prefer, or what is readily available, and follow the manufacturer's directions. Be sure, however, that you pick up a can of the thinner that is recommended for each. You'll need this to prepare your work surface.

All wax, dirt, etc., must be removed from the surface to be repaired. Clean, with the thinner, a large area surrounding the site.

If attempting to patch a deep scratch, wrap some fine sandpaper around a narrow round rod (the thin shank of a screwdriver) and sand the scratch lightly to remove sharp ridges or discolorations.

Working temperatures are important with resin finishes so it's a good idea to store both the stock and the finish in a heated room before attempting application.

When ready, mask a rather large area around the fault. Don't shake or stir your resin too vigorously because this will create an abundance of air bubbles in the finished surface. You can't brush heavily either. Use only a soft camel's hair brush (not nylon) and flow a thin coat of resin over the surface.

When working on a deep scratch, pour a little resin into a bottle cap after coating the damaged area. The material in the bottle cap will harden quickly so you'll have to watch it closely to determine when it has formed into a heavy, but workable, putty-like substance. With the softened tip of a toothpick, lay a ridge of this putty mix down the center of the scratch. Upon drying, this should help restore the level. Buff it down with a fine wet sandpaper.

Let the work dry overnight and apply two coats of finish the following day, with about six hours between coats.

Complete curing will now take at least 24 hours. For final polishing, to blend the new surface with the old, use rottenstone and water. Rub it down vigorously, especially around the outer edges of the patch.

COMPLETE STOCK FINISHING

Regardless of the type of finish you wish to employ, the quality of the finished job is largely dependent upon your willingness to prepare the stock properly.

When shaping is completed, sand all surfaces thoroughly with successively finer grits of paper. Use fine files, flat and round, to smooth rough areas before sanding. Pay special attention to edge grain areas—under the lip of the cheek piece, around the pistol grip, the leading edge of the fore-end.

Upon achieving a glass-smooth surface, wet a sponge in a mixture of water and alcohol, lightly wet all external surfaces and immediately expose them to heat (from a stove or propane torch) to force rapid drying. Take care to avoid scorching the surface of the wood.

This will raise "whiskers" in the wood grain. Rub them off with fine steel wool followed by extra fine sandpaper. Repeat the whiskering process as often as necessary until the grain refuses to raise any further.

Now we can get on with the finishing.

Oil Finish—Talk to ten gunsmiths and you'll get ten different formulas for a "genuine oil finish." I've never seen one that I could call bad, thought I've seen some that I liked better than others, so you needn't view my own, eleventh, formula with apprehension.

First, thin some shellac with about an equal volume of alcohol. This really has to be thin and mixed well. With a soft brush, paint it over *all* stock surfaces—don't forget the butt and inletted areas. When dry, sand lightly.

Use a good commercial wood filler next. Pack it into the pores of the wood with your fingertips by rubbing across the grain. Wait until it sets up and wipe it off, lightly, with a coarse rag. Let dry and, again, buff it cross-grain fashion.

Mix some good, clear, marine varnish with turpentine to make a thin solution. Paint this on with a soft brush to bind the filler and prepare a base for the oil. Be sure to cover the butt and inletted areas too. After it has had adequate time to dry, sand lightly and repeat.

When the second coat has dried fully, sand the entire stock vigorously with very fine paper.

Now you're ready for the boiled linseed oil (such as G. B. Linspeed Oil) but, first, find a rather warm work area. Store the stock and oil in that area overnight before commencing oiling operations.

Apply a liberal coating of oil to the stock and rub it in with your fingertips and the palms of your hands until the wood feels hot. Wait about an hour and wipe the surface down with a clean, heavy rag. Let stand until dry. This, unfortunately, seems to take forever. Linseed oil dries so doggone slowly it takes ten days to two weeks to get any semblance of a real stock finish. Quit when you've had enough.

Epoxy Finishes—These require the same preparatory steps as an oil finish, up to the completion of the whiskering process. Then instead of an alcohol and shellac sealer, use the sealer and filler recommended by the manufacturer, buy the suggested epoxy thinner and mix up a very thin coat of the epoxy for the base. When this has dried, follow it with the wood filler, wipe off the surplus, and apply another thin coat of your homemade sealer when the filler has dried. Remember, too, to sand lightly between each coat.

Follow the manufacturer's directions for applying the epoxy. Avoid creating air bubbles by stirring or shaking it too vigorously. Also, use a fine

soft brush, or a spray, to apply it. Don't brush too energetically either; instead, flow the liquid on the surface. Runs, sags, bubbles, etc. can be removed between coats by light sandings with #400 wet or dry paper and water.

When completed, buff down exterior surfaces with rottenstone and water to get a smooth satin-gloss finish.

One word of caution: individual coats of epoxy have surprising thickness. Be careful around inletted areas where only a thinned solution should be employed. Two very thin coats will suffice in these areas. Checkered patterns should be handled in the same manner.

REPLACING PARTS

With pump or autoloading models the parts most likely to require replacement are the extractors and ejectors. Often these are fitted into the breech block via a spring and plunger retainer. You need only a sharp pointed awl to get between the tail surface of the extractor (or ejector) to compress the plunger against its spring, freeing the part in question. Installation of the new replacement is easily accomplished and the procedure rather obvious.

With autoloading models the ejector is often built into the barrel extension as a rather rigidly mounted appendage. Manufacturers use a variety of techniques for installing these—some are screwed into place but most are pinned and some pinned and silver-soldered. When ordering such an ejector be sure to order a new ejector pin at the same time.

Remove the broken ejector by filing off the expanded end of the pin. If some solder is present it will have to be melted before the pin can be tapped out. Pin the new ejector into place and peen the pin against a hard work surface until it is pretty much flattened at both ends. Dress the raw ends with a fine metal file and emery. A high heat, applied quickly, will enable you to add a drop of

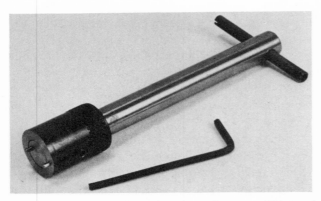

Only a gunsmith will appreciate the versatility and usefulness of this adjustable spanner-wrench for firing pins that have been set into the face of the breech. (Tool is offered by B-Square Company.)

silver solder to the joint to secure the new ejector.

Be careful with heat when working on the barrel extension because you certainly don't want to soften this component. Wrap the bulk of the extension in cold wet rags before removing or adding solder and use only as much heat as you need to get the job done quickly.

FIRING PINS

These should always be tested after installation to determine that they are of the proper length. Too long, or too pointed, and they'll puncture primers, resulting in some gas leakage through the breech. Firing pins are easy to replace in pump and auto models; in double guns, of any kind, they're usually difficult.

The owner of a side-by-side or over and under gun should not be encouraged to attempt repairs in the area of the breech. Guns of this type are intricately designed and require assembly through a series of special tools and jigs. Also, there is a specific balance in the way components function. Give such jobs to a specialist.

Some years back, on the night before the opening of duck season, a friend popped up at my door with the butt end of his double gun in pieces. He

had taken it apart that afternoon to replace a badly worn firing pin and couldn't get it back together. Since he was one of the group that I planned to hunt with the next day I had no choice but to tackle the reassembly job, in spite of the fact that my home workshop lacked the tools commonly used for this work. To avoid repeating the frustrating experience he had already endured that afternoon, I started by fashioning a crude hammer key from a scrap of hardwood. An old carriage bolt was reduced in diameter to serve as a slave pin and a small vise-grip was used as a clamp.

It took about an hour to fashion the make-do tools but, with them, we were able to reassemble that old double gun in about fifteen minutes. This is another reason why you should give these jobs to your gunsmith—he has the tools to do them properly.

BARREL BENDING

While the B-square Company makes a simplified form of barrel bending tool, only a skilled technician should attempt such work because it requires a trained and practiced eye. The odds are high against the amateur's success.

Single barrel guns (pumps, autos, etc.) often have their barrels bent to shoot on target. Patterning tests generally point up faults in this area and, when the shooter finds himself saddled with a gun that simply won't shoot where it's aimed, he'd be wise to write the manufacturer. Barrels for double guns are "trued" *before* they are joined.

CHOKE CORRECTIONS

The overly tight choke can be opened by polishing with a fine grade of crocus cloth wrapped around a steel rod or hardwood dowel. Find a rod or dowel that is considerably smaller than choke diameter and cut a longitudinal slot in it to accept one end of a strip of crocus. Chuck the rod in a drill or lathe, note the direction of its spin and wrap the crocus around it, starting with one end

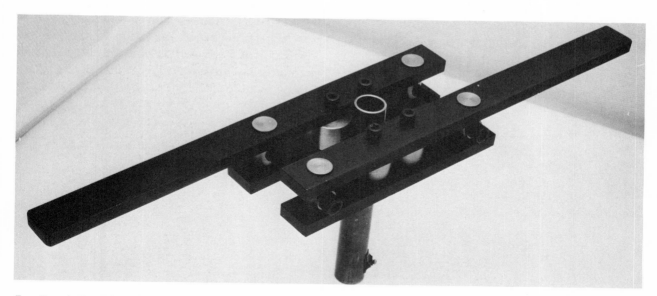

For the shotgun barrel that has lost its choke, or the swaged choke that has worn away, B-Square makes this special swaging tool.

in the slot. Simply slide the muzzle end of the barrel over the fixture and roll it, *gently* against the abrasive surface.

Be careful here because a little polishing often makes dramatic changes in the pattern. It's best to polish a little at a time, testing at frequent intervals.

This same technique can be used to make small corrections in the point of impact. If a given barrel throws a pattern that favors one side of the aiming point, simply polish the opposite wall of the barrel in the choke area. Bear in mind, however, that you'll be opening the pattern a bit with this solution—determine if it has room to spread.

Barrels that throw overly large patterns cannot be corrected by the hobbyist—these are best taken to a gunsmith (who'll tell you he can't guarantee success either because jug-choking is, at best, unpredictable).

Incidentally, barrels that are chrome lined can-not be altered by polishing. With these the only possible answer to a patterning problem is the installation of an adjustable choke device.

INSTALLATION OF THREE SHOT PLUGS

To comply with the Federal Migratory Bird Act, repeating shotguns having a capacity for more than three shells must be equipped with a magazine limiting device. Assuming the gun will carry one shell in the chamber, the plug should reduce the magazine capacity to two. The problem here is that plugging devices cannot be easily re-movable, nor easily reinstallable. Essentially, we're concerned only with pump action and auto-loading models having tubular magazines.

Generally made with a five shot capacity, these models are usually furnished with a plastic or wooden magazine plug by their makers. Some-times, too, plugs are factory installed in the mag-azine; when they're separately packed, the water-fowl hunter will have to open the magazine (to-wards the muzzle end of the gun) remove the cir-cular spring retainer and slip the plug down inside the magazine spring. Compress the magazine spring and reinstall the split lock ring.

Violation of this regulation carries a fairly stiff penalty so waterfowl hunters should be darned sure their shootin' iron is properly equipped.

The firearm is deceptively simple in appearance and extremely complex in fact. For this reason we have excluded countless gunsmithing tasks that, it was felt, were beyond the realm of the average layman. If a given task is not outlined here, the shooter is best advised to give it to a professional.

CHAPTER 17

Muzzle-Loading Shotguns

In my "Book of the Rifle," published last year, I found it necessary to include a rather comprehensive chapter on muzzle-loading rifles—"their care and feeding," so to speak, because the revival of interest in these old smoke-poles has been dramatic.

Black powder scattergunning is not far behind.

Actually, there's no great trick to loading and firing a muzzle-feeding shotgun. The biggest problem is in finding wads that fit the bore tightly; though most shooters soon learn to make their own when commercially produced wads are unavailable. When hard pressed, I've even used crumpled bits of newspaper for wadding purposes, but I can't say much for resulting performance.

SAFETY FIRST

There are a few basic dangers inherent to black powder scatterguns, so we'll discuss these to clear the slate. First, black powders are far more sensitive to sparks, heat and flame than smokeless powders so they must be handled carefully. When handling this stuff *one does not smoke!*

Many resurrected old specimens should be left hanging over the fireplace. Attempts to use grandpappy's quail gun should be preceded by a visit to the local gunsmith. Let him determine if the thing is safe enough to return to service.

Double-barrel front enders pose a number of threats: realizing that your hands will often be in close proximity to a fully loaded tube (when loading the second one) you'll have to take special pains to prevent accidental discharges. Make sure *neither* barrel is outfitted with a percussion cap or priming charge when undertaking loading operations. If you've only fired one shot, and want to reload the empty barrel, you'll have to remember to clear the firing mechanism of the loaded barrel before proceeding. Next, you'll often find that the discharge of the first barrel will loosen the charge of the second. If the second barrel is subsequently fired, it is almost certain to be bulged—or worse! Alternate barrels so that one charge is not subjected to more than one firing from its mate, and then tamp down *both* charges, in spite of the fact that you've only fired one! Recharging an empty barrel, soon after it has been fired, is especially hazardous—be sure to dis-arm the opposite tube and clear the fired barrel so that no smouldering remnants remain in the breech.

Under no circumstances should you attempt to use smokeless powder in a gun intended for black

Russ Dunham's old smooth-bore musket cannot be used safely with a solid projectile but it serves very well as a shotgun. Roughly 14 gauge in bore size, it handily accepts 12 gauge wads.

powder. Muzzle-loading guns *are strictly black powder guns.*

Finally, use only lead shot in muzzle-loading shotguns; do not attempt to fire these with solid projectiles.

PREPARING THE MUZZLE-LOADER

To start with, you need a perfectly clean blunderbuss—no grease, fowling, dirt or debris can be tolerated, particularly not in the ignition channels. So, remove the stock and scrub down metal components with hot, soapy water. Examine flash holes and nipples with special care and be sure they provide unimpeded access to the breech area. Dry all metal parts carefully and wipe with a good grade of gun oil. Re-assemble the shotgun and we're ready to go on:

If operating a percussion gun, work with the empty bore and fire a couple of caps, preliminarily, to clear and dry the powder end of the barrel. With a flintlock, you can simply clean the flash hole before loading.

Next, take a good long look at the business end

of your ramrod. This should be almost (but not quite) bore diameter in size. If the tip of the ramrod is too small, too narrow, it will encourage wads to tip in the bore. Replace the ramrod tip, if necessary, to get a good, broad, wad-compressing surface.

Now that we're set up and ready to go, examine the loading tables that follow and determine the proper load for the gauge you are using and select the load you want to start with.

Recommended Shotgun Loads

(Note: these charges, particularly the heaviest loads shown for each gauge, are intended for use only in newly manufactured muzzle-loaders. Antique guns should be examined by a competent gunsmith and thoroughly tested before use.)

Gauge	Powder	Powder Charge	Filler Wad*	Weight of Shot Charge
.410	FFG	1¼ drams	⅜″	½ oz.
.410	FFG	1½ drams	⅜″	⅝ oz.
.32	FFG	1½ drams	⅜″	½ oz.
.32	FFG	1¾ drams	⅜″	½ oz.
.28	FFG	2 drams	⅜″	⅝ oz.
.28	FFG	2¼ drams	⅜″	⅝ oz.
.28	FFG	2⅜ drams	⅜″	⅞ oz.
.20	FFG	2 drams	⅜″	¾ oz.
.20	FFG	2¼ drams	½″	⅞ oz.
.20	FFG	2½ drams	½″	1 oz.
.16	FFG	2¼ drams	½″	1 oz.
.16	FFG	2½ drams	½″	1 oz.
.16	FFG	2¾ drams	½″	1⅛ oz.
.14	FFG	2⅜ drams	½″	1 oz.
.14	FFG	2¾ drams	½″	1⅛ oz.
.12	FFG	2½ drams	½″	1⅛ oz.
.12	FFG	3 drams	½″	1⅛ oz.
.12	FFG	3¼ drams	½″	1¼ oz.
.12	FG	3½ drams	½″	1⅜ oz.
.10	FG	3¾ drams	⅝″	1⅜ oz.
.10	FG	4 drams	⅝″	1½ oz.
.10	FG	4¼ drams	⅝″	1⅝ oz.

*Don't forget to use a card wad over the powder before loading filler wad.

The following tables can be used to convert ounces to grains (when weighing shot) and drams to grains (when weighing powder).

To Weigh on a Grain Scale

Ounces of Shot	Grains
½ oz.	218 grs.
¾ oz.	328 grs.
1 oz.	437 grs.
1⅛ oz.	492 grs.
1¼ oz.	547 grs.
1½ oz.	656 grs.
1⅝ oz.	711 grs.
1¾ oz.	765 grs.
2 oz.	875 grs.

To Weigh Black Powder on a Grain Scale

Drams of Powder	Grains
1 dram	27.4 grs.
1¼ drams	34.2 grs.
1½ drams	41.1 grs.
1¾ drams	47.9 grs.
2 drams	54.8 grs.
2¼ drams	61.6 grs.
2⅜ drams	65.1 grs.
2½ drams	68.5 grs.
2¾ drams	75.3 grs.
3 drams	82.2 grs.
3⅛ drams	85.6 grs.
3¼ drams	89.0 grs.
3½ drams	95.9 grs.
3¾ drams	102.7 grs.
4 drams	109.6 grs.
4⅛ drams	113.0 grs.
4¼ drams	116.4 grs.
4½ drams	123.4 grs.

WADS

Load efficiency hinges on the wadding used. If the wads are too loose in the bore, or of an inadequate thickness, they will not contain the powder well enough to achieve any real pressure and velocity. If a commercially made wad combination can be found to fit the bore tightly, you're in luck. On the other hand, when commercial wads of the appropriate size are simply unavailable, the shooter will have to resign himself to the task of making them by hand.

The first thing to do is "mike" the bore. (If your muzzle-loader is made with a choke, you'll have to be careful to take your measurement from an area before the start of the choke.)

Now you'll have to look for assorted pieces of pipe or tubing having inside diameters measuring about two-thousandths (.002″) larger than your bore diameter, preferably of steel. Bevel the outer wall of one of these on a grinder and sharpen it to a knife edge on the I. D. Cut to about six inches in overall length and you'll find yourself equipped with a home-made wad cutter.

If you can't find suitable pipe material, visit your local gunsmith and ask him to make up a couple of wad cutters for you. He can turn these out easily on his lathe and the cost should be modest.

Equipped with cutting tools, you now turn your attention to wad materials: the substance and fit of the powder wad is most important—if it fits the bore too loosely gases will slip around it, into the shot charge, and pressures will drop off greatly. Conventional shotshell loading wads rarely work out simply because they're too small. Some muzzle-loaders get around this by using twelve-gauge wads in a sixteen-gauge gun and sixteen-gauge wads in a twenty bore, etc. etc. Equipped with a rubber or leather mallet, the shooter simply hammers the oversized wad into the muzzle so that the barrel, itself, cuts the wads to bore size.

Here we're talking about cardboard over-powder wads and fibre filler wads. Plastic wads are next to useless in a muzzle-loader simply because they rarely fit the bore tightly.

Since the over-powder wad is our first concern, we'll deal with materials for that before going on to the filler wad: here shooters have tried everything from tarpaper to milk cartons and plastic cup wads. I've always gotten the best performance

from commercial cardboard wads marketed for "over-powder" or "over-shot." With a twelve-gauge gun, for example, I try to get a total thickness approximating .200.″ With a twenty-gauge gun, the over-powder wad can be as thin as .135.″ If need be, I'd glue wads together to get close to these dimensions. Commercial wads are generally found in thicknesses of .070,″ .135,″ and .200.″ The problem is that a .200″ wad is danged difficult to cut down to size. It's easier to work with thinner materials, glueing them together after cutting them to size.

Bob Steindler (the well-known firearms writer) swears by cup-like wads made from old milk cartons. The cup idea has merit—I just think they'd be devilishly tricky to load—unless one is equipped with something resembling a false muzzle, tapered quite a bit larger than bore diameter at one end for easy starting of the cup.

Richard Horlacher, the current international Percussion Claybird Champion, told me that many European shooters use a form of roofing paper (tar paper?) for the over-powder function. Assuming that he's referring to the heavier form of tar paper (that we use on flat roofs) the idea sounds quite logical; this would be easy to cut and load and would appear to provide some heat and flame resistance with a good bore seal. I'm anxious to try it.

Obviously, some experimentation is necessary here, especially in light of the fact that some barrels are choked (what fits tightly at the muzzle may not fit very well when pushed down over the powder). Just don't get carried away by putting *too much* over-powder wadding in the bore because it can start to influence pressures if weight gets excessive.

FILLER WADS

Appropriate material for filler wads is harder to come by; here it pays to search commercial sources—such as Alcan, Dixie Gun Works, Lyman Gun Sight, and Navy Arms—before resigning yourself to the task of creating them from basement scraps.

Some use heavy felt purchased from the local soft goods outlet. This, however, is usually so soft it has to be treated with a stiffener of some sort. One friend used melted paraffin, but it created an awesome sludge in the barrel. Another dipped the cut felt wads in a mixture of shellac and alcohol (equal parts) and let them dry overnight. (This seemed to work better.) Others have simply cut filler wads from scrap ceiling tiles (Celotex?). One shooter I ran into claimed he used laminated pieces of corrugated cardboard packed with Crisco but I can't imagine what kind of performance he got with that formula.

If you've already made up a homemade wadcutter to match your bore size, the best bet would be to buy oversize commercial shotshell-loading filler wads—like Alcan's Feltan—and cut them down to size. On the other hand, you can use the European trick of hammering a ten-gauge felt wad into a twelve-gauge bore, using a rubber or leather mallet.

Filler wads are generally lubricated in some fashion—try liquid soap, patch lubricant, Crisco or what-have-you until you find something that works well for you.

OVER-SHOT WADS

Over-shot wads pose no problem because there's an unlimited supply of pressed board readily available in thicknesses from .050" to .135." Just make sure the over-shot wad fits tightly too!—especially if using a double barrel.

LOADING THE BLACK POWDER SCATTERGUN

Now, consult the loading table, at the beginning of this chapter, and find a suitable, *light* load for the gauge you're using. With the proper *dram-measure scoop*—appropriately adjusted—charge the bore with black powder. Tap the butt of the gun once or twice to settle the powder to the base of the breech.

Start your over-powder wad into the muzzle (you may have to tip it slightly to get it going) and press it home with the ramrod—snug against the powder.

In the field, the muzzle-loading hunter prefers to carry his black powder in a traditional flask or steer horn. Numrich Arms offers this one, complete with carrying strap for $6.55.

Muzzle-loading "fowling pieces," in flintlock or percussion, are offered by several suppliers. This one is Dixie Gun Works Model #79F.

A cushioning filler wad goes in next. This should measure no less than ⅜ of an inch in thickness and, again, it has to be a bit larger than the bore in diameter. Grease the edges if it gives you feeding problems and seat it snugly against the over-powder wad.

Dippers graduated for ounces of shot are made in the same pattern as powder dippers. These are usually the least expensive and the easiest to use. Lacking a proper dipper you'll have little choice but to weigh your charges on a grain scale; plastic pill bottles from a pharmacy can be used for pre-weighing and storing a number of charges. (Some hunters go into the field with their pockets full of plastic-bottled loads.)

Now that you've got that smoke-pole stuffed with the appropriate recipe, you'll have to find a way to hold the shot tightly against the filler wad. This calls for another cardboard wad (the over-shot wad) one considerably thinner than the first. Try a tight-fitting specimen that mikes from .070″ to .135″ in thickness. See that it's positioned flat against the shot (not tipped) and that none of the individual lead pellets have managed to get over the wad, towards the muzzle. I generally tip the muzzle of the gun down after loading: if anything is not as it should be portions of the load will drop to the ground and, for safety's sake, I'll pull the charge rather than attempt to fire it.

Assuming you have a proper load, and that you're ready to shoot, you now need only to rig up your ignition system. With a flintlock gun, set the hammer on half-cock, raise the striker, and fill the flashpan with the finest black powder available—preferably 4 Fg (FFFFg.) Close the striker over the flashpan, cock the hammer, take aim and let fly.

With a percussion lock, set the hammer at half-cock, affix a cap to the exposed nipple, move the hammer to full cock, take aim, and fire!

Before reloading, take pains to make sure no smouldering remnants remain in the bore. If you

Note how Russ leans the muzzle away from the face and body during loading. Here he's loading powder into the bore from a steer horn measure.

should immediately throw another powder charge into the barrel there exists a very good possibility that it will flash back into your hand. For this reason, never load powder directly from the flask, always use the scoop and be sure to keep the barrel anagled *away* from your face and body.

Some shooters blow into the flash hole after firing to clear smouldering debris; others insert the ramrod while they're measuring a new powder charge. You can experiment with bore clearing methods until you find one that works well for you, meanwhile however, guard against flashbacks!

Whatever you come up with, it will pay you to

A leather or rubber mallet will simplify wad loading. Here Russ is loading a half-inch fibre filler wad. Wads that fit tightly do much to improve performance.

test components and loads on a patterning board, especially if you intend to do some serious bird-shooting with your front-ender. Keep records on your test results so you won't find yourself chasing down the same blind alleys a year later.

In conclusion, don't overlook these basic safety precautions:

1. Have old muzzle-loaders examined and tested by a competent gunsmith before attempting to use them.
2. Start with *light* loads, whether the gun is old or new!
3. Don't smoke when handling black powder.
4. Never load powder directly from the flask or container; use a dipper.
5. Keep the gun angled away from the face and body during loading operations.
6. *Never* place your hand over the muzzle during loading. Hold the rod from the side, between your thumb and forefinger.
7. Never attempt to charge a barrel when a percussion cap or priming charge is in place.
8. Don't set up the ignition system until you're ready to shoot.
9. Be especially careful with double-barrel models.
10. *Never, never attempt to use a muzzle-loading gun with smokeless powders!*

With muzzle-loading scatterguns the tip of the ramrod should be very close to bore size to prevent tipping wads in the bore.

Hold the ramrod between the thumb and forefinger when seating the over powder wad and tamp it into place firmly.

CHAPTER 18

Shotgun Accessories

In this somewhat brief chapter we'll describe some of the accessories that are common to shotgunning and, whenever possible, we'll also mention sources of supply for the convenience of the interested reader.

ADJUSTABLE CHOKE DEVICES

There are two basic patterns to the choke devices commonly marketed; with one form of muzzle attachment a base collar is fitted with interchangeable tubes. One simply equips the device with the desired tube by screwing it into the base which is rigidly attached to the muzzle of the barrel. These devices may be had with, or without, ventilated sleeves.

Manufacturers, such as Winchester and Mossberg (among others) have regularly featured the interchangeable tube choke on specific models.

Pachmayr Gun Works, at one time, sold a similar interchangeable tube device but we could find no mention of it in current literature so it is very likely out of production at this writing.

Undoubtedly the most popular of the assorted interchangeable tube chokes is Lyman's Cutts Compensator. This has been on the market, without interruption, for as long as the author can remember. (It is especially popular among skeet

shooters although many a duck gun has been equipped with the Cutts extra-full tube.)

The second pattern of choke device is one that uses a segmented inner element which, under spring tension, can be made to contract or expand under the pressure of a rotating outer sleeve. The Polychoke is the most popular of these though there are a considerable number currently offered—including one that automatically changes from an open to a tighter choke after passage of the first shot.

As for advantages and disadvantages, the adjustable choke should, theoretically, give the shooter some flexibility in applying one shotgun to assorted targets. The reliability of the device, however, is largely dependent upon a number of contributing factors: first, existing bore diameter often influences the performance of the adjustable muzzle. For this reason, some makers offer bases in assorted sizes, thereby enabling installers to match specific bore dimensions. The problem, here, is that only sophisticated gunsmith's shops are equipped to do the work properly. When the bore diameter is not "miked" and matched properly, the adjustable choke will tend to throw only one pattern, regardless of how it is adjusted.

Choke devices equipped with ventilated sleeves

Polychoke's lightweight, add-on, ventilated rib.

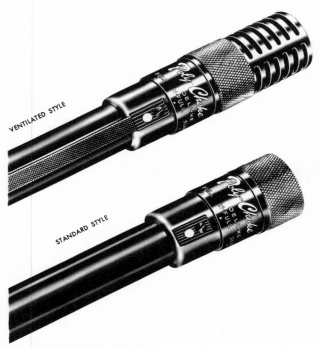

Polychoke (adjustable choke devices) with and without ventilated sleeve.

are *not* ideally suited to recoil operated autoloading shotguns because they interfere with the recoil energy that is used to operate the mechanism. With such models a vent-less device is much preferred.

The shooter who, by some mishap, damages the choke end of his barrel, can often minimize his loss by installing a choke device—assuming that he has not lost too much barrel length.

The ideal barrel length, incidentally, for a multi-purpose shotgun equipped with an adjustable choke, would lie between twenty-seven and twenty-eight inches (with choke fitted).

One last point on this subject—when fitting an adjustable choke to a barrel that is equipped with a ventilated rib, one should not demand a specific finished length because the gunsmith may be forced to cut the barrel in such a way that a large segment of the rib will be left unsupported. It's

best to discuss this with the gunsmith so that a compromise length can be worked out to result in cutting close to the vertical support.

RIB INSTALLATIONS

Owners of plain-barreled shotguns can now have a ventilated rib fitted to their existing barrels at modest cost.

Polychoke (Hartford, Connecticut) makes an add-on rib from a lightweight alloy that can be installed with an epoxy cement. Simmons Gun Specialties (Olathe, Kansas) is also a specialist in this area.

RECOIL REDUCERS

Frankly, in shotguns, the most effective recoil reducer I have found (strictly my own opinion) is the gas-operated autoloading design. Next best, for recoil reduction, is the recoil operated auto. Nevertheless, makers of adjustable choke devices often claim recoil-reducing powers for their ventilated-sleeve muzzle attachments and, while they may come up with some lower butt-end test numbers, I can't honestly say that I've ever felt much of a difference.

Some later-day gadgets touted to tame that

This Wesson Brno shotgun, handled by Bob Steindler, is equipped with a form of ventilated sleeve muzzle device, apparently for recoil-reducing purposes.

shoulder crunch are simply spring loaded weights mounted in a cylinder for installation in the butt-stock. I did run some tests with one of these and can report that I was sorely disappointed. In fairness to the maker I may have had a defective specimen, or one that I adjusted improperly. Nevertheless, those interested in one of these would be well advised to "try before you buy!"

Winchester has a plastic, two-piece, recoil reducing stock that is made with an internal piston. This, I know, does a creditable job of reducing recoil but it offers another problem: A shooter with flabby cheeks could be painfully pinched if a portion of his cheek managed to overlap the joint. For whatever it's worth, one well-known skeet shooter, who was forced to abandon his favorite sport because of a severe bursitis condition in his right shoulder, was able to resume shooting when equipped with the Winchester-style two-piece stock.

SHOOTING GLASSES

There are shooting glasses and there are sunglasses—don't confuse the two!

Shooting glasses are made with special impact-resistant and shatterproof lenses to protect the eyes in the event of a mishap. They're also made with rims that position the lenses high over the eyes so as to avoid obstructing the shooter's vision when his face is canted forward in an aiming altitude. The lower rim of each eyepiece is also mounted high and away from the cheek because—as will be seen with ordinary sunglasses—a rim that bears on the cheek will often pinch or cut when the gun recoils.

Buy shooting glasses through your local firearms dealer to be sure you're getting the real article and look for those made by Bushnell (Bausch & Lomb), Mitchell, May or Willson.

GUN CASES

There are no less than fifty or sixty manufac-turers in the gun case field so we can't possibly mention them all here. We can, however, describe certain forms of construction, calling your attention to advantages and disadvantages.

Soft cases are made with outer covers of cloth, vinyl, canvas, or leather. The genuine leather case would, of course, be the best and no doubt the most expensive. Canvas cases are next best, though not very attractive. Vinyl is the principle material used in inexpensive cases and it has good water-shedding qualities when properly designed.

Zippers can be a problem when they're not of the heavy-duty type or when they open only one end of the case. Check this feature looking for a heavy zipper and one that opens the case full length.

Inner linings run from simple padded cloth to fleece and foam rubber. The important thing here is to have enough padding to protect the firearm from knocks and bumps—check the thickness of the padding.

Inner linings, incidentally, must be kept perfectly dry. One can't store a firearm in a case that has been dampened by a rain-soaked gun because rust deposits will start to form almost immediately. Fleece linings are particularly problematical in this area.

The best cases are equipped with carrying straps as well as normal luggage handles. A case made without a shoulder strap is pure aggravation, though you probably won't miss the strap until you've tried to jockey a pile of luggage through a busy terminal.

Rigid gun cases should be made with at least *two* lockable hasps (one at each end) and should be made with soft, foam-rubber interiors. A piano-hinge running the length of the spine is also better than the small, separated hinges.

Compartmented hard cases are best, especially if they have a good leather outer covering. However, these really should be fitted to a particular firearm so that each piece is held snugly in place.

When components have room to rattle around inside their compartments you'll quickly find signs of wear.

SNAP CAP

This is a device that is loaded into the chamber, in place of a real shell, for the purpose of protecting the firing pin when dry-firing. Usually sold in sets of two, the snap cap is made with a spring loaded plunger or cushioning material in the area usually occupied by the shotshell primer.

Found in all better gun shops, snap caps are made by a number of factories but the only source we could find in current reference material is Pachmayr's (Los Angeles).

TRIGGERS

This is a subject that is best discussed with your local gunsmith. There are many trigger sources—too many to mention here—and each has some unique specialty. The Timney Company, for example, is now offering an interchangeable, adjustable, trigger unit for Remington's Models 870 and 1100, together with an all-steel guard. Release triggers, too, can be had from a number of sources. A knowledgeable gunsmith will no doubt be able to advise you better after learning what your problem is or what it is that you are looking for.

SCOPES AND SIGHTS

Descriptive information can be obtained readily by writing to Bushnell, Leupold, Williams, Lyman or Redfield. When you have some idea of what you need, visit your local gunsmith to arrange the purchase and installation.

Slug guns, used for big game hunting, should be equipped with some form of rifle sight. However, if the same gun is to be used for wingshooting, perhaps with an interchangeable barrel, it would be desirable to have sighting equipment that is easily detachable. One may select any form of

rear sight from an open notch to a peep, or even a scope sight.

With a scope, one should favor the lower magnifications in order to get the largest possible field of view. Some even prefer the long eye-relief scopes for this form of hunting. Another point one might consider, if the same shotgun is to be used for wingshooting, is that prominent top mount bases may obstruct the sighting plane when the scope is removed. The side mounted scope is preferred for obvious reasons. If one must go with a top-mounted scope, look for a mount having a small inconspicuous base.

As for reticles, the conventional crosswire does not show well against the heavily shadowed backgrounds common to brush country hunting. A solid post would be considerably easier to define.

INTERCHANGEABLE BARRELS

Interchangeable barrels, or sets of barrels, are generally available for better-grade guns.

Today, most makers of automatic shotguns produce barrels that are readily interchangeable (without factory fitting) on all receivers (of the same gauge) of a given model. Barrels are also easily interchanged on most take-down model pumpguns.

Side-by-side and over and under double guns invariably must be ordered with the interchangeable barrel sets.

One frame, or receiver, for which the shooter has a number of interchangeable barrels, results in a truly versatile shotgun with a number of advantages. For one thing, the shooter will find that his performance will improve simply because he's continuously working with the same stock and trigger. Also, when two or more barrel sets are available to him, he'll find that he'll be able to outfit the rig ideally for most any form of hunting or shooting. Finally, if one considers the cost of a battery of shotguns, for a variety of shooting endeavors, he'll find the interchangeable-barrel route an inexpensive way to accomplish the same objective.

Assuming that we're discussing the conventional twelve-gauge pump or auto, one would need three barrels to cover the shooting spectrum and these would be: a 26-inch bored improved cylinder, a 28-inch bored modified and a 30-inch bored with a full choke. Specialty barrels for sophisticated forms of target shooting are excluded from this example but, if one is interested in handicap Trap shooting, he could easily substitute, or add, the appropriate barrel to this grouping.

The thirty-inch full-choke barrel is generally not made for the smaller gauges, i.e., .410, 28, 20 and 16 so one could "batterize" these with just two barrels.

In twelve-gauge double guns the complete battery would consist of sets of barrels in: 26-inch bored improved cylinder and modified; 28-inch bored modified and full; and 30-inches bored modified (or improved modified) and full. Some waterfowl hunters would ask the manufacturer for a set in the thirty-inch length bored full and full, for pass shooting. Similarly, pigeon guns are often ordered with barrels measuring 28-inches bored improved cylinder and full or improved-cylinder and improved modified.

The trap shooter may elect to go with a thirty-inch set bored modified or improved modified (for sixteen-yard events) in combination with a full or extra-full choke (for handicap shooting). On the other hand, trap shooters are usually very fussy about their special stock dimensions and any interchangeable barrels would invariably be tailored for other forms of trap competition, not field use.

With some guns—and you'd have to check this out with your local firearms dealer—it is possible to change *gauge* when switching barrels, though there are, understandably, some strict limitations on what can, or cannot be done in this area.

Skeet shooters, incidentally, often have one high grade double gun (usually an O/U) made up with *four* sets of barrels covering all skeet classes, i.e., .410, 28, 20 and 12 gauges. Some, too, have differing barrels for the international as well as American forms of the game.

Concluding this chapter on accessories, some mention has to be made on the subject of clothing for hunting and shooting. Like any other sport shooting and hunting puts some special demands on the participant insofar as his togs are concerned.

Hunting gear should be water repellant and fairly durable. For some species of game (notably waterfowl) clothing should also offer some degree of camouflage and this goes double for those hunting the wild turkey. The hunter who works thickets and thorny tangles must give some thought to special outfits, most especially—brush trousers.

When big game hunting is contemplated, be sure to examine your local hunting laws because some areas now stipulate that the hunter *must* wear a certain percentage of outer clothing in blaze orange or red.

For ease of carrying, and to free the hunter's hands for gun handling, many hunting outfits are made with a built-in game bag having a plasticized liner. This is a very convenient accessory, don't overlook its importance.

Target shooting outfits are made in a wide variety of styles and from materials patterned for varying temperatures. Shooting vests for summer, sweaters for spring and fall, heavy kapok lined jackets for the cold months. Generally, target outfits have smooth panels on the gun-mounting side, large pockets, and a cushioned shoulder pad. Special garments are made for international skeet and trap having a full-length panel on the gun-mounting side to facilitate shouldering when the butt of the gun is held low.

Foot gear is especially important; boots should be soft, comfortable and waterproof or warm, depending upon the climate and terrain. At times, too, knee boots or hip boots would be required for the waterfowl hunter or upland-gunner working marshy bottom lands.

Special gloves and mittens are available with cutouts for the trigger finger or slotted palms (in mittens) for the entire trigger hand. These are much more practical than ordinary hand coverings.

The long and the short of it is that the average haberdashery or shoe outlet does not handle shooter's gear. The reader is best advised to shop for clothing, boots, etc., at his local firearms emporium.

CHAPTER 19

Catalog Section

SINGLE BARREL SHOTGUNS

In single-barrel, single-shot shotguns there are a number to choose from:

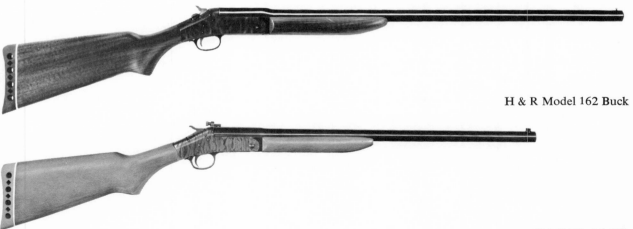

H & R Model 162 Buck

H & R Model 490

H&R: (otherwise known as Harrington & Richardson) offers four models of their well known "Topper."

MODEL 162: in 12 gauge with 3″ chamber for all commercially loaded 12 gauge shells. Cylinder bored with walnut stock and overall length of 40″. Weight 5½ lbs. Blade front sight with folding leaf rear sight for slug use.

MODEL 490: in .410 or 20 gauge with 3-inch chamber. Walnut stock. Length 40″. Weight 5 lbs. Barrel, 26 inches in both gauges. Twenty gauge with modified choke, .410 bored full. Brass front sight.

MODEL 058: in 12, 20 or .410 gauge with 3-inch chambers or, 16 gauge with 2¾-inch chamber. Walnut stock. Length 41″ to 51″. Weight, 6 lbs. average. Brass bead front sight. Barrels & chokes: 12/36″F, 12/32″F, 12/30″F, 12/28″F, 12/28″M, 20/28F, 20/28″M, 16/28″M, 410/26″F.

MODEL 098: also in .410 or 20 gauge with 3-inch chamber. Ebony finished hardwood stock. Length 41″. Weight 5½ lbs. Receiver brightly polished. Barrel length 26 inches bored full in the .410 gauge and modified in 20 gauge. Brass front sight.

It should be noted here that H&R also offers their "Topper" in the Model 158C which is a 20 gauge single shot shotgun provided with an interchangeable rifle barrel in choice of .22 Hornet or .30–30 caliber.

ITHACA SINGLE-SHOT: Ithaca offers their popular Model 66 Supersingle in six versions:

MODEL 66 Supersingle: in choice of 12, 20 or .410 gauges with 3-inch chamber. Under-lever action opener. Straight grip stock. Weight 7 lbs. Rebounding hammer. Gauges and lengths are— 12/30″F, 12/28″F, 12/28″M, 20/28″F, 20/28″M, .410/26″F.

MODEL 66 Supersingle Vent-Rib: the 12 or 20 gauge models (listed above) may also be had with ventilated rib barrels at about $10.00 additional.

MODEL 66 STANDARD YOUTH: similar to the above but in only .410 or 20 gauge with shortened (13½″) stock and 26-inch barrel bored 20/26″M or .410/26″F.

MODEL 66 LONGTOM: "turkey" gun in 12 gauge with 36-inch barrel chambered for all 2¾- or 3-inch loads. 7 lbs. length of pull, 14″.

MODEL 66 BUCKBUSTER: in 12 gauge at 6½ lbs. or 20 gauge at 5½. Special slug bore barrel of 22 inches for 2¾- or 3-inch shells. Length of pull 14″.

IVER JOHNSON: The Champion Model may be had in 12, 20 or .410 gauges with 3″ chambers. Full choke barrels in 12/28″, 12/30″, 20/28″, .410/26″. Walnut stock with broad fore-end. Weight about 6½ lbs. Take-down action with automatic ejection.

Stevens Model 94-C

Stevens 94-Y Youth's Model

SAVAGE-STEVENS: Offers two versions of their popular Model 94, i.e., a standard man-sized, 94-C and M94-Y Youth's Model.

MODEL 94-C: in 12, 16, 20, and .410 gauges; all with 3-inch chambers except the 16 gauge which is bored with the conventional 2¾" chamber. With external hammer, auto-ejector, top-lever, break-open action. Barrels of 12/28", 12/30", 12/36", 16/28", 20/28", .410/26". Full chokes only. Walnut finished stock with checkered grip surfaces. Weight, approximately 6 lbs. Length 42 inches (with 26" barrel.) Case-hardened frome. (36-inch barrel at slight extra cost.)

MODEL 94-Y YOUTH'S GUN: same as 94-C except that it is offered only in .410 or 20 gauge with 26-inch barrel and length of pull of 12½ inches. Equipped with recoil pad. Length, overall, 40½".

GALEF: Galef's famous Companion single barrel shotgun is a folding model (the barrel is hinged to swing completely rearward for easy portability.) With 3-inch chambers this model may be had in 12, 20 or .410 gauge. The 16 gauge is made only with 2¾-inch chamber. Barrels are 12/30", 16/28", 20/28" and .410/26" and all are full choked.

Winchester Model 37A

WINCHESTER: Continues to offer their ever-popular Model 37 in the standard 37 and 37A Youth version.

37A: in 12, 20 or .410 gauge with 3" chamber, 28 and 16 gauge with 2¾" chamber. Barrels are .410/26", 28/28", 20/28"F, 16/30"F, 12/30"F, 12/32"F, and 12/36"F. Weight 5½ to 5¼ lbs. Length 42¼" overall with 26-inch barrel. Walnut stock measures 14" × 1⅜" × 2⅜". Gold plated trigger, decorated receiver, auto-ejector, white line spacers. Top lever opens left or right.

37A YOUTH MODEL: only in .410 or 20 gauge with 26-inch barrel and 12½" length of pull. Overall length 40¾".

KLEINGUNTHER: The Daino single-barrel is made only in 12 or 20 gauge with 27½-inch barrel, full choked. Weight 5½ lbs. Length 44½. Hand checkered walnut stock with pistol grip. (Also a "folding" model.)

MONTGOMERY WARD: Western Field Model 100 single barrel in 12, 16, 20, and .410 which is bored with 3" chamber. Barrels are 12/30"F, 16/28"F, 20/28"F, and .410/26"F. Weight 6¼ to 7 lbs. Auto safety and auto ejector.

BOLT ACTION SHOTGUNS

The bolt action shotgun is peculiarly American, in fact, to the best of our knowledge, no foreign maker has ever ventured into this unique market area. For that matter, few American producers turn out bolt-scatterguns.

Following is a rundown on those currently offered:

Savage-Stevens Model 58

SAVAGE ARMS CORP.: produces the popular lines sold under the names: "Savage," "Stevens," and "Fox." Savage also functions as the U. S. distributor for Anschutz firearms.

Only under the Stevens label, however, do they offer one model of bolt action shotgun:

MODEL 58: A .410 gauge with a plain barrel, 3-shot clip magazine, self-cocking bolt, bead sight, thumb safety, steel receiver, and checkered hardwood stock and fore-end. Length, overall—43-inches. Average weight 5½ lbs. Stock measures 14″ × 1½″ × 2½″. A versatile model for all ages.

Marlin Model 55 Goose Gun

MARLIN FIREARMS COMPANY: offers two versions of their popular Model 55 bolt action shotguns. These sell for a bit less than $100.00:

MODEL 55 GOOSE GUN: 12 gauge bolt action chambered for all 2¾- and 3-inch 12 gauge shells, magnum and standard. With a detachable two-shot clip magazine total capacity is three shots. Equipped with a 36-inch plain barrel, bored

full choke and fitted with a bead front sight. Overall length is 57 inches; weight—about 7¼ lbs. Walnut stock with fitted recoil pad and sling.

MODEL 55S SLUG GUN: same as the Model 55 Goose gun (above) but equipped with a 24-inch slug barrel and rifle sights. Also tapped and drilled for a long eye-relief scope. Overall length 45-inches; weight 7 lbs.

Mossberg Model 183K

Mossberg Model 385K

Mossberg Model 395S

O. F. MOSSBERG & SONS, INC.: Bolt-action shotguns are made by Mossberg, in 12, 20 gauge and .410 bore. Proof-tested and chambered for all standard and 3″ magnum loads. Three-shot capacity, two in the magazine plus one in the chamber. A modern self-cocking action with positive safety on top, under the thumb. All Mossberg shotguns shoot rifled slugs accurately, for hunting deer or other big game.

Specifications: MODEL 395K: 12 gauge. Detachable box magazine for quick loading and unloading. With 3″ magnum shells and number 2 shot, this makes a great goose gun.

Action: Strong bolt, chambered for 3″ magnum as well as 2¾″ factory-loaded shells. Double-locking lugs for added strength. Positive safety.

Barrel: 26″ including C-LECT-CHOKE.

Sights: Grooved rear sight. Shotgun type front bead.

MODEL 385K: Same as Model 395K except in 20 gauge, with 26″ barrel, including C-LECT-CHOKE. Chambered for 3″ magnum as well as 2¾″ factory-loaded shells.

MODEL 385T: Same as 385K, but without C-LECT-CHOKE feature or recoil pad.

MODEL 183K: The only .410-bore shotgun with the advantage of a finger-operated adjustable choke.

Action: Fixed-type loading magazine holds two shells, plus one in the chamber. Chambered for all factory-loaded 2½″ and 3″ shells. Convenient thumb-operated safety, with red button indicator inlaid in stock.

Stock: Walnut finish, Monte Carlo design. Rubber recoil pad with white-line spacer.

Barrel: 25″ tapered blued-steel barrel, with factory-installed Mossberg C-LECT-CHOKE. Gold bead front sight. Weight—About 6¾ lbs. Length overall: 43½″.

MODEL 183T: Same as 183K, but without C-LECT-CHOKE feature.

MODEL 395S: A popular deer and bear gun. Same specifications as Model 395K, but equipped with 24″ Slugster barrel with sights. Front sight is partridge type on ramp and rear sight is adjustable folding leaf. Receiver is drilled and tapped for scope mounting. Gun is equipped with web sling and swivels.

MODEL 183K: .410 bore with C-LECT-CHOKE
MODEL 183T: .410 Bore
MODEL 385K: 20 ga. with C-LECT-CHOKE
MODEL 385T: 20 ga.
MODEL 395K: 12 ga. with C-LECT-CHOKE
MODEL 395T: 12 ga.
MODEL 395S: 12 ga. with 24″ Slugster barrel

Montgomery-Ward Model 172

MONTGOMERY-WARD: Offers three bolt action models as follows:

WESTERN FIELD MODEL 172: in 12 gauge with 3-inch chamber for all 2¾- and 3-inch 12 gauge shells. Self-cocking bolt. Thumb safety. Double lugs, detachable clip magazine. 28-inch barrel with adjustable choke. Monte Carlo style walnut stock with recoil pad.

WESTERN FIELD MODEL 175: similar to above but in 20 gauge.

WESTERN FIELD MODEL 150C: a .410 gauge bolt action with a 3-inch chamber. Self-cocking. Three-shot capacity. Thumb safety. Full choke barrel measures 24 inches. Weight 5½ lbs. Length, overall 44½″. Monte Carlo style hardwood stock.

SLIDE ACTION SHOTGUNS

The slide action shotgun (colloquially referred to as the "pump gun") is a uniquely American type of scattergun that probably exceeds all others in popularity. It is durable and reliable, yet an inexpensive rapid-firing repeater. Winchester, Remington, Savage, and Ithaca are traditional pump gun makers. In recent years, however, they've been joined by Mossberg, Marlin, and High-Standard, so the shooter has a broad assortment to choose from today.

High-Standard Flite-King

HIGH STANDARD: The Flite-King series produced by High-Standard embraces standard and deluxe grades in 12, 20, 28 and .410 gauges and in target versions for skeet and trap.

Essentially, the Flite-King shotgun is a side-ejecting pump action with a five-shot capacity. (Three-shot plugs are provided for migratory bird hunting.) Both plain and ventilated rib barrels are offered in all conventional length and choke combinations. Their brush gun version, however, is made only in 12 gauge with a 20-inch cylinder bored barrel. Most models are equipped with factory-fitted recoil pad. Weights run from 6 lbs. (in the smaller gauges) to 7¼ lbs. (in the 12 gauge). Skeet and trap models are slightly heavier.

Walnut stocks and fore-ends are impressed-checkered and generally measure 14″ × 1½″ × 2½″. The trap stock, however, is a bit higher and ⅜″ longer. Prices range from about $150 to two hundred some odd dollars.

A deluxe grade Flite-King is also offered with a factory-fitted adjustable choke.

Ithaca Model 37 Deerslayer

ITHACA: Ithaca's traditional Model 37 series pump gun is offered in seven different styles in the conventional 12, 16, and 20 gauges. Prices range from about $150 (for a plain barrel) to something approaching $200 for a ventilated rib version. Special custom finished and decorative grades, however, can be special ordered.

The Model 37 is a perennial best seller. It is a bottom-ejecting five-shot repeater furnished with a 3-shot plug. In all conventional barrel lengths and choke combinations it also features a push-button safety (in the trigger guard) a Raybar front sight and tastefully decorated walnut stock and fore-end. Barrels are easily interchangeable so it is possible to convert one gun for other applications by simply installing another, appropriate, barrel.

Field model stocks measure 1⅝″ drop at comb, 2⅝″ drop at heel, and 14″ length of pull.

A special slug gun model, called the "Deer-slayer," is offered in choice of 12 or 20 gauge and is equipped with rifle sights and grooved for easy scope installation.

Marlin Model 120 Trap Gun

Marlin Model 120 Magnum

MARLIN: Marlin makes only four versions of their famous Model 120 pump gun, but these have some unique, special applications.

The Model 120 boasts the interchangeable barrel feature, is made in 12 gauge only (though it is chambered to accept 3-inch shells as well as 2¾" types), has a five-shot capacity (plug furnished), and right-side ejection port. With factory-fitted recoil pad, the field stock measures 1½" drop at comb, 2⅜" drop at heel, and 14" length of pull. Push-button safety is located in the leading edge of the trigger guard. Fore-ends are semi-beavertail type. Variations follow:

MODEL 120 MAGNUM: with ventilated rib, 12 gauge only (for 2¾" & 3" shells). Choice of 26" I.C., 28"M or 30"F choke barrels.

MODEL 120 SLUG GUN: in 12 gauge with 26" cyl. slug barrel equipped with rifle sights and tapped for easy scope mounting.

MODEL 120 40" MXR MAGNUM: a special 3" 12 gauge Magnum version with a 40-inch barrel for turkety shoots or pass shooting of waterfowl. Extra full choke.

MODEL 120 TRAP GUN: in 12 gauge with a 30" full choke, ventilated rib barrel. Equipped with a deluxe grade Monte Carlo style stock measuring 1¼" drop at comb, 1¾" drop at Monte Carlo, 1¼" drop at heel and 14¼" length of pull.

Mossberg Model 500

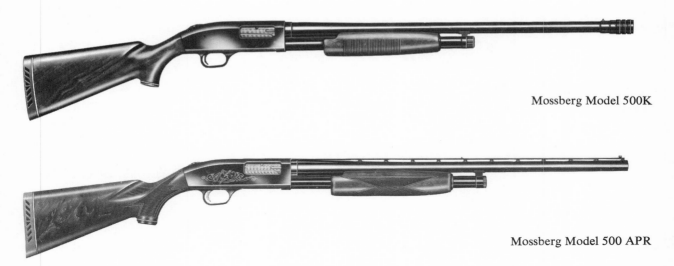

Mossberg Model 500K

Mossberg Model 500 APR

MOSSBERG: This well-known American producer offers about a dozen different versions of their now famous Model 500 pump gun. These are made in choice of 12, 20, or .410 bore and cover plain barrel types as well as some equipped with ventilated ribs and/or adjustable chokes.

At the top of the 500 line is their new Model DSPR which is a limited edition Commemorative 12 gauge Magnum in an ultra-deluxe styling. This one honors the waterfowl shooting fraternity and the Migratory Bird Act. Only 1,000 pieces of this model will be offered in 1975.

The basic Model 500 features are encompassed by all: barrels are interchangeable; six-shot capacity (2¾″ shells) and five-shot capacity when using 3″ shells; furnished with 3-shot magazine plug.

With steel receiver, right-side ejection, chrome damascened bolt, sliding thumb operated safety on tang, and factory-fitted recoil pad.

Stocks are of high quality walnut, handsomely checkered and attractively finished. With fluted combs and semi-beavertail fore-end. Field model stocks measure 1½″ × 2½″ × 14″. The deluxe trap stock, found on the Model 500 APTR Pigeon Grade Trap Gun, is made with a Monte Carlo and measures 1½″ × 1½″ × 2″ × 14½″.

All traditional barrel length and choke combinations are offered in 12, 20 or .410 gauges. A special slug model is made with a 24″ cyl. bore barrel.

Prices range from slightly under $150 to about $200.

Remington Model 870

REMINGTON: Remington's Model 870 is offered in the 12, 16, 20, 28 and .410 gauges in a host of different stylings—including a left-hand version with the left-side ejection port in the 12 and 20 gauges only. Other special models include a standard and deluxe "Deer gun," a 3″ Magnum Duck Gun (in 12 or 20 ga.), a Police gun, and a number of target guns for skeet and trap. In all, there are twenty-eight differing styles and grades up to the "870F Premier" which is priced over $2,000.-oo. Standard grades range from about $150 to $200 plus.

All Model 870's are five-shot repeaters (furnished with 3-shot plugs) and range in weight from 6½ to about 7 lbs. (in 20-12 ga.) depending upon barrel length. Produced in all traditional barrel and choke combinations, the Model 870 also offers a 20-inch barrel in its deer and police grades,

however, an 18-inch barrel may be had in police grade as well. Skeet guns are made with 26-inch skeet choke barrels; Trap guns with 30″ full choke barrels.

Available only as an extra barrel, a 34-inch full choke tube may be had for 12 gauge receivers.

Field stocks measure 1⅝″ drop at comb, 2½″ drop at heel and 14″ length of pull. Trap guns are available with standard or Monte Carlo stocks and measure 1½″ × 1⅞″ × 13⅜″ (standard) or 1½″ × 1½″ × 1⅞″ × 14⅜″ (Monte Carlo) Stocks and semi-beavertail fore-ends are made from fine American walnut and exceptionally attractive grains are selected for deluxe versions. Most models are attractively impressed checkered; higher grades, however, are hand checkered.

In 20, 28 and .410 gauges, weights range from 5½ to 6 lbs.

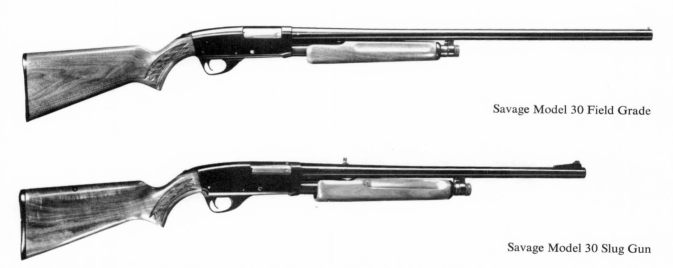

Savage Model 30 Field Grade

Savage Model 30 Slug Gun

SAVAGE: Savage Arms Corp. offers only the Model 30 to the pump gun market, however, this is made in three versions in choice of 12, 20 or .410 gauge.

MODEL 30D: with 26-, 28- or 30-inch barrel for all standard or 3-inch shells in all three gauges. This deluxe style also includes a ventilated rib barrel (in all conventional lengths and chokes) as well as a factory fitted recoil pad.

MODEL 30 FG: "Field Grade" model comparable to the above but with plain round barrel and composition butt plate.

MODEL 30 FG-SLUG: the deer hunter's shotgun with 22-inch cylinder-bored barrel and rifle sights.

The basic spec's for the Model 30 are common to the three types, i.e.—top tang safety, interchangeable barrels (in the same gauge), semi-beavertail fore-end and walnut butt stock.

Weights range from 7 to 7¾ lbs. depending upon gauge and barrel length.

All versions are made with a rugged all-steel receiver, forged and machined.

SMITH & WESSON: This famous handgun manufacturer has now branched into the shotgun field with their Model 916 "Eastfield": pump. In 12, 16 or 20 gauge, the Eastfield is offered with 26- or 28-inch barrels bored improved cylinder (26″ only), modified or full. The 12 gauge version is also available with a 30-inch barrel. Barrels may be had plain or with ventilated ribs.

Deluxe versions are made up with factory-fitted recoil pad.

Pistol grip stock and semi-beavertail fore-end are made from walnut.

WEATHERBY: Offers their "Patrician Pump" in 12 gauge only with 2¾″ chamber. All conventional barrel and choke combinations. Stock measures 1⅜″ × 1¼″ × 14¼″. With push-button safety, reversible. Extra interchangeable barrels also available. Weight about 7½ to 7¾ lbs. depending upon barrel length. Prices under $300.00. Special trap version also available.

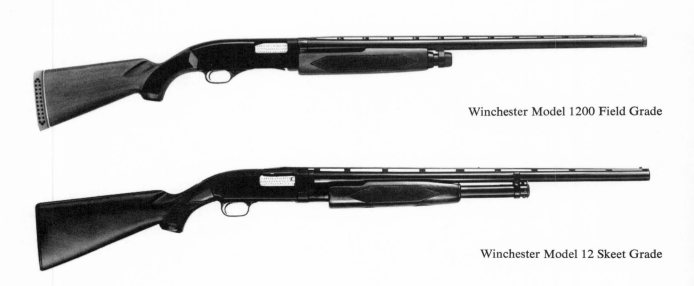

Winchester Model 1200 Field Grade

Winchester Model 12 Skeet Grade

Winchester Model 12 Super-Pigeon **Grade**

Winchester Model 12 Field Grade

WINCHESTER: This famous producer of pump guns has only recently revived their time-honored Model 12, however, this is offered only in 12 gauge. Their Model 1200, on the other hand, is offered in 12 and 20 gauges. Details follow:

MODEL 1200 FIELD GRADE: in 12 or 20 gauge with 26″ IC or 28″M plain, or 30″F barrel in 12 gauge only. Five-shot capacity with 3-shot plug furnished. Alloy receiver with trigger-guard push-button safety. Take-down style. Stock measures 1⅜″ × 2⅜″ × 14″. Impressed checkered. Recoil pad. Steel pistol grip cap. Weight, approximately 6½ lbs. depending upon gauge and barrel length.

MODEL 1200 DEER GUN: Same as above but with 22″ barrel, cylinder bored for slug shooting. Equipped with rifle sights.

MODEL 1200 3-INCH MAGNUM: Same as field model but chambered to accept 3-inch magnum shells as well as standard 2¾″ 20 gauge with 28-inch full choke barrel. 12 gauge with 30-inch full choke barrel. Weights range from 7¾ to 8 lbs. Overall length 48⅝″. Ventilated rib barrels available at slight extra cost.

All model 1200's are designed to accept interchangeable barrels (in the same gauge).

MODEL 12 FIELD GRADE: in 12 gauge only with 6-shot capacity (3-shot plug furnished.) Choice of 26″ I.C., 28″M or 30″F choke barrels. Stock measures 1½″ × 2½″ × 14″. Semi-fancy walnut with checkered grip surfaces on pistol grip and semi-beavertail fore-end. Weight about 7¾ lbs.

MODEL 12 SKEET GRADE: Same as above but equipped with ventilated rib skeet choked barrel of 26 inches. Recoil pad.

MODEL 12 TRAP GRADE: Same as field grade but with 30-inch full choke ventilated rib-barrel. Choice of standard stock (1⅜″ × 1⅞″ × 14⅜″) or Monte Carlo stock (1½″ × 1½″ × 2⅛″ × 14⅜″).

Price-wise, the Winchester 1200 ranges from $135.00 to about $170.00. The Model 12 ranges from $400.00 upward; target grades about $450.00. Special deluxe grades on quotation.

Browning Auto-5

BROWNING: Browning Arms Co. still offers their famous "Auto-5" in 12, 16 and 20 gauges, the sixteen gauge version has long been called "Sweet 16." Special magnum models for 3-inch 12 and 20 gauge shells are called "Auto-5 Magnum 12 or 20." In the same series there will be found a "Buck Special" and "Skeet" autos.

Browning, who originally created the recoil-operated autoloader, has long been famous for this durable scattergun. It will be found on bird fields, in salt marshes and on skeet ranges from coast to coast.

AUTO-5 LIGHT 12, 20 & SWEET 16: chambered for 2¾-inch shells. Recoil operated. Takedown. Interchangeable barrels. All conventional barrel lengths and choke combinations. Weights— 12 ga. 7¼ lbs.; 16 ga. 6¾ lbs.; 20 ga. 6⅜ lbs. Stock with modified pistol grip, of French walnut, checkered, measures 1⅝″ × 2½″ × 14¼″. Scroll engraving, double extractors, magazine cut-off

and push-button safety. Prices start at about $300.00. Ventilated rib models about $20.00 higher. Five-shot capacity, plug furnished.

AUTO-5 BUCK SPECIAL: two versions of this are offered—a standard at 7⅝ lbs. and a lightweight at 7 lbs. (12 gauge). Also may be had in 16 gauge and 12 gauge Magnum. Specifications generally the same as above except equipped with 24″ slug barrel and rifle sights. Lightweight 12 is approximately $10.00 higher than standard. May also be ordered with detachable swivels and sling.

AUTO-5 LIGHT SKEET: offered only in 12 or 20 gauge with choice of 26″ or 28″ skeet choked barrel and plain or vent rib barrel. Other details same as "AUTO-5 LIGHT" shells. May be had with plain barrel or vent rib. 12 gauge version weighs between 8¾ and 9 lbs., depending upon barrel length and presence of rib. 12 gauge barrel choices are 28″ and 26″. Weight 7½ lbs.

CHARLES DALY: The Daly autoloading shotgun is imported in 12 gauge only with barrels chambered for 2¾-inch shells. Barrel choices are 26″ I.C., 28″M, 28″F and 30″F. (all with ventilated rib). Stock is hand-checkered walnut with pistol grip. Five-shot capacity (plug furnished). Barrels are interchangeable. Push-button safety in trigger guard. In appearance, this model resembles the Browning.

F.A.R.M.S.: Information on this well-made line of recoil-operated autoloaders was not available at this writing. Trusting to memory the F.A.R.M.S. auto is made in Italy with a light-alloy receiver in both 12 and 20 gauge and with all conventional combinations of chokes and barrel lengths. Five-shot capacity. Checkered walnut stock and fore-end. May be had with vent rib.

FRANCHI: An Italian import with a light alloy receiver in 12 and 20 gauge; all standard barrel lengths and chokes. Special 3-inch models also available along with deluxe grades. Impressed checkered stock and fore-end. Slug gun with 22″ barrel and rifle sights. Vent ribs available. Barrels interchangeable. Five-shot capacity. Weight range from 5 lbs. to 8¼ lbs. depending upon gauge and barrel.

TRADEWINDS: MODEL H-170 AUTO: this lightweight import is offered in 12 gauge only, chambered for 2¾-inch shells. Choice of 26″ I.C., 28″M or 28″F barrels with chrome lined bores, with or without ventilated rib. Attractive walnut stock and fore-end are hand-checkered. Five-shot capacity with 3-shot plug furnished. Pistol grip. Weight, approximately 7 lbs.

GAS-OPERATED AUTOLOADING SHOTGUNS

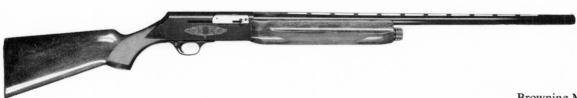

BROWNING: MODEL B/2000: this new Browning gas-operated auto was first introduced to the market in 1974 and it excited considerable attention. Initially available only in 12 gauge (choice of 2¾″ or 3″ chamberings), the Model B/2000 has a self-cleaning gas system, a left-side loading port, and an interchangeable barrel feature together with a unique unloading system.

Plain barrels are generally supplied on field grades but ventilated rib barrels may also be had at slight additional cost. Magazine capacity for 2¾-inch shells is five. (Magnums-four.) Choice of 26″, 28″ or 30″ barrel in standard 12 gauge; 32″ barrel also available for magnum. Weight, approximately 7½ lbs. Hand-checkered French walnut stock measures 1⅝″ × 2½″ × 14¼″.

Special models for slug, skeet and trap are expected to be announced in the near future.

High-Standard Supermatic

HIGH STANDARD: SUPERMATIC GAS-OP-ERATED AUTO: in the field grade, is made in 12 and 20 gauges. The former with a 5-shot capacity and the latter with 3-shell capacity. 12 gauge is chambered for 2¾″ shells; 20 gauge—3″.

Barrel choices are 26″ I.C., 28″M or 30″F in 12 gauge; 20 gauge only 28″M. Stock measures 1½″ × 2½″ × 14″. Walnut checkered. Recoil pad fitted. Weight, about 7½ lbs. (12 ga.)

SUPERMATIC 12 GA. DUCK: similar to above but chambered for 3″ Magnum shells and equipped with vent rib barrel.

SUPERMATIC SKEET: similar to field model (above) but made with 26″ skeet choke barrel.

SUPERMATIC TRAP: similar to field model but in 12 gauge only with 30″ full choke barrel. Stock—1½″ × 1⅞″ × 14⅜″. Weight 8 lbs.

HIGH-STANDARD SHADOW SHOTGUN: an imported gas-operated auto in 12 or 20 gauge with 2¾″ or 3″ chambers. All popular barrel and choke combinations. Skeet and Trap models too. Weight, about 7 lbs. (Checkered walnut wood.)

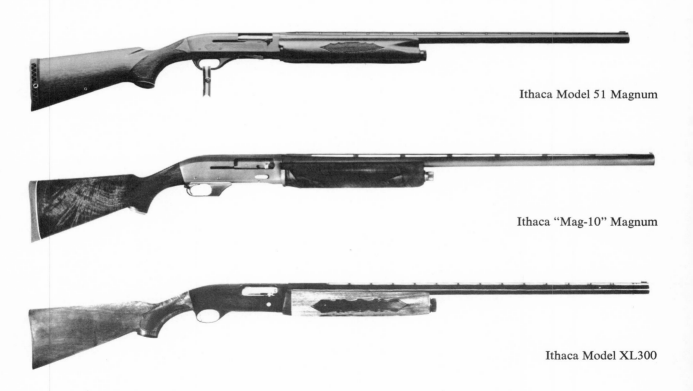

Ithaca Model 51 Magnum

Ithaca "Mag-10" Magnum

Ithaca Model XL300

ITHACA: MAG-10: Ithaca's new "MAG-10" gas-operated auto caused a sensation in waterfowl circles when it was announced. Designed to digest the 3½-inch 10 gauge magnum shell, this model will surely find a following among pass shooters.

Offered only with a vent-rib-equipped, full-choke, 32-inch barrel the "MAG-10" weighs about 11¼ lbs. It has an American walnut stock measuring 1½″ × 2⅜″ × 14⅛″. With recoil pad. Reversible push-button safety.

MODEL 51 FEATHERLIGHT AUTO: at last count, there were about a dozen different versions of Ithaca's famous Model 51 currently in production.

Made in 12 and 20 gauge, these may be had chambered for 2¾″ or 3″ shells—(the latter will handle both.) Barrels are interchangeable and safeties (push-button type) are reversible. All conventional combinations of barrel length and choke are available. Stocks are made from fine American walnut and are hand-checkered. Field dimensions are: 1½″ drop at comb, 2¼″ drop at heel and 14″ length of pull. Weights range from 7¼ to 8 lbs. May be had with plain barrel or vent rib (at slight additional cost).

Unique self-cleaning gas-piston action is self-adjusting to compensate for differing-velocity shotshells. Easy take-down and minimum mainte-

nance requirements make the Model 51 unique among gas-operated shotguns. Generally equipped with Raybar front sight. Target models have floating ribs. Top plane of receiver Parkerized to reduce glare.

As for a run-down on the differing grades, the shooter can choose from a 2¾″ field model (in 12 or 20) with plain or vent rib barrel; magnum (3″) versions of 12 and 20; four trap grades (12 ga.) one of which is made with a Monte Carlo stock, and two skeet grades with vent rib, skeet choke, barrels. Prices start at about $200.00 and approach $300.00.

Ithaca also functions as the U. S. distributor for the Japanese firm of SKB. Under this label Ithaca offers the Models XL300 and XL900 gas-operated autos; lightweight five-shot repeaters with dial-a-load valving. Safeties are reversible. Barrels are hard chrome lined and black chrome finished externally. In 12 or 20 gauge, choose from field, slug, trap or skeet models weighing from 6 to 7¾ lbs.

The Model XL300 has a roll-engraved blue-black receiver. The Model XL900 (deluxe version) has etched game scenes on the receiver flats which are bright natural-metal finished.

Field stock dimensions are 1½″ × 1⅞″ × 14½″. Prices range from $200.00 to $300.00.

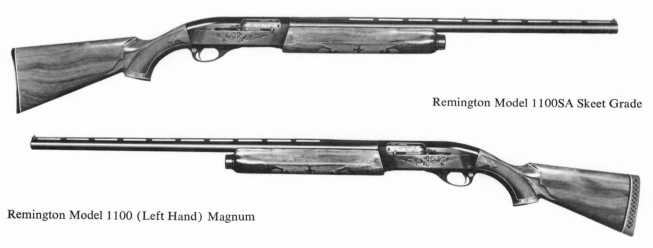

Remington Model 1100SA Skeet Grade

Remington Model 1100 (Left Hand) Magnum

Remington Model 1100 20 Ga. Magnum

REMINGTON: The Model 1100 needs little introduction to American wingshooters: it has been well-accepted by both field and skeet enthusiasts.

The 1100 is a five-shot auto (plug furnished) in 12, 16 and 20 gauge. Available in all conventional combinations of barrel length and choke. Checkered American walnut stock measures 1½″ × 2½″ × 14″. Weight ranges from 7¼ to 7½ lbs., depending upon gauge and barrel. Standard models come with plain barrels but vent ribs available at slight extra cost. Barrels are interchangeable. Push button safety. Prices start at about $200 and range up to $2,100 for special custom versions.

MODEL 1100 SMALL GAUGE: same as above but made in 28 and .410 gauges with 25-inch barrel (I.C., M. or F.). Left-hand model available.

MODEL 1100 MAGNUM: same as field 1100 but in 12 and 20 gauge Magnum—for 3″ shells. 12 gauge in 30″ full. 20 gauge in choice of 28″ or 30″ full. Also available for left-hand.

MODEL 1100 DEER GUN: same as field 1100 but in 12 gauge only, with 22″ I.C. barrel and rifle sights. With recoil pad. Weight, 7¼ lbs.

MODEL 1100 SA SKEET: same as field 1100 but in 12 and 20 gauge with 26″ barrel, skeet choked. Weight, 7½ lbs. Ivory bead front sight with metal bead middle sight. May also be had in 28 or .410 gauge.

MODEL 1100 TB-TRAP: same as field 1100 but with deluxe wood and recoil pad. 12 gauge only with 30″ full choke barrel, vent rib. Recoil pad. Ivory bead front sight with white metal middle sight. Stock measures 1⅜″ × 1¾″ × 13⅜″. Also available for left hand and with Monte Carlo stock. Prices start at about $270.

MODEL 1100 20 GAUGE LIGHTWEIGHT: a special weight-saving version that tips the scales at about 6½ lbs. Plain or vent rib. Spec's generally same as 1100 field model. Also available with 3″ chamber.

Remington also maintains a special custom-gun department that will make up conventional actions with special customized and decorative wood and engravings.

Winchester Model 1400 Deer Gun

Winchester Model 1400 Field Grade

Winchester Model 1400 Skeet Grade

Winchester Model 1400 Trap Grade

Winchester Super-X Model 1 Field Grade

Winchester Super-X Model 1 Trap Grade

WINCHESTER: MODEL 1400 MARK II: in 12 or 20 gauge, a 3-shot autoloader with choice of 26″, 28″ or 30″ barrels bored I.C., M. or F. Alloy receiver. Push button safety. Stock measures 1½″ × 2⅜″ × 14″. Interchangeable barrels. Prices start at about $170. Weights range from 6½ to 6¾ lbs., depending upon gauge and barrel.

SUPER-X MODEL 1: the latest addition to the Winchester line is this superbly crafted gas-operated autoloader made entirely from forged and machined steel components. Produced only in 12 and 20 gauge, the Super-X has a four-shot capacity and may be had with barrel combos of 26″ I.C., 28″M, 28″F and 30″F (12 ga. only). American walnut stock has pistol grip and semi-beavertail fore-end, hand checkered. Dimensions are 1½″ × 2½″ × 14″. With plain barrel prices start at about $260.00; vent ribs approximately $20.00 higher.

SUPER-X, MODEL 1, TRAP & SKEET: these are essentially similar to the field model described above but tailored for special-purpose target use. Trap model may be had with conventional or Monte Carlo stock and 30″ modified or full ventilated rib barrel. Receiver is engraved; stock with black rubber recoil pad. Red bead front sight. Skeet model equipped with 26-inch vent-ribbed skeet barrel, otherwise similar to trap gun but with skeet stock dimensions.

SUPER-X MODEL 1 DEER GUN: same as field model described earlier but in 12 gauge only with 22″ barrel, cylinder choke and rifle-type sights. Price, approximately $270.

SMITH & WESSON: MODEL 1000: a 12 gauge autoloader chambered for 2¾-inch shells and having a four-shot capacity. Vent rib barrels only in 26″ Skeet, 26″ I.C., 28″ I.M., Mod. or Full and 30″ Full. Weight about 7½ lbs. Stock 1½″ × 2⅜″ × 14″. Reversible push-button safety. Front and middle sights. Alloy receiver. Prices start at about $235.00.

WEATHERBY: The Centurion Auto is in 12 gauge only, with 2¾″ chamber. Choice of 26-, 28- or 30-inch barrels bored I.C., M., or F. Weight about 7½ lbs. Walnut stock with recoil pad. Interchangeable barrels. Gold plated trigger. Starts at $270.00.

BERETTA: Beretta guns are imported from Italy. The line encompasses the below-described autoloading shotgun, an assortment of side-by-side and O/U doubles and a broad selection of handguns for which Beretta is well known.

BERETTA AL-2 AUTOLOADER: in 12 or 20 gauge only with 2¾ - or 3-inch chambers (the latter in Magnum models). Shell capacity is four with 3-shot plug furnished. Barrel choices are— 30″F, 28″F, 28″M, 26″ I.C. in 12 gauge, and 28″F, 28″M, 26″ I.C. in 20 gauge. Trap gun, 30″F. Skeet guns (12 or 20) with 26″ Skeet barrels. Magnum models 12/30″F and 20/28″F.

Weights range from 6½ to 7½ lbs., depending upon model, gauge and barrel. Hand checkered walnut stock and fore-end Monte Carlo available for trap model. Prices start at about $300.00.

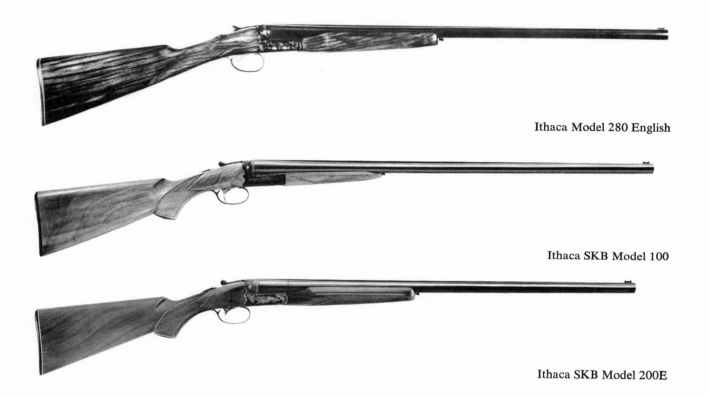

Ithaca Model 280 English

Ithaca SKB Model 100

Ithaca SKB Model 200E

ITHACA: SKB MODEL 100 FIELD GRADE: imported from Japan in 12 ga. (2¾″) and 20 ga. (3″). Hammerless box lock with auto safety, selective single trigger and non-auto extractor. Barrel offerings are—12/26″ IC&M, 12/28″ (or 30″) M&F, 20/28″ M&F, 20/25″ IC&M. Walnut checkered stock measures 1½″ × 2⅝″ × 14″. European splinter fore-end. Weights range from 6 to 7 lbs. Prices start at about $250.

SKB 200E FIELD GRADE: same as model 100 but with beavertail fore-end, selective automatic ejectors and twin bead sights. Priced about $340.

SKB 200E SKEET GRADE: same as 200E except with non-auto safety and recoil pad. Skeet choked barrels measure 25″ in 20 gauge and 26″ in 12. Weights 6½ lbs. (20) 7¼ lbs. (12). Priced about $350.

SKB MODEL 280 QUAIL DOUBLE: in 20 gauge only, with 3″ chambers and 25-inch barrels bored I.C.&I.C. Weight, 6½ lbs. English-style stock and fore-end. Stock measures 1½″ × 2⅝″ × 14″.

SKB MODEL 280 ENGLISH DOUBLE: similar to Model 200E but with typical English styling (straight grip, small splinter fore-end). In 12 ga. (2¾″ and 20 ga. (3″.) Choice of 25- or 26-inch barrels bored I.C.&M or 28″ M&F. Weights from 6½ to 7⅛ lbs.

BROWNING: MODEL B-SS: in 12 gauge with 2¾″ chamber, or 20 gauge with 3″ chamber. Box lock action with tang safety and single trigger. Barrel choices—26″ IC&M, 26″ M&F or 28″ M&F. Weight from 6¾ to 7 lbs. Stock 1⅝″ × 2½″ × 14¾″. Engraved receiver, auto ejectors mechanical single trigger, auto safety. Priced to start at about $280. Modified beavertail fore-end.

Pedersen Series 2500

PEDERSEN CUSTOM DOUBLES: The custom gun division of O. F. Mossberg turns out a broad assortment of really fine custom doubles. Because certain models are custom-made, to order, the customer can get almost any reasonable variation he desires. One grade, however, the 2500 Series, Grade III, is produced in quantity, unadorned, to conventional field gun specs. This one is considerably cheaper than the customized versions.

2000 SERIES DOUBLE, GRADE I: a box-lock side by side in choice of 12 or 20 gauge. Stock, weight, length and barrels to customer's specs (within manufacturing limitations). Selec-tive auto ejectors, gold-filled engraving, auto safety, selective single trigger. Price, approximately $1,800.

2000 SERIES DOUBLE, GRADE II: same as the previously described Grade I but somewhat less decorated and with slightly plainer conventional stock measuring 1½″ × 2½″ × 14″. Priced at approximately $1,400.

2500 SERIES GRADE III: comparable to series 2000 but in plain field gun version with standard stock and lacking engraving. Beavertail fore-end and pistol grip are hand checkered. Priced about $300.

Savage-Fox Model B-SE

Stevens Model 311

SAVAGE: Savage Arms Corp., makers of Savage, Stevens and Fox guns, has long been famous for their broad line of inexpensive, but sturdy, and reliable doubles.

MODEL 311: marketed under the Savage-Stevens label, this model is made in 12, 16, 20 and .410 gauges. (12, 20 and .410 with 3″ chambers.) A top lever, hammerless, box-lock equipped with double triggers and tang safety. All popular barrel and choke combinations. Weight ranges from 7 to 8 lbs. Stock 1½″ × 2½″ × 14″. Case-hardened frame. Priced at about $116.

SAVAGE-FOX MODEL B-SE: produced in 12, 20 and .410 gauges. Hammerless, take-down, box-lock with non-selective single trigger, auto safety and auto ejectors. All popular barrels and chokes. Checkered walnut stock and beavertail fore-end. Case-hardened frame. Priced about $175. May also be had with double triggers for a bit less.

SAVAGE-FOX MODEL B, 24″ LIGHT-WEIGHT: 12 or 20 gauge, choice of chambers. Comparable to above with double triggers only. Popular barrels. Priced about $150.

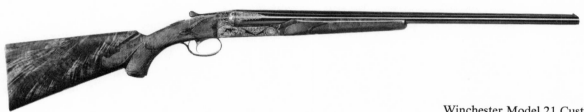

Winchester Model 21 Custom Grade

WINCHESTER: Winchester still offers their time-honored Model 21 on a custom order basis in a number of grades ranging in price from about $3000 to $7000. These may be had in 12, 16 or 20 gauge with choice of chambers, barrel lengths, chokes, triggers, stock, fore-end, engraving, etc. It would serve no purpose to go into all the possible variables here; it suffices to say that the interested wingshooter can get most any combination of features in a shotgun built to his specifications with a stock tailor-made to his physical requirements.

IMPORTED DOUBLES

There's a host of these on the American market; shotguns coming from England, Japan, Belgium, Germany, Italy, Spain, and France. We could also add a large selection from Iron-Curtain countries but space doesn't permit us to cover this field in detail.

ENGLISH DOUBLES

The famous side-by-sides made by Holland & Holland, Purdey, Greener and Webley & Scott are still available to American shooters but some are now offered only on a special order basis and prices start at about $2,000 and can easily exceed $8,000. Most any gauge and type of double can be had tailored to the individual's physical requirements and hunting needs but allow at least two years for fabrication. Orders should be placed through a reputable American firearms importer or agent.

WEST GERMAN DOUBLES

Sauer & Sohn is the only West German maker producing in quantity and exporting to the U. S. Line includes a number of models in 12, 16 and 20 gauge as well as an assortment of rifle-shotgun combinations.

ITALIAN DOUBLES

Beretta makes a number of 12 and 20 gauge doubles. These are generally offered under the model designations "GR" and "SO". Boxlock actions are the rule and prices start at about $500.

Franchi makes a few custom class doubles at prices ranging upward from $1,200. Distributed by Stoeger.

Vincenzo Bernardelli of Gardone, V. T. makes a number of fine doubles, some closely patterning the English style and quality. In 12 or 20 gauge, these may be had with box-locks or side-locks and prices start at about $500.

Umberto Bernardelli is another Italian double gun maker whose products are offered in the U. S. by Harden & Knight of Miami, Florida.

Though we couldn't get confirmation in time for this edition, we suspect that the firms of Zoli and Gamba (Gardone, V.T.) are also producing some double guns in limited quantities.

SPANISH DOUBLES

AYA is probably the largest of Spanish double gun makers. In 12 or 20 gauge their Models 56, 53E, XXX/SL and No. I are made on sidelock actions with prices starting at about $800. Distributed by JBL Arms Co., AYA makes all of the customary barrel and choke combinations and prefers to produce stocks to the customer's specifications.

VICTOR SARASQUETA: this well-known firm, headed by Spain's famous shooting champion, has long been known for their broad variety of double guns. They produce all popular gauges in box-

locks as well as side-locks and prices can easily range to $4,000. Models retailing for $600 or more show excellent quality. Current American distributor is unknown.

UGARTECHEA: is one of Spain's foremost custom gun builders with a well equipped plant in Eibar. Distributed by American Import Co., current offering consists of 12, 20, 28 and .410 gauge models 1302, 1303, 1304 and 1305. Prices start at about $200.

AUSTRIAN DOUBLES

The many small custom gun makers of Ferlach are syndicated. Their specialty is combination rifle-shotguns but some undoubtedly will produce custom side-by-sides to order. The problem here is that quality is not uniform from one maker to another so the would-be purchaser would be wise to place his order with a U. S. agent working with one specific builder of known quality.

BELGIAN DOUBLES

The gun makers of Liege also function along the lines of a syndicate or cooperative. Quality varies from one firm to another though generally ranging from good to excellent. On a special order basis most any form of double gun may be had; prices, however, would start at about $500. Again, work through a U. S. agent or distributor working with one specific, known, manufacturer.

FRENCH DOUBLES

In the gun making center of St. Etienne, there are a number of small firms who produce shotguns. Prices are high and designs are uniquely French. From existing records we could find only one builder who is exporting to the U. S. in quantity. This is the firm of Darne (pronounced Darn) who builds an unusual sliding breech double of very light weight that is distributed in the U. S. by Firearms Center, Inc. Prices start at about $500.

IRON CURTAIN DOUBLES

A number of famous gun houses fell into Russian hands at the end of WWII and have since resumed production of sporting shotguns. Those located in East Germany are most conspicuous by their absence but others may be found in Czechoslovakia, Poland and Hungary. Their products are *not* generally available in the U. S. at this writing.

BRAZILIAN DOUBLES

The Rossi firm of Brazil produces a couple of comparatively inexpensive side-by-sides that are imported into the U. S. by Garcia Corp. These sell for under $200 and are offered only in 12 or 20 gauge with a limited selection of barrels and chokes.

OVER & UNDER GUNS

Browning Citori Trap Model

BROWNING: Browning's Superposed line of over and unders embraces about thirty different versions ranging from the "Super-Light" field model (priced from $820) to cased-set combinations having interchangeable barrels and priced up to $5000 in deluxe grades. Space won't permit us to describe them all in detail here, we will, however, outline each series briefly.

SUPERPOSED FIELD GUNS: available in Grade I, and deluxe grades called "Pigeon," "Diana," and "Midas." These are found in 12 or 20 gauge with 26½″ barrels and are made on boxlock actions with auto ejectors, single trigger, auto safeties, etc. With straight grip stocks, weights start at about 6 lbs. 6 oz. With vent rib.

SUPERPOSED MAGNUM: a three-inch 12-gauge Magnum version with 30″ M&F or F&F barrels. Recoil pad. Weight 8 lbs.

SUPERPOSED LIGHTNING SKEET in 12 or 20 gauge (only) with skeet chokes and choice of 26″ or 28″ barrels. Weight 6½ to 7¾ lbs.

SUPERPOSED ALL-GAUGE SKEET SET: is made with four matched sets of barrels in 12, 20, 28 and .410 gauges. With 26½″ barrels, weight is approximately 7 lbs. 10 ozs. With 28″ bbls., weight is 7¾ lbs.

SUPERPOSED LIGHTNING TRAP: in 12 gauge only with stock measuring 1⁷⁄₁₆″ × 1⅝″ × 14⅜″. Weight 7¾ lbs. with 30-inch F&F, I.M.&F or M&F barrels. Non-auto safety and ivory sights.

SUPERPOSED LIGHTNING: generally the same as the "Superlight" field model with pistol grip stock and heavier fore-end. Weighs from 7 to 7¼ lbs. in 12 gauge; 6-6¼ lbs. in 20 gauge. Prices start at $780.

SUPERPOSED BROADWAY TRAP in 12 gauge, similar to "Lightning Trap" but with ⅝"-wide ventilated rib.

SUPERPOSED COMBINATIONS: both the "Super-light" and "Lightning" models may be ordered with factory-fitted interchangeable barrel sets, in any of the four grades, with prices starting at $1,250 for one extra barrel set.

BROWNING CITORI O/U SHOTGUN: a comparatively new and inexpensive O&U addition to Browning's line. Starts at $300 plus. 12 or 20 gauge, all popular chokes and lengths. Weight, about 7½ lbs. Vent rib. Single trigger. Auto ejectors and auto safety. Available in field, skeet and trap grades.

BROWNING "LIEGE": another imported O&U, in 12 gauge only with 2¾" or 3" chambers. All popular chokes and lengths. Single trigger (mechanical) manual safety, auto ejectors, p.g. stock, priced from about $500.

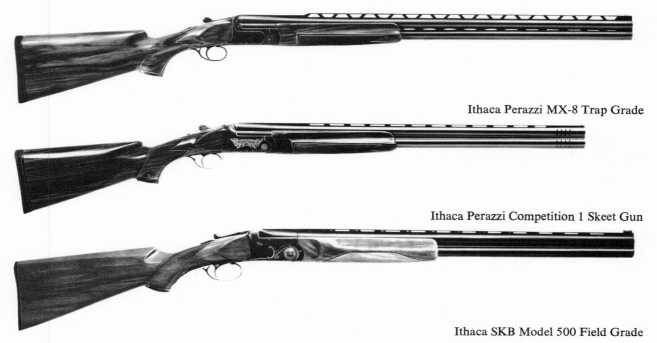

Ithaca Perazzi MX-8 Trap Grade

Ithaca Perazzi Competition 1 Skeet Gun

Ithaca SKB Model 500 Field Grade

ITHACA: Ithaca imports and distributes a number of O&U guns from both Italy and Japan.

PERAZZI MIRAGE O&U: in 12 gauge only with 2¾" chambers. Box-lock. Selective single trigger has interchangeable feature. Vent rib barrels are offered in skeet or trap patterns with lengths to 32". Weight 8¼ lbs. A target gun, priced about $1,700.

PERAZZI MX-8 TRAP GUN in 12 gauge only with choice of 30" or 32" barrels. Bored for international trap competition. Non-selective single trigger (interchangeable). Stock to order. Weight 8 lbs. Also $1,700.

PERAZZI MX-8 COMBINATION: similar to above but with interchangeable *single* barrel in 32" or 34" length. Priced at $2,300.

PERAZZI COMPETITION I SKEET O&U: in 12 gauge only with 26¾" skeet bored barrels. Vent rib, interchangeable single trigger. Stock 1½" × 2⅜" × 14½". Weight 7¾ lbs. Prices start at $1,100.

ITHACA SKB OVER & UNDERS: these are offered in the Models 500, 600, 700, and 880 in field, skeet, trap and deluxe grades. Some models offered only in 12 gauge and others in choice of 12 or 20 gauge. Skeet guns, however, are available in 28 and .410 gauge as well. Skeet barrels are 26″ or 28″. Trap barrels are 32″. All models with ventilated ribs, checkered walnut stocks and fore-ends, selective single trigger, box-lock actions. Target models with non-auto safety. Field models $350; Magnums—$360; Skeet guns $400, $410 & $500; Trap models $400, $500 and $1,200. Crown grade, approx. $1,000.

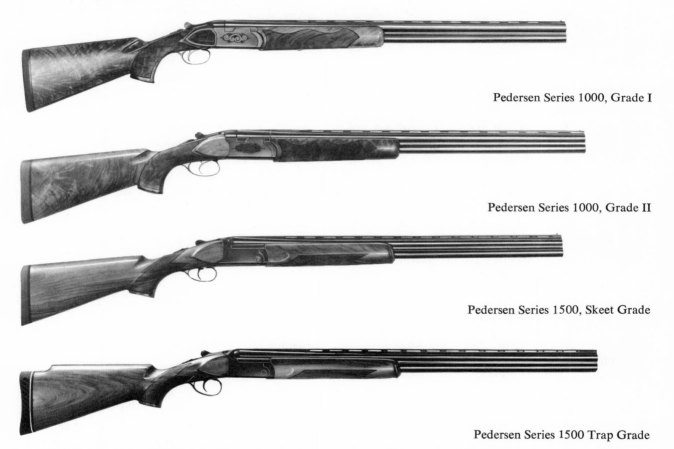

Pedersen Series 1000, Grade I

Pedersen Series 1000, Grade II

Pedersen Series 1500, Skeet Grade

Pedersen Series 1500 Trap Grade

PEDERSEN CUSTOM GUNS: offers their Series 1000 in grades II, III and "Custom" at prices ranging from $1,200 to $1,800. These are 12 or 20 gauge over and unders with barrels, chokes and stocks to customer's specifications. Vent ribs, selective single triggers, auto ejectors, checkered walnut stocks and fore-ends, engraved receivers. Special skeet and trap versions also may be had at comparable prices.

PEDERSEN 1500: a 12 gauge (only) O&U with choice of barrels from 26″ to 32″. Weight 7 to 7½ lbs. Checkered walnut stock (with recoil pad) and fore-end. Auto ejectors, vent rib, selective single trigger. Field, skeet and trap configurations. Priced from $450 to $475.

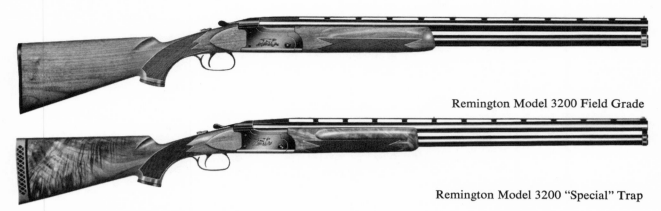

Remington Model 3200 Field Grade

Remington Model 3200 "Special" Trap

REMINGTON: MODEL 3200: this is probably the *only* mass-produced over and under gun on the market that is American-made. Announced late in '73, the 3200 boasts a number of interesting new features and has quickly moved to the top of the market.

At this writing the 3200 is available only in 12 gauge, but we expect some additional gauges to be announced at any time. With 2¾" chambers, the 3200 has a purely mechanical selective single trigger, top-lever box-lock frame, ventilated rib, auto ejectors, target trigger, shielded breech, modi-fied beavertail fore-end and pistol grip stock of checkered American walnut.

Barrel choices are 26″ I.C.&M., 26″ Skeet & Skeet; 28″ M&F, 28″ SK&SK, 30″ M&F, 30″ F&F and 30″ I.M.&F. Weight ranges from 7¾ lbs.

Firing pins will not fall when chambers are empty so the 3200 can safely be dry-fired. Lock time is exceptionally fast. Target models with wide trigger. Approximate prices are: Field grade $485; Skeet $530; Trap $550; and Model "one of 1000 Skeet" $1,050.

ROTTWEIL OLYMPIA: This is a German-import—the gun that won the Skeet Olympics at Munich (1972). Until recently, so few of these guns were produced that there were none available for export to the U. S. We've recently learned, however, that they're now being made in both field and target grades and that they'll soon appear on the American market at around $1,500 per copy. With Bohler steel barrels, chrome-steel forged and machine frame, interchangeable single trigger units, the Olympia will be available in all field and target versions.

The Olympia Skeet Gun (which attracted all the attention to begin with) is made with the newly-developed "TULA CHOKE." This is an unusual skeet choke that provides good uniform patterning with a longer than usual shotstring. (See "chokes" in our chapter on barrels.)

Savage Model 330 Field Grade

SAVAGE: Savage Arms Corp. offers three models of over and under shotguns; these are made in Europe to Savage's specs and are popularly priced.

MODEL 333: In 12 and 20 gauge with vent rib, selective single trigger and auto ejectors. With checkered p.g. and fore-end. Barrel choices, in 12 ga., are 26″ Sk & Sk, 26″ I.C.&M., 28″ M&F, and 30″ M&F. 20 gauge choices are 26″ Sk & Sk, 26″ IC&M, 28″ M&F. Priced at about $340.

MODEL 333T: a special 12 gauge Trap Model with selective single trigger, Monte Carlo stock, manual safety, and 30-inch barrels bored improved modified and full. Weight 7¾ lbs. Also priced at $340.

MODEL 330: a field model in choice of 12 or 20 gauge with selective single trigger, extractors, auto safety, checkered walnut stock and fore-end. 20 gauge models chambered for 3″ as well as 2¾-inch shells. Available in all standard lengths and chokes. Priced at $270.

WEATHERBY: This well-known rifle builder is now offering a deluxe over and under gun under the name "Regency." In 12 or 20 gauge, this is a box-lock style with 28-inch barrels bored I.C.&M., M.&F. or Skeet & Skeet. Selective auto ejectors, selective single trigger, American walnut stock and fore-end. Greener-type crossbolt. Weight ranges from 6⅞ to 7⅜ lbs. Priced from $600 to $650 in field, skeet and trap grades.

Winchester Model 101 Field Grade

Winchester Model 101 Skeet Grade

Winchester Model 101 Trap Grade

WINCHESTER: Winchester offers five versions of their Model 101 over and under, as follows:

101 FIELD GRADE O&U: in 12, 20, 28 or .410 gauge with manual safety, selective single trigger, vent rib and auto ejectors. Barrels are: 26″ or 28″ in all gauges, however, 12 gauge may also be had with 30-inch tubes. Choke combo's are I.C.&M, or M.&F. Bores and chambers chrome plated. Weights are 6¼ to 7¾ lbs. Prices from $430 to $460.

101 MAGNUM: same as field gun but chambered for 3-inch 12 or 20 gauge and with 30-inch barrels bored M&F or F&F. Price about $440.

101 SKEET: same as field model but with non-auto safety in 12, 20, 28 or .410 gauges. 26″ or 28″ skeet barrels. $470 to $500.

101 SKEET COMBINATION: 20 gauge skeet gun with two additional sets of interchangeable barrels in 28 and .410 gauges. Includes trunk case. $1,100.

101 PIGEON GRADE TRAP GUN: same as field grade but in 12 gauge only with choice of 30″ or 32″ barrels bored I.M.&F. Weight 8¼ lbs. Standard trap stock 1⅜″ × 1⅞″ × 14⅜″. Monte Carlo also available at slight additional cost. Standard grade sells for $670.

Beretta Model BL-6

BERETTA: Offers three models of over and under.

MODEL BL-2/S: a 12 gauge with 26″ IC&M, 28″ M&F or 30″ M&F vent rib barrels. Selective single trigger with unusual selector built into face of trigger itself. Also available with 3-inch chambers. Weight, 7 to 7¼ lbs. Priced from $400.

MODEL BL: in 12, 12 Mag, 20 or 28 gauge in all popular lengths and chokes. In four grades (BL, BL-3, BL-4 and BL-6.) Selective single trigger, auto ejectors, vent rib, checkered stock and fore-end. Priced from $400 to $900.

MODEL SO: a slidelock over and under in 12 gauge only with 26″, 28″ or 30″ barrels. Chokes, stock, decorations to customer's spec's. This is a custom grade only.

DALY: Sloan's of New York imports the Japanese-made Daly line. These are offered in six grades for field, skeet or trap and in all of the usual lengths and chokes. Gauges generally limited to 12 and 20 and there are some 3-inch models available. Prices from $420 to $900.

FRANCHI: Offers about a dozen differing versions of their Falconet series O/U in 12, 16, 20, 28 and .410 gauges. Prices from $500 to $1,800. Field models generally with lightweight alloy re-ceiver. Target versions with steel receiver. All conventional chokes and lengths. Inertia-block single triggers, auto ejectors, auto safeties (except on target grades). Made in Italy.

HIGH-STANDARD: The Japanese Shadow Indy O/U is offered by High-Standard in 12 gauge only with 2¾″ chambers in most barrel and choke combinations. Priced at $500 to $600. Weight 8 lbs. Selective single trigger. Auto ejectors and auto safety. Aluminum (lightweight) rib.

KRIEGHOFF: One of the better lines of imported over and under guns, Krieghoff's are priced from $700 to $11,000. In two models ("TECK" and "MODEL 32") these may be had in many different grades embracing side-lock as well as box-lock actions. Choice of lengths from 28″ to 34″ and chokes in 12, 20, 28 and .410 gauges. 3-inch chambers also available. Weights from 7 lbs.

Krieghoff's Model 32 has a purely mechanical single trigger which is adjustable for weight of pull. Unusual safety device is selective—shooter can choose manual, auto or inoperative settings. Auto ejectors and vent ribs.

Attractive walnut stocks are hand checkered and finished. Special customizing division will work to customer's specs.

MIIDA: This Japanese import is distributed by Marubeni America Corp. in about six grades priced from $400 to $1,200. Available only in 12 gauge with usual assortment of chokes and lengths. Selective single triggers and auto ejectors.

ZOLI: Imported by J. L. Galef Co., of New York, the ZOLI Silver Snipe O/U is made with 3-inch chambers in 12 and 20 gauges. It has a crossbolt together with a Purdey-type box-lock. Choice of 26″ I.C.&M., 28″ M&F, and 26″ Sk&Sk barrels. In the 12 gauge, may also be had with 30″ M&F or 30″ F&F barrels. Weights from 6 to 7¾ lbs. Auto safety on field models. Non-auto safety in skeet and trap grades. Extractors, vent ribs, single trigger, and chromed bores. Priced from $330 to $390.

GOLDEN SNIPE O/U: same as above but with selective auto ejectors priced from $380 to $450. Also imported by J. L. Galef Co.

SINGLE-BARREL TRAP GUNS

This type of target gun virtually disappeared from the market after WWII but has been making a comeback in recent years due to the greatly intensified interest in trap shooting.

Tops in this field are those models produced by Ithaca, so we'll cover them first before going on to the imports.

Ithaca Model 4E Single Barrel Trap Gun

Ithaca Perazzi Single Barrel Trap

Ithaca Century SBT Trap Gun

ITHACA 4E: $2,250 in 12 gauge with choice of 32″ or 32″ ribbed barrel. Stock measures, 1⅜″ × 1⅜″ × 14⅜″. Weight 8½ lbs. With crisp target trigger.

ITHACA 5E: similar to above but more highly decorated and priced at $3,000.

ITHACA $5,000 GRADE: priced as it is titled, this is an exquisitely decorated version of the Model 4E. With very fancy-figured wood.

Beretta Mark II Trap Gun

BERETTA: The Mark II Beretta single barrel is made in 12 gauge with 32″ or 34″ full choke, matted rib, barrels and Monte Carlo stock. Priced about $450.

DALY: Distributed by Sloan's, N. Y., the Charles Daly single barrel is also a 12 gauge in choice of 32″ or 34″ full choked, ribbed barrel at $450.

KRIEGHOFF: Distributed by Krieghoff Gun Co., in the U. S. the Krieghoff trap gun may be had with 32″ or 34″ barrels in five grades priced from $1,295 to $5,700. Also made in Vandalia Model with 30″, 32″ & 34″ barrels at $1,695 to $7,000.

GALEF: Offers their Monte Carlo single barrel trap gun at $170. This is in 12 gauge with 32″ full-choke barrel and stock measuring 1⅛″ × 1⅝″ × 14½″. Hand checkered with beavertail fore-end and auto ejector. Weight 8¼ lbs.

LJUTIC: Ljutic Industries Inc. of Yakima, Washington is a custom gun builder that produces target grade shotguns as a specialty. These are primarily trap models in O&U, single barrel and autoloading configurations.

MONO GUN: with 34″ barrel and overall weight of 8⅝ lbs. Custom choke, stock and trigger are to customer's specs. Prices start at $1,995.00.

LJUTIC X73: a single-barrel trap gun that holds the woman's long-run record. With 33-inch barrel, Ljutic choke, tapered rib, pushbutton opener, pull or release trigger, prices start at $1,195.

LJUTIC DYN-A-TRAP: a production grade single-barrel trap gun with 33-inch barrel, push-button opener, pull trigger, conventional trap stock with Monte Carlo, recoil pad. Priced at $895.